Other Books and Series by Jeff Bowen

Applications for Enrollment of Choctaw Newborn Act of 1905 Volumes I thru XX

Choctaw By Blood Enrollment Cards 1898-1914 Volumes I thru XIX

Oglala Sioux Indians Pine Ridge Reservation 1932 Census Book I

Visit our website at **www.nativestudy.com** to learn more about these and other books and series by Jeff Bowen

CHOCTAW BY BLOOD ENROLLMENT CARDS 1898-1914

VOLUME XX

TRANSCRIBED BY

JEFF BOWEN

NATIVE STUDY
Gallipolis, Ohio
USA

Native Study LLC
Gallipolis, OH
www.nativestudy.com

Library of Congress Control Number: 2020911767

ISBN: 978-1-64968-116-4

Made in the United States of America.

**This series is dedicated to
Mike Marchi,
who keeps my spirits up.**

CREEK CENSUS.

SECOND NOTICE.

Members of the Dawes Commission will be present at the following times and places for the purpose of enrolling Creek citizens, as required by Act of Congress of June 10, 1896:

At Muskogee, Nov. 8 to 30, 1897, inclusive.
At Wagoner, Nov. 8 to 13, " inclusive.
At Eufaula, Nov. 8 to 13, " inclusive.
At Sapulpa, Nov. 15 to 20, " inclusive.
At Wetumpka, Nov. 15 to 20, " inclusive.
At Okmulgee, Nov. 22 to 30, " inclusive.

All persons who have not heretofore enrolled before the Dawes Commission should appear and enroll. Parents and guardians can enroll their families and wards.

TAMS BIXBY,
FRANK C. ARMSTRONG,
A. S. McKENNON,
THOS. B. NEEDLES,
Commissioners.

The above illustration is similar in nature to what was found throughout Indian Territory for different tribes as far as postings on bulletin boards, public centers, or wherever they could be read so people would be notified of where and when they needed to be for enrollment with the Dawes Commission.

This is a picture of the Dawes Commission at Camp Jones in Stonewall, Indian Territory on September 8, 1898.

The images below are of two of the original cards given on the microfilm. The cards given in this book have been formatted to fit on one page and still give all the information found on the original cards.

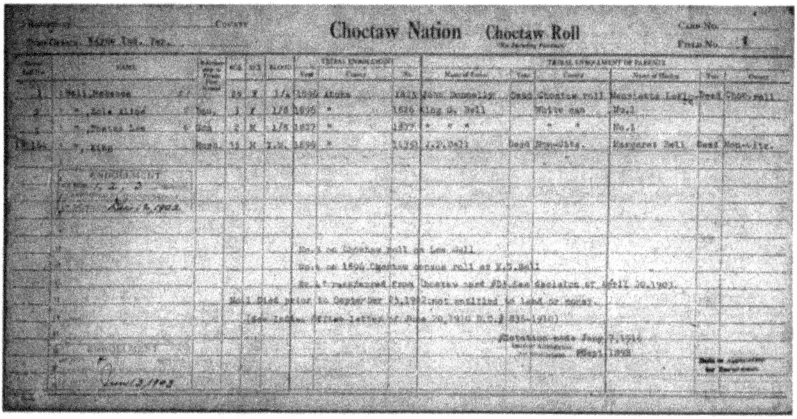

Choctaw Nation Choctaw Roll

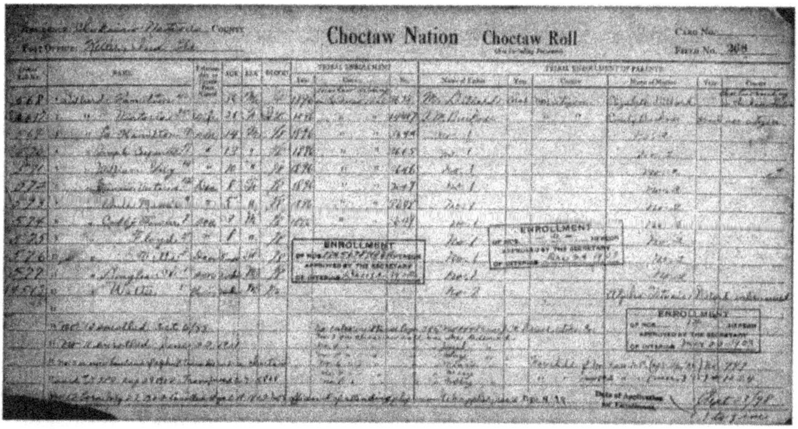

Choctaw Nation Choctaw Roll

ENROLLMENT

Introduction

This series of Choctaw Enrollment Cards for the Five Civilized Tribes 1898-1914 has been transcribed from National Archive Film M-1186 Rolls 39-46.

The series contains more than 6100 Choctaw enrollment cards. All of the cards list age, sex and degree of blood, the parties' Dawes Roll Numbers, and date of enrollment by the Secretary of Interior for each person. The contents also give the enrollee's parents' names as well as miscellaneous notes pertaining to the enrollee's circumstances, when needed. Most entries indicate whether or not a spouse is an Intermarried White, with the initials I.W.

Enrollment wasn't as simple a process as most would think just by going through these pages. The relationships between the Five Tribes and the Dawes Commission were weak at best. There were political battles going on between the tribes and the U.S. Government as it was, but the struggles didn't stop there. Each tribe had its own political factions pulling it from every direction. On top of everything else, people from every corner of the United States were trying to figure how to get in on the spoils (Money and Land Allotment) by means of political favor. Kent Carter, author of *The Dawes Commission*, describes the continuous effort required to enroll the different tribes and the pressure the Commission incurred from people all over the country who tried to insinuate themselves into the equation:

"In May 1896 the Dawes Commission Returned To Indian Territory for its third visit, establishing its headquarters at Vinita in the Cherokee Nation. It now had to process applications for citizenship in addition to negotiating allotment agreements; these circumstances make the narrative of events more confusing because the commission attempted the two tasks concurrently. The commissioners resumed making their usual speeches to tribal officials and public gatherings to promote negotiations, but now they inevitably had to respond to questions about how the application process for citizenship would work. They also began receiving letters from people all over the United States asking how they could 'get on the rolls' so they could 'get Indian land'."[1]

For the actual process of Choctaw enrollment, "A commission was appointed in each county of the Choctaw Nation under an act of September 18 to make separate rolls of citizens by blood, by intermarriage, and freedmen; it was to deliver them to recently elected Chief Green McCurtain by October 20, but he rejected them even before they were completed because of charges that people were being left off for political reasons. On October 30, the National Council authorized establishment of a five-member

---

[1] *The Dawes Commission* by Kent Carter, page 15, para. 1

commission to revise the rolls within ten days and then directed McCurtain to turn them over to the Dawes Commission on November 11, 1896. The Choctaws hired the law firm of Stuart, Gordon, and Hailey, of South M^c^Alester to represent the tribe at all proceedings held by the Dawes Commission,"[2] another indication that throughout the Commission's efforts there was always controversy between the tribes and the negotiators.

When completed, this multi-volume series will contain thousands of names, all of them accounted for in the indexes carefully prepared by the author. Hopefully this work will help many researchers find their ancestors and satisfy the questions that so many have had about their Native American heritage.

Jeff Bowen
Gallipolis, Ohio
NativeStudy.com

---

[2] *The Dawes Commission* by Kent Carter, page 16, para. 5

Choctaw By Blood Enrollment Cards 1898-1914

RESIDENCE: Choctaw Nation ~~COUNTY.~~ **Choctaw Nation** **Choctaw Roll** *(Not Including Freedmen)* CARD NO.
POST OFFICE: Caddo I.T. FIELD NO. 5751

Dawes' Roll No.		NAME	Relationship to Person First Named	AGE	SEX	BLOOD	TRIBAL ENROLLMENT Year	County	No.
15271	1	Carroll, Earnest		20	M	1/32	1893	Kiamitia	112
IW1361	2	" Laura L	Wife	18	F	I.W.			
15272	3	" Elanor[sic]	Dau	6w	F	1/64			
15273	4	" Stanton B	Son	1mo	M	1/64			
	5								
	6								
	7								
	8								
	9	ENROLLMENT							
	10	OF NOS. 1 - 3 & 4 HEREON APPROVED BY THE SECRETARY							
	11	OF INTERIOR MAY 9 1904							
	12								
	13								
	14	ENROLLMENT							
	15	OF NOS. 2 HEREON APPROVED BY THE SECRETARY							
	16	OF INTERIOR MAR 14 1905							
	17								

TRIBAL ENROLLMENT OF PARENTS

	Name of Father	Year	County	Name of Mother	Year	County
1	George Carroll	Dead	non citizen	Lizzie Booker		Blue
2	Frank Brown	"	" "	Ella Brown		non-citz
3	No1			No2		
4	No1			No2		
5						

6 No3 born Dec 13, 1900, enrolled Feby 3, 1901
7 No4 born Jany 10, 1902, enrolled Feby 20, 1902
Transferred from Choctaw Card # D. 372
8 ~~No1 is great grandson of John Null, who was~~
9 admitted by decision of Supreme Court of Choctaw
10 Nation in October, 1872
For child of Nos 1 & 2 see NB (March 3, 1905) #1196
11
12
13
14
15
16 Date of Application for Enrollment. Aug 25/99
17 PO Caddo I.T. 11/25/04 transfer to this card MAR 18 1904

Choctaw By Blood Enrollment Cards 1898-1914

Choctaw Nation
tringtown I.T.

~~COUNTY.~~ **Choctaw Nation** **Choctaw Roll** *(Not Including Freedmen)* CARD NO. FIELD NO. 575

Dawes' Roll No.	NAME	Relationship to Person First Named	AGE	SEX	BLOOD	TRIBAL ENROLLMENT Year	County	No.
IW783	1 , James H		49	M	I.W.	1896	Kiamitia	14826

ENROLLMENT
OF NOS. 1 HEREON
APPROVED BY THE SECRETARY
OF INTERIOR MAY 7 1904

TRIBAL ENROLLMENT OF PARENTS

Name of Father	Year	County	Name of Mother	Year	County
1 S.G. Miller	Dead	Non-Citz	Calistey F Miller	Dead	Non-Citz

~~No1 is husband of Ella J Miller, Choctaw Card #4242 Roll #11879~~

Transferred from Choctaw Card # D.394. See decision of Feby 27, 1904

~~Date of Application~~ for Enrollment.

Aug 31/99

transfer date to this card MAR 17 1904

RESIDENCE: Choctaw Nation ~~COUNTY.~~ **Choctaw Nation** Choctaw Roll (Not Including Freedmen) CARD NO.
POST OFFICE: Goodwater I.T. FIELD NO. 5753

Dawes' Roll No.	NAME	Relationship to Person First Named	AGE	SEX	BLOOD	TRIBAL ENROLLMENT Year	County	No.
IW 1362	1 Randolph, Ed		26	M	I.W.	1896	Red River	14972
15522	2 " Anna E	Wife	23	F	1/8	1896	" "	7584
15523	3 " Lee	Son	4	M	1/16	1896	" "	10812
15524	4 " Leonard	"	2	"	1/16			
15525	5 " Oda Olline	Dau	7wks	F	1/16			

No4 Proof of birth filed May 6, 1899

ENROLLMENT OF NOS. 2-3-4-5 HEREON APPROVED BY THE SECRETARY OF INTERIOR MAY 9 1904

ENROLLMENT OF NOS. 1 HEREON APPROVED BY THE SECRETARY OF INTERIOR MAR 14 1905

TRIBAL ENROLLMENT OF PARENTS

Name of Father	Year	County	Name of Mother	Year	County
1 M.O. Randolph	1896	Non-citz	Anna Randolph	1896	non-citz
2 White Kirby		" "	Kizzie Kirby	Dead	Red River
3 No1			No2		
4 No1			No2		
5 No1			No2		

No2 on 1893 Leased district pay roll Red River County #679 as Ama Kirby
No2 on 1896 Choctaw roll as Annie E Kirby
No5 Born June 1, 1901 enrolled July 15, 1901
~~Transferred from Choctaw Card # D. 129 March 21, 1904~~
For child of Nos 1&2 see N.B. (Apr 26, 1906) Card No. 205

~~April 27/99~~
Date of Application for Enrollment.

transfer date ~~on this card~~ MAR 21 1904

PO [Illegible] IT 3/15/04

Choctaw By Blood Enrollment Cards 1898-1914

: Choctaw Nation ~~COUNTY.~~ **Choctaw Nation** **Choctaw Roll** *(Not Including Freedmen)* CARD NO.
CE: Glover I.T. FIELD NO. 5754

	NAME	Relationship to Person First Named	AGE	SEX	BLOOD	TRIBAL ENROLLMENT Year	County	No.
1	Merry, Louis		27	M	I.W.	1896	Eagle	14822
2	" Bessie	Wife	19	F	3/4	1896	"	8644
3	" Ida May	Dau	1	"	3/8			
4								
5								
6								
7								
8								
9								
10								
11								
12								
13								
14								
15								
16								
17								

ENROLLMENT
OF NOS. 2 - 3 - HEREON
APPROVED BY THE SECRETARY
OF INTERIOR MAY 9 1904

ENROLLMENT
OF NOS. 1 HEREON
APPROVED BY THE SECRETARY
OF INTERIOR MAR 14 1905

TRIBAL ENROLLMENT OF PARENTS

	Name of Father	Year	County	Name of Mother	Year	County
1	Calvin Merry	Dead	Non-citz	Elizabeth Merry	Dead	non-citz
2	Peter Durant	"	Boktuklo[sic]	Ellen Durant	"	Boktuklo
3	No1			No2		
4						
5						

6 ~~No1 on 1896 Choctaw roll as Lewis Merry~~
7 No2 on 1896 " " " Betsy "
8 No3 Born June 12, 1898 proof of birth filed May 9 1899
Transferred from Choctaw Card # D.128
9
10
11 See letters from Green Mc Curtain and Peter J Hudson referring to 1893
12 Leased district money for No2 filed April 2, 1904.
13
14
15 4/26/99
16 **Date of Application for Enrollment.** transfer date on this card
17 MAR 21 1904

RESIDENCE: Chickasaw Nation COUNTY. **Choctaw Nation** **Choctaw Roll** *(Not Including Freedmen)* CARD NO.
POST OFFICE: Pauls Valley I.T. FIELD NO. 5755

Dawes' Roll No.	NAME	Relationship to Person First Named	AGE	SEX	BLOOD	TRIBAL ENROLLMENT Year	County	No.
15599	1 Hewlett, Sarah C		49	F	1/16	1896	Choctaw residing in Chickasaw Dist	6171
	2							
	3							
	4							
	5							
	6							
	7							
	8							
	9							
	10							
	11							
	12							
	13							
	14							
	15							
	16							
	17							

ENROLLMENT
OF NOS. 1 HEREON
APPROVED BY THE SECRETARY
OF INTERIOR Sep 22 1904

TRIBAL ENROLLMENT OF PARENTS

Name of Father	Year	County	Name of Mother	Year	County
1 Cornelius Lane	Dead	Non citizen	Letha H Lane	Dead	Choctaw
2					
3					
4					
5					
6					
7					
8					
9					
10					
11					
12					
13					
14					
15					
16					
17					

No1 Adopted by Choctaw Council as Sarah C. Cunningham, copy of Act filed with Dawes Com Case No 431. Act approved Oct. 21, 1885
Transferred from Choctaw Card # D27

Sept 16/98
Date of Application for Enrollment.

transfer date to this card
Mar 28 1904

RESIDENCE: Chickasaw Nation ~~COUNTY.~~
POST OFFICE: Ardmore I.T.

Choctaw Nation

Choctaw Roll
(Not Including Freedmen)

CARD NO.
FIELD NO. 5756

Dawes' Roll No.	NAME	Relationship to Person First Named	AGE	SEX	BLOOD	TRIBAL ENROLLMENT Year	County	No.
15947	1 James, Jesse Albert	First Named	4	M	1/2			
	2							
	3							
	4							
	5							
	6							
	7							
	8							
	9							
	10							
	11							
	12							
	13							
	14							
	15							
	16							
	17							

ENROLLMENT
~~OF NOS.~~ 1 ~~HEREON~~
APPROVED BY THE SECRETARY
OF INTERIOR Nov 24 1905

TRIBAL ENROLLMENT OF PARENTS

	Name of Father	Year	County	Name of Mother	Year	County
1	Charley James	1896	Eagle	Nannie James		white woman
2						
3						
4						
5						

6 No1 Born April 23, 1894 Application made Sept 19, 1898 Proof of birth filed April 3, 1905
7 Father of No1 is Charles James on Choctaw card #1302 No. 3543 on final roll.
~~Transferred from Choctaw Card # D. 36~~
8 ~~See testimony in Choctaw #D36~~
9 Application for the Enrollment of No1 made Sept 19 1898

Sept 19/98
Date of Application for Enrollment.

Enrolled Sep 19, 1899

Mar 31 1904

RESIDENCE: Choctaw Nation ~~COUNTY.~~ **Choctaw Nation** **Choctaw Roll** *(Not Including Freedmen)* CARD NO.
POST OFFICE: Antioch, I.T. FIELD NO. 5757

Dawes' Roll No.	NAME	Relationship to Person First Named	AGE	SEX	BLOOD	TRIBAL ENROLLMENT Year	County	No.
15600	1 Davis, Charley L		20	M	1/8	1896	Blue	3552
IW 1149	2 Damron, Mary A	Mother	58	F	I.W.	1896	"	14476

ENROLLMENT OF NOS. 1 HEREON APPROVED BY THE SECRETARY OF INTERIOR Sep 22 1904

ENROLLMENT OF NOS. 2 HEREON APPROVED BY THE SECRETARY OF INTERIOR Nov 16 1904

TRIBAL ENROLLMENT OF PARENTS

Name of Father	Year	County	Name of Mother	Year	County
1 George Davis		Choctaw	Mary Davis		non-citz
2 Chas Seagoe	dead	Non-Citz	Polly Seagoe	dead	" "

On 1896 Choctaw census roll as Charles Davis
Transferred from Choctaw Card # D. 997

No.2 transferred from Choctaw Card # D.341 Oct 31, 1904: See decision of Oct 15, 1904
No2 on 1896 Choc census roll as Mary Ann Davis.

No2 P.O. Durant 3/12/04
P.O. Roberta I.T. 8/8/04

Date of Application for Enrollment. Aug 21/99
transfer date to this card Apr 9-1904

RESIDENCE: Chickasaw Nation ~~COUNTY~~.
POST OFFICE: Fitzhugh, I.T.

Choctaw Nation

Choctaw Roll *(Not Including Freedmen)*

CARD NO.
FIELD NO. 5758

Dawes' Roll No.	NAME	Relationship to Person First Named	AGE	SEX	BLOOD	TRIBAL ENROLLMENT Year	County	No.
IW797	1 Cope, A. W.		43	M	I.W.	1896	Tobucksy	14404

ENROLLMENT
OF NOS. 1 HEREON
APPROVED BY THE SECRETARY
OF INTERIOR May 9 1904

TRIBAL ENROLLMENT OF PARENTS

Name of Father	Year	County	Name of Mother	Year	County
1 John Cope	Dead	non-citizen	Catherine Cope	Dead	Non-citizen

Admitted as an intermarried citizen in 1896 by Dawes Commission Case #730
Children are on Choctaw card #462
On 1896 Choctaw roll as A.W. Coke
~~on appeal judgment was sustained in this case by U.S. Court~~
Central Dist Ind Ter in Court Case #167

Judgment of U.S. Ct set aside and vacated by decree of C.C.C.C. Dec. 19, 1902.
~~admitted by C.C.C.C. Case #59 March 28, 1904~~

Transferred from Choctaw Card # D. 115

March 20/99
~~Date of Application~~
for Enrollment.

transfer date
~~to this card~~
~~Apr 11 1904~~

RESIDENCE: Choctaw Nation ~~COUNTY.~~ **Choctaw Nation** **Choctaw Roll** *(Not Including Freedmen)* CARD NO.
POST OFFICE: Allen, I.T. FIELD NO. 5759

Dawes' Roll No.	NAME	Relationship to Person First Named	AGE	SEX	BLOOD	TRIBAL ENROLLMENT Year	County	No.
15528	1 Dendy, Annie L	First Named	24	F	1/8			
15529	2 " Samuel M	Son	8	M	1/16			
15530	3 " Minnie J	Dau	5	F	1/16			
15531	4 " James L	son	3	M	1/16			
15754	5 " Ozella	Dau	1	F	1/16			

ENROLLMENT OF NOS. 1-2-3-4 HEREON APPROVED BY THE SECRETARY OF INTERIOR May 9 1904

ENROLLMENT OF NOS. 5 HEREON ~~APPROVED BY THE SECRETARY~~ OF INTERIOR Dec 15 1904

For child of No1 see N.B. (Apr 26-06) Card #390
" " " " " " (March 3-05) " #968

TRIBAL ENROLLMENT OF PARENTS

Name of Father	Year	County	Name of Mother	Year	County
1 Samuel C Williams	Dead	Choctaw	Paralee Williams	Dead	Non citizen
2 D. B. Dendy		non-citizen	No1		
3 "		"	No1		
4 "		"	No1		
5 "		"	No1		

Nos 1 and 2 admitted by Commission in 1896 Choctaw case #634

~~Nos 1-4 inclusive transferred from Choctaw Card R535~~
~~See decision of March 15,1904~~

No. 5 was born July 31, 1901: application for enrollment alleged to have been made Nov 4, 1902. Commission directed by Department to receive and consider application ~~by letters of Aug 4, 1904 and Oct. 3, 1904~~
No.5 enrolled on this card Oct 3, 1904, under resolution of Commission of that date.

~~Date of Application~~ for Enrollment.
~~June 7, 1900~~
Date of Transfer to this Card
Apr 13 1904

RESIDENCE: COUNTY. **Choctaw Nation** #5760 **Choctaw Roll** *(Not Including Freedmen)*

POST OFFICE: Caddo I.T.

Dawes' Roll No.		NAME	Relationship to Person First Named	AGE	SEX	BLOOD	TRIBAL ENROLLMENT Year	County	No.
15532	1	Adams, John S		33	M	1/8	1896	Atoka	87
	2								
	3								
	4								
	5								
	6								
	7								
	8								
	9								
	10								
	11								
	12								
	13								
	14								
	15								
	16								
	17								

ENROLLMENT OF NOS. 1 HEREON APPROVED BY THE SECRETARY OF INTERIOR MAY 9 1904

TRIBAL ENROLLMENT OF PARENTS

	Name of Father	Year	County	Name of Mother	Year	County
1	Hugh N Adams		Intermarried	Polly Adams	Dead	Skullyville
2						
3						
4						
5						
6	No1 on 1896 Choctaw roll as Jno S. Adams					
7						
8	No1 transferred from Choctaw Card D. 398 See decision of March 15, 1904					
9						
10						
11						
12						
13						
14						
15						
16						transfer date to this card
17			Sept 1/99 Date of Application for Enrollment.			APR 13 1904

RESIDENCE: Choctaw Nation ~~COUNTY.~~ **Choctaw Nation** Choctaw Roll (Not Including Freedmen) CARD NO.
POST OFFICE: Valliant I.T. FIELD NO. 5761

Dawes' Roll No.	NAME	Relationship to Person First Named	AGE	SEX	BLOOD	TRIBAL ENROLLMENT Year	County	No.
IW 1949	1 Fowler, Hosea L		43	M	I.W.	1896	Towson	14527
15533	2 " Josephine	Wife	35	F	Full	1896	"	12603
15534	3 " John	Son	18	M	1/4	1896	"	4125
15535	4 " David	Son	16	M	1/4	1896	"	4126
15536	5 " Moses	Son	14	M	1/4	1896	"	4127
15537	6 " Sarah	Dau	3	F	1/2			
15538	7 " Rosetta	Dau	1	F	1/2			
15539	8 Wilson, George	StepSon	18	M	1/2			
	9							
	10							
	11							
	12							
	13							
	14							
	15							
	16							
	17							

ENROLLMENT OF NOS. 2-3-4-5-6-7-8 HEREON APPROVED BY THE SECRETARY OF INTERIOR May 9, 1904

ENROLLMENT OF NOS. 1 HEREON APPROVED BY THE SECRETARY OF INTERIOR Aug 3, 1904

TRIBAL ENROLLMENT OF PARENTS

	Name of Father	Year	County	Name of Mother	Year	County
1	N. M. Fowler		non citizen	Margaret C. Fowler		non-citizen
2	Geo Williams	Dead	Towson	Sallie Williams	Dead	Towson
3	No.1			Minerva Fowler	"	
4	No.1			" "	"	
5	No.1			" "	"	
6	No.1			No.2		
7	No.1			No.2		
8	Louie Wilson	Dead	Towson	No.2		
9						

10 No2 on 1896 roll as Josephine Victor
11 No2 on 1893 roll as Josephine Victor Towson Co No 399
No3 on 1893 roll Towson Co as Johnny Fowler No 105
12 No4 on 1893 roll Towson Co No 106
13 No5 on 1893 roll Towson Co No 107
14 No8 on 1893 roll Towson Co No 480
15 Nos 7and8 Evidence of birth filed
Nos 108 inclusive transferred from Choctaw Card D127
16 See decision of March 15, 1904
17 6/10/15 Ages hereon are calculated to Sept 25, 1902

Date of Application for Enrollment. April 26/99

For child of No3 see NB (Apr 26 1906) #23
" " " Nos1&2" " (March 3, 1905) #1106

Date of transfer to this card. Apr 13, 1904

RESIDENCE: COUNTY. **Choctaw Nation** Choc[redacted]ll [redacted]
POST OFFICE: Summerfield, I.T. (Not Includ[redacted]) [redacted]762

Dawes' Roll No.	NAME	Relationship to Person First Named	AGE	SEX	BLOOD	T[redacted]ROLLMENT Year	County	No.
15540	1 Russell, Minnie		21	F	1/2	1893	Sugar Loaf	330
	2							
	3							
	4							
	5							
	6							
	7							
	8							
	9							
	10							
	11							
	12							
	13							
	14							
	15							
	16							
	17							

ENROLLMENT
OF NOS. 1 HEREON
APPROVED BY THE SECRETARY
OF INTERIOR MAY 9 1904

ENROLLMENT OF PARENTS

	Name of Father	Y[redacted]	[redacted]nty	Name of Mother	Year	County
1	Sampson Holson	189[redacted]		Sallie Holson		Cherokee
2						
3						
4						
5						
6						
7						

8 No1 on 1893 roll as Minnie Holson
9 No1 is wife of George Russell a Cherokee citizen
No1 transferred from Choctaw Card # D. Choctaw card D666
10 ~~See decision of March 15, 1904~~

~~Oct 7/01~~ Date of Application for Enrollment.

~~transfer date~~ to this card APR 13 1904

RESIDENCE: Cherokee Nation ~~COUNTY.~~ **Choctaw Nation** **Choctaw Roll** *(Not Including Freedmen)* CARD NO.
POST OFFICE: Hanson I.T. FIELD NO. 5763

Dawes' Roll No.	NAME	Relationship to Person First Named	AGE	SEX	BLOOD	TRIBAL ENROLLMENT Year	County	No.
15541	1 Seabolt, Mollie Ann		23	F	1/2	1896	Gaines	5317
	2							
	3							
	4							
	5							
	6							
	7							
	8							
	9							
	10							
	11							
	12							
	13							
	14							
	15							
	16							
	17							

ENROLLMENT
OF NOS. 1 HEREON
APPROVED BY THE SECRETARY
OF INTERIOR MAY 9 1904

TRIBAL ENROLLMENT OF PARENTS

Name of Father	Year	County	Name of Mother	Year	County
1 Sampson Holson	1896	Gaines	Sallie Holson		Cherokee
2					
3					
4					
5					

6 No1 is wife of John Ellis Seabolt

7 No1 on 1893 roll Sugar Loaf County Page 32 No 329 as Mollie Holson

8 ~~No1 on 896 roll as Mollie A Holson~~

9

10 No1 transferred from Choctaw Card D 665

See decision of March 15, 1904

Date of Application for Enrollment: Oct 2/01

transfer date to this card APR 13 1904

RESIDENCE: Cherokee Nation ~~COUNTY.~~ **Choctaw Nation** Choctaw Roll (Not Including Freedmen) CARD NO.
POST OFFICE: Gann I.T. FIELD NO. 5

Dawes' Roll No.	NAME	Relationship to Person First Named	AGE	SEX	BLOOD	TRIBAL ENROLLMENT Year	County	No.
15542	1 Holson, Ida May		18	F	1/2	1893	Sugar Loaf	331
15543	2 " Lula Belle	Sis	14	F	1/2	1893	" "	332
15544	3 " William H H	Bro	11	M	1/2	1893	" "	333
15545	4 " Sampson S.N.	Bro	10	M	1/2	1893	" "	334
	5							
	6							
	7							
	8							
	9							
	10							
	11							
	12							
	13							
	14							
	15							
	16							
	17							

ENROLLMENT OF NOS. 1-2-3-4 HEREON APPROVED BY THE SECRETARY OF INTERIOR MAY 9 1904

TRIBAL ENROLLMENT OF PARENTS

Name of Father	Year	County	Name of Mother	Year	County
1 Sampson Holson	1896	Gaines	Sallie Holson		Che
2 " "	"	"	" "		
3 " "	"	"	" "		
4 " "	"	"	" "		
5					

6 No1 on 1893 roll as Ida Holson
7 No3 on 1893 roll as H. Holson
No4 on 1893 roll as S.S. Holson
8 ~~Nos 1-4 inclusive transferred from Choctaw Card D664~~
9 See decision of March 15, 1904
10 For child of No.1 see N.B. (Apr 26, 1906) Card No 175

transfer date ~~to this card~~ APR 13 1904

Date of Application for Enrollment. Oct 2/01

RESIDENCE: Choctaw Nation COUNTY. Cho[redacted] Nation **Choctaw Roll** [redacted]
POST OFFICE: Garretts Bluff, Texas *(Not Including Freedmen)* FIELD NO. 5765

Dawes' Roll No.	NAME	Relationship to Person First Named	AGE	SEX	BLOOD	TRIBAL ENROLLMENT Year	County	No.
15546	1 Crowder, Ida	First Named	9	F	1/8	1893	Jackson	113
IW 1563	2 Buckhanon, Nanie[sic]	Mother	23	F	I.W.			
	3							
	4							
	5							
	6							
	7							
	8							
	9							
	10							
	11							
	12							
	13							
	14							
	15							
	16							
	17							

ENROLLMENT OF NOS. 1 HEREON APPROVED BY THE SECRETARY OF INTERIOR MAY 9 1904

ENROLLMENT OF NOS. 2 HEREON APPROVED BY THE SECRETARY OF INTERIOR AUG 2 - 1906

TRIBAL ENROLLMENT OF PARENTS

Name of Father	Year	County	Name of Mother	Year	County
1 Richard Crowder	Dead	Jackson	Nannie Keaton		noncitizen
2 Hiram Hankins			Mattie Hankins	Dead	noncitizen

No2 was formerly wife of Richard Crowder, deceased whose name appears in 1893 Leased District Pay Roll, Kiamitia County No. 110

No.1 transferred from Choctaw Card # D.581
See decision of March 15 1904

No2 placed hereon March 14, 1906 under order of Commissioner to the Five Civilized Tri[redacted] date holding application was made for her enrollment within the time provided by Act of Congress approved July 1, 1902 (32 Stat 641)

No2 GRANTED APR 16 1906

Date of Application for Enrollment. 8/22/1900

transfer date to this card APR 13 1904

Choctaw By Blood Enrollment Cards 1898-1914

RESIDENCE: Choctaw Nation COUNTY. **Choctaw Nation** **Choctaw Roll** *(Not Including Freedmen)* CARD NO.
POST OFFICE: Muldrow I.T. FIELD NO. 5766

Dawes' Roll No.	NAME	Relationship to Person First Named	AGE	SEX	BLOOD	TRIBAL ENROLLMENT Year	County	No.
16647	1 Fargo, Isaac	First Named	21	M	3/16			
	2							
	3							
	4							
	5							
	6							
	7							
	8							
	9							
	10							
	11							
	12							
	13							
	14							
	15							
	16							
	17							

ENROLLMENT
OF NOS. 1 HEREON
APPROVED BY THE SECRETARY
OF INTERIOR MAY 9 1904

TRIBAL ENROLLMENT OF PARENTS

Name of Father	Year	County	Name of Mother	Year	County
1 Chas A Fargo		Cherokee	Narcis Fargo	Dead	
2					
3					
4					
5					

6 No1 admitted by Commission in 1896 Choctaw Case #489

7

8 No1 transferred from Choctaw Card # D. 490
~~See decision of March 15, 1904~~

9

10 For child of No1 see NB (Apr 26-06) Card #839

~~9/14/99~~ Date of Application for Enrollment.

~~Transfer date~~ to this card APR 13 1904

RESIDENCE: COUNTY. **Choct[redacted]w Roll** (Not Including Freedmen) CARD NO.

POST OFFICE: Durant I.T. FIELD NO. 5767

Dawes' Roll No.	NAME	Relationship to Person First Named	AGE	SEX	BLOOD	TRIBAL ENROLLMENT Year	County	No.
IW855	1 McCurtain, Clara E		28	F	I.W.			
	2							
	3							
	4							
	5							
	6							
	7							
	8							
	9							
	10							
	11							
	12							
	13							
	14							
	15							
	16							
	17							

ENROLLMENT OF NOS. 1 HEREON APPROVED BY THE SECRETARY OF INTERIOR MAY 21 1904

TRIBAL ENROLLMENT OF PARENTS

Name of Father	Year	County	Name of Mother	Year	County
1 Geo M Hagood		noncitizen	Anna Hagood		noncitizen

No1 is now the wife of Ben Mc Curtain on Choctaw card #5394

No1 transferred from Chickasaw card D 366

See decision of March 15, 1904

Date of Application for Enrollment: Aug 25/99

transfer date to this card: APR 13 1904

RESIDENCE: COUNTY. **Choctaw Nation** **Choctaw Roll** *(Not Including Freedmen)* CARD NO.
POST OFFICE: Purcell, I.T. FIELD NO. 5768

Dawes' Roll No.	NAME	Relationship to Person First Named	AGE	SEX	BLOOD	TRIBAL ENROLLMENT Year	County	No.
15548	1 Hammons, Czarena		29	F	1/4	1896	Tobucksy	10243
15549	2 Parnell, Hoyt	Son	10	M	1/8	1896	"	10244
15550	3 " , Ewing	Son	7	M	1/8	1896	"	10245

ENROLLMENT OF NOS. 1 - 2 - 3 HEREON APPROVED BY THE SECRETARY OF INTERIOR MAY 9 1904

TRIBAL ENROLLMENT OF PARENTS

Name of Father	Year	County	Name of Mother	Year	County
1 Milo A Hoyt	Dead	Sans Bois	Harriet Mattix	1896	Tobucksy
2 Jesse Parnell		noncitizen	No.1		
3 " "		"	No.1		

~~No1 on 1896 roll a Serena Parnell~~
No2 on 1896 roll as White Parnell

~~Nos 1 and 2 transferred from Choctaw Card D465~~
~~No3 transferred from Choctaw Card # D. Choctaw card #4529~~
See decision of March 15, 1904.

April 24, 1902

~~Sept 81/99~~ Date of Application for Enrollment. ~~transferred to~~ this card APR 13 1904

Choctaw By Blood Enrollment Cards 1898-1914

RESIDENCE: Choctaw Nation ~~COUNTY.~~ **Choctaw Nation** **Choctaw Roll** *(Not Including Freedmen)* CARD NO.
POST OFFICE: Red Oak Ind Ter FIELD NO. 5769

Dawes' Roll No.	NAME	Relationship to Person First Named	AGE	SEX	BLOOD	TRIBAL ENROLLMENT Year	County	No.
15601	1 Suddith, Ben		26	M	Full	1896	Skullyville	8487

ENROLLMENT
~~OF NOS. HEREON~~
APPROVED BY THE SECRETARY
OF INTERIOR SEP 22 1904

TRIBAL ENROLLMENT OF PARENTS

Name of Father	Year	County	Name of Mother	Year	County
1 Don't know	Dead	Mississippi	Lue Suddith	Dead	Choctaw

6 On 1893 Leased district pay roll Sugar Loaf County as Ben Sakke
On 1896 Choctaw census roll as Ben Mose
7 ~~Claims to have been admitted by Choctaw Council about 1892.~~
8 Transferred from Choctaw Card # D994

12/16/16

~~Date of Application~~ for Enrollment.
Dec 16 1902

RESIDENCE: Choctaw Nation ~~COUNTY.~~ **Choctaw Nation** Choctaw Roll (Not Including Freedmen) CARD NO.
POST OFFICE: Towson County Cairo I.T. May 7/04 FIELD NO. 5770

Dawes' Roll No.	NAME	Relationship to Person First Named	AGE	SEX	BLOOD	TRIBAL ENROLLMENT Year	County	No.
15602	1 Harris, Annie		24	F	Full	1896	Towson	5482
	2							
	3							
	4							
	5							
	6							
	7							
	8							
	9							
	10							
	11							
	12							
	13							
	14							
	15							
	16							
	17							

ENROLLMENT
OF NOS. 1 HEREON
APPROVED BY THE SECRETARY
OF INTERIOR Sept 22, 1904

TRIBAL ENROLLMENT OF PARENTS

Name of Father	Year	County	Name of Mother	Year	County
1 King Harris	Dead	Towson	Elizabeth Harris	Dead	Towson
2					
3					
4					

5 Transferred from Choctaw Card # D927.
6 See testimony of No1 taken at Atoka I.T. April 25, 1904.
7 ~~*Duplicate enrollment of No 15602: "Not entitled to land or money under this number"~~
8 ~~See I O L G.F #916 194~~ Notation hereon placed through error, see Choctaw
9 Census card 4184

Date of Application for Enrollment: Dec 24/02

Transfer date ~~on this card~~ May 7, 1904

RESIDENCE: Blue COUNTY. **Choctaw Nation** **Choctaw Roll** *(Not Including Freedmen)* CARD NO.
POST OFFICE: Caddo, Ind Ter FIELD NO. 5771

Dawes' Roll No.	NAME	Relationship to Person First Named	AGE	SEX	BLOOD	TRIBAL ENROLLMENT Year	County	No.
15603	1 Colbert, Elijah Ruben		14	M	Full	1896	Tobucksy	2378
	2							
	3							
	4							
	5							
	6							
	7							
	8							
	9							
	10							
	11 ENROLLMENT							
	12 OF NOS. 1 HEREON APPROVED BY THE SECRETARY							
	13 OF INTERIOR Sept 22 1904							
	14							
	15							
	16							
	17							

TRIBAL ENROLLMENT OF PARENTS

Name of Father	Year	County	Name of Mother	Year	County
1 Ruben Colbert	Dead	Gaines	Sissie Colbert	Dead	Gaines
2					
3					
4					
5					
6 Also on 1893 leased district payment roll Gaines County page 7 #65 as Elijah Colbert					
7 Transferred from Choctaw Card # D. 926					
8					
9					
10					
11					
12					
13					
14				Date of Application for Enrollment.	12/24/02
15					
16				transfer date to this card	May 14, 1904
17					

RESIDENCE: Choctaw Nation COUNTY. **Choctaw Nation** Choctaw Roll *(Not Including Freedmen)* CARD NO.
POST OFFICE: Chula, I.T. FIELD NO. 5772

Dawes' Roll No.	NAME	Relationship to Person First Named	AGE	SEX	BLOOD	TRIBAL ENROLLMENT Year	County	No.
IW950	1 Woolery, Dona		16	F	I.W.			
	2							
	3							
	4							
	5							
	6							
	7							
	8							
	9							
	10							
	11							
	12							
	13							
	14							
	15							
	16							
	17							

ENROLLMENT OF NOS. 1 HEREON APPROVED BY THE SECRETARY OF INTERIOR AUG 3 1904

TRIBAL ENROLLMENT OF PARENTS

Name of Father	Year	County	Name of Mother	Year	County
1 Albert Cherry		non-citizen	Julia Cherry		non-citizen
2					
3					
4					
5					
6 No.1 is wife of James Woolery on Choctaw card #1373					
7 No.1 transferred from Choctaw Card # D. 847. See decision of May 28-1904.					
8					
9					
10					
11					
12					
13					
14					
15					
16					transfer date ~~on this card~~
17		Nov 28/02	Date of Application for Enrollment.		June 13-1904

Choctaw By Blood Enrollment Cards 1898-1914

RESIDENCE: Choctaw Nation COUNTY. **Choctaw Nation** **Choctaw Roll** *(Not Including Freedmen)* CARD NO.
POST OFFICE: Massey, Ind. Ter. FIELD NO.

Dawes' Roll No.	NAME	Relationship to Person First Named	AGE	SEX	BLOOD	TRIBAL ENROLLMENT Year	County	No.
IW951	1 Massey, Arizona C		21	F	I.W.			

ENROLLMENT OF NOS. 1 HEREON APPROVED BY THE SECRETARY OF INTERIOR AUG 3 1904

TRIBAL ENROLLMENT OF PARENTS

	Name of Father	Year	County	Name of Mother	Year	County
1	James Crouch	dead	non-citizen	Lucy Crouch	dead	non-citizen

6 No.1 is the wife of Oliver Massey on Choctaw card #4452
7 No.1 transferred from Choctaw Card D-795. See decision of May 27-1904
For child of No1 see N.B. (Apr 26, 1906) Card No. 194
8 " " " " " " (Mar. 3, 1905) " " 628

Date of Application for Enrollment. Sept 20/02

transfer date to this card June 12-1904

RESIDENCE: Pontotoc COUNTY. **Choctaw Nation** Choctaw Roll (Not Including Freedmen) CARD NO.
POST OFFICE: Center, Ind. Ter. FIELD NO. 5774

Dawes' Roll No.	NAME	Relationship to Person First Named	AGE	SEX	BLOOD	TRIBAL ENROLLMENT Year	County	No.
IW952	1 Long, Charley C		27	M	I.W.			
	2							
	3							
	4							
	5							
	6							
	7							
	8							
	9							
	10							
	11							
	12							
	13							
	14							
	15							
	16							
	17							

ENROLLMENT OF NOS. 1 HEREON APPROVED BY THE SECRETARY OF INTERIOR AUG 3 1904

TRIBAL ENROLLMENT OF PARENTS

Name of Father	Year	County	Name of Mother	Year	County
1 William H. Long		non-citizen	Lou Long		non-citizen
2					
3					
4					
5					

6 No.1 was married to Veda Long, identified on 1893 and 1896 Choctaw rolls Atoka Co
7 who died on February 19, 1900.
8 No.1 transferred from Choctaw Card # D. 57. See decision of May 27-1904

Date of Application for Enrollment. 10/11/98

Transfer date to this card June 12-1904

17 P.O. Ada, I.T. 7/20/04

Choctaw By Blood Enrollment Cards 1898-1914

RESIDENCE: Sugar Loaf COUNTY. **Choctaw Nation** **Choctaw Roll** *(Not Including Freedmen)* CARD NO.
POST OFFICE: Red Oak, I.T. FIELD NO. 5775

Dawes' Roll No.	NAME	Relationship to Person First Named	AGE	SEX	BLOOD	TRIBAL ENROLLMENT Year	County	No.
IW953	1 Ish, William W		62	M	I.W.			
	2							
	3							
	4							
	5							
	6							
	7							
	8							
	9							
	10							
	11							
	12							
	13							
	14							
	15							
	16							
	17							

ENROLLMENT OF NOS. 1 HEREON APPROVED BY THE SECRETARY OF INTERIOR AUG 3 1904

TRIBAL ENROLLMENT OF PARENTS

Name of Father	Year	County	Name of Mother	Year	County
1 John Ish	Dead	Non-citizen	Cyntha Ish	Dead	Non-Citizen
2					
3					
4					
5					
6 No1 was admitted in Choctaw 1896 case No 1103					
7					
8					
9 No 1 transferred from Choctaw Card # D. 264. See decision of May 27-04					
10					
11					
12					
13					
14					
15					transfer date
16		6/21/99	Date of Application for Enrollment.		to this card
17					June 12-04

RESIDENCE: Skullyville COUNTY. **Choctaw Nation** **Choctaw Roll** *(Not Including Freedmen)* CARD NO.
POST OFFICE: Fort Smith, Ark. FIELD NO. **5776**

Dawes' Roll No.		NAME	Relationship to Person First Named	AGE	SEX	BLOOD	TRIBAL ENROLLMENT		
							Year	County	No.
15604	1	Le Flore, Chester H		26	M	1/16	1896	Skullyville	7748
IW986	2	" Florence H	wife	23	F	I.W.			
15605	3	" Chester H, Jr	Son	1	M	1/32			

ENROLLMENT OF NOS. 2 HEREON APPROVED BY THE SECRETARY OF INTERIOR SEP 22 1904

ENROLLMENT OF NOS. 1 and 3 HEREON APPROVED BY THE SECRETARY OF INTERIOR SEP 22 1904

TRIBAL ENROLLMENT OF PARENTS

	Name of Father	Year	County	Name of Mother	Year	County
1	Campbell Le Flore	dead	Skullyville	Ida L. Le Flore now Foucar	1896	Intermarried
2	J.B. Harwood		non-citizen	Sarah Harwood		non-citizen
3	No.1			No.2		

Nos. 1 and 3 transferred from Choctaw Card D188. See decision of May 27-04
No.2 " " " " D623 " " " " "
~~No.3 Born July 20, 1902; enrolled Aug. 26, 1902~~

~~5/31/99~~ Date of Application for Enrollment.

Date of Transfer to this Card. June 12-1904

Choctaw By Blood Enrollment Cards 1898-1914

RESIDENCE: Chickasaw Nation ~~COUNTY.~~ **Choctaw Nation** **Choctaw Roll** (*Not Including Freedmen*) CARD NO.
POST OFFICE: Stuart, Ind. Ter. FIELD NO. 5777

Dawes' Roll No.	NAME	Relationship to Person First Named	AGE	SEX	BLOOD	TRIBAL ENROLLMENT Year	County	No.
15606	1 Jones, John F.	First Named	25	M	1/8	1885	Sugar Loaf	518
15607	2 " Loney Ann	Dau	2	F	1/16			
15608	3 " Lafayette	Son	6mo	M	1/16			
15609	4 " Josephine	Dau	5mo	F	1/16			
IW 1227	5 " Mary	Wife	27	F	I.W.			
	6							
	7							
	8							
	9							
	10							
	11							
	12							
	13							
	14							
	15							
	16							
	17							

ENROLLMENT OF NOS. 5 HEREON APPROVED BY THE SECRETARY OF INTERIOR DEC 13 1904

ENROLLMENT OF NOS. 1,2,3 and 4 HEREON APPROVED BY THE SECRETARY OF INTERIOR SEP 22 1904

TRIBAL ENROLLMENT OF PARENTS

	Name of Father	Year	County	Name of Mother	Year	County
1	Daniel Jones		non citizen	Emily Jones	Dead	Choctaw
2	No.1			Mary Jones		
3	No.1			" "		
4	No.1			" "		
5	Wiley Brown		non citizen	Angeline Brown		non citizen
6						
7						

8 No.4 Born Sept. 7-1901. Enrolled Feby 15-1902
9 Nos. 1,2,3 and 4 transferred from Choc Card # D-304. See decision of Jun. 16-04
Wife of No1 on Choctaw card #D304
10 ~~No.5 transferred from Choctaw Card # D. 304 Nov. 26, 1904; see decision of Nov. 3, 1904~~
11 No 5 originally listed for enrollment on Choctaw card #D-304 Aug. 8/99
12 For children of Nos 1&5 see NB (March 3-1905) #799

transfer date to this card
July 2-1904

17 PO Celestine I.T. 4/5/05 Aug 8/99 **Date of Application for Enrollment.**

RESIDENCE: Sugar Loaf COUNTY. **Choctaw Nation** **Choctaw Roll** *(Not Including Freedmen)* CARD NO.
POST OFFICE: Caston, I.T. FIELD NO. 5778

Dawes' Roll No.	NAME	55	AGE	SEX	BLOOD	TRIBAL ENROLLMENT Year	County	No.
IW954	1 Jones, Daniel		M	I.W.				
	2							
	3							
	4							
	5							
	6							
	7							
	8							
	9							
	10							
	11							
	12							
	13							
	14							
	15							
	16							
	17 No.1 now in House of Correction, Detroit Mich. 12/17/05							

ENROLLMENT ~~OF NOS.~~ 1 ~~HEREON~~ APPROVED BY THE SECRETARY OF INTERIOR AUG 3 1904

TRIBAL ENROLLMENT OF PARENTS

Name of Father	Year	County	Name of Mother	Year	County
1 John Jones	Dead	Non citizen			non citizen
2					
3					
4					
5					
6 Sent to penitentiary for life					
7 No.1 transferred from Choctaw Card # D214. See decision of June 16-1904					
8					
9 First married in 68 to Lucrec[illegible] Folsom who died in 69					
10 Feb. 16-72 married Emily Choat [illegible] Sugar Loaf #516					
11					
12					
13					
14					
15					
16		~~6/6/99~~	~~Date of Application~~ for Enrollment.		~~transfer date to this card~~
17					7/2/04

RESIDENCE: Sugar Loaf COUNTY. **Choctaw Nation** **Choctaw Roll** *(Not Including Freedmen)* [redacted]9

POST OFFICE: Thomasville I.T.

Dawes' Roll No.		NAME	Relationship to Person First Named	AGE	SEX	BLOOD	TRIBAL ENROLLMENT Year	County	No.
15610	1	Davis, Marshall A	Named	30	M	1/4	1896	Sugar Loaf	3263
15611	2	" William Z	Son	4	M	1/8			
15612	3	" Oria	Dau	2	F	1/8			
15613	4	" Marshall Joseph	Son	1	M	1/8			

ENROLLMENT OF NOS 1,2,3 and 4 HEREON APPROVED BY THE SECRETARY OF INTERIOR SEP 22 1904

TRIBAL ENROLLMENT OF PARENTS

	[redacted]	Year	County	Name of Mother	Year	County
1	Zach Davis	Dead	noncitizen	Emily Davis	Dead	Eagle
2	No.1			Emma Davis		noncitizen
3	No.1			" "		"
4	No.1			" "		"

Nos 1,2,3 and 4 enrolled by Decision of Commission of July 20, 1903
Record and decision with protest of attorneys for Choctaw and Chickasaw Nations
forwarded Department Aug [illegible]

~~Nos.1to4 inclusive transferred from Choctaw Card D191~~
See decision of Commission of July 20, 1903 affirmed
by Department July 14, 1904 (I.T.D. 8291-1903)

~~No3 Enrolled Aug. 29, 1900~~
No4 Born Aug 10, 1902 Enrolled Dec. 24, 1902
For child of No1 see NB (Apr 26-06) Card #431
ages given hereon as of September 25, 1902.

Date of Application for Enrollment.
6/5/99

Date of Transfer to this Card.
JUL 26 1904

RESIDENCE: Sugar Loaf COUNTY. **Choctaw Nation** **Choctaw Roll** *(Not Including Freedmen)* CARD NO.
POST OFFICE: Page, I.T. FIELD NO. 5780

Dawes' Roll No.		NAME	Relationship to Person First Named	AGE	SEX	BLOOD	TRIBAL ENROLLMENT Year	County	No.
15614	1	Davis, Burk		32	M	1/4	1896	Sugar Loaf	3251
IW987	2	" Sarah Ann	Wife	27	F	I.W.			
15615	3	" Lillie M	Dau	9	F	1/8	1896	Sugar Loaf	3252
15616	4	" Vinan J	Son	7	M	1/8	1896	" "	3253
15617	5	" Mary J	Dau	6	F	1/8	1896	" "	3254
15618	6	" John R	Son	4	M	1/8			
15619	7	" Sherm Henry	Son	1	M	1/8			

Nos. 1to7 incl. enrolled by decision of Commission of July 20, 1903
Record and decision with protest of attorneys for Choctaw and Chickasaw Nations
forwarded Department

ENROLLMENT
OF NOS. 2 HEREON
APPROVED BY THE SECRETARY
OF INTERIOR SEP 22 1904

ENROLLMENT
OF NOS. 1,3,4,5,6 and 7 HEREON
APPROVED BY THE SECRETARY
OF INTERIOR AUG 3 1904

TRIBAL ENROLLMENT OF PARENTS

	Name of Father	Year	County	Name of Mother	Year	County
1	Zack Davis	Dead	noncitizen	Emily Davis	Dead	Eagle
2	David Brewer	"	" "	Elizabeth Brewer	"	noncitizen
3	No1			No2		
4	No1			No2		
5	No1			No2		
6	No1			No2		
7	No1			No2		

No4 on 1896 roll as Vinnen J Davis
No7 Born Sept. 25, 1901. Enrolled Dec. 24, 1902

Nos 1-7 inclusive transferred from Choctaw Card # D. 192. See decision of July 20, 1903
Affirmed by Department July 14, 1904 (I.T.D. 8291-1903 etc.)
For child of Nos 1 and 2 see NB (Mar 3 '05) #428.

Heavener I.T. 9/23/04

Date of Application for Enrollment 6/5/99

Date of Transfer to this Card. JUL 26 1904

RESIDENCE: Chickasaw Nation COUNTY. **Choctaw Nation** **Choctaw Roll** *(Not Including Freedmen)* CARD NO.
POST OFFICE: Ardmore, I.T. FIELD NO. 5781

Dawes' Roll No.		NAME	Relationship to Person First Named	AGE	SEX	BLOOD	TRIBAL ENROLLMENT Year	County	No.
IW 1957	1	Blake, L. L.		58	M	I.W.	1896	Chick Dist	14365
	2								
	3								
	4								
	5								
	6								
	7	ENROLLMENT							
	8	OF NOS. 1 HEREON							
	9	APPROVED BY THE SECRETARY OF INTERIOR Aug 20 1904							
	10								
	11								
	12								
	13								
	14								
	15								
	16								
	17	See Pet #C-55 as to children							

TRIBAL ENROLLMENT OF PARENTS

	Name of Father	Year	County	Name of Mother	Year	County
1	T.K. Blake	Dead	non-citizen	Clara T. Blake	Dead	non-citizen
2						
3						
4						
5						
6	No.1 denied by Commission in 1896 Choctaw Case #902					
7	No.1 admitted by U.S. Court Ardmore, I.T. Dec 21, 1897 Court Case #122					
8	~~No. 1 admitted by Choctaw and Chickasaw Citizenship Court~~					
9	Case 98 T June 30, 1904					
10						
11	No.1 transferred from Choctaw Card # 5091					
12						
13						
14						
15						~~Date of transfer~~
16			~~9/22/98~~	Date of Application for Enrollment.		to this card
17						Jul 29 1904

RESIDENCE: Choctaw Nation COUNTY. **Choctaw Nati[redacted] Choctaw Roll** (Not Including Freedmen) CARD NO.
POST OFFICE: Paula Valley I.T. FIELD NO. 5782

Dawes' Roll No.	NAME	Relationship to Person First Named	AGE	SEX	BLOOD	TRIBAL ENROLLMENT Year	County	No.
IW958	1 Brooks, G.W.		36	M	I W			
	2							
	3							
	4							
	5							
	6							
	7							
	8							
	9							
	10							
	11							
	12							
	13							
	14							
	15							
	16							
	17 See Petition No C-18							

ENROLLMENT
OF NOS. 1 HEREON
APPROVED BY THE SECRETARY
OF INTERIOR AUG 20 1904

TRIBAL ENROLLMENT OF PARENTS

Name of Father	Year	County	Name of Mother	Year	County
Brooks	Dead	noncitizen	Ada Brooks		noncitizen

7 No1 denied [by] Commission in 1896 Choctaw case #899
8 No.2 admitted by U.S. Court Southern District March 12, 1898
Court Case [illegible]
9
10 No1 admitted by Choctaw and Chickasaw Citizenship Court
11 Case No 47 January 30 1905
12 No1 transferred from Choctaw Card D# 14
13
14
15
16
17 Sept 12/98 Date of Application for Enrollment. JUL 29 1904

RESIDENCE: Chickasaw Nation COUNTY. **Choctaw Nation** **Choctaw Roll** (*Not Including Freedmen*) CARD NO.
POST OFFICE: Ardmore, I.T. FIELD NO. 5783

Dawes' Roll No.	NAME	Relationship to Person First Named	AGE	SEX	BLOOD	TRIBAL ENROLLMENT Year	County	No.
15555	1 Boyd, John T.		27	M	1/16	1896	Atoka	2001
15556	2 " Louis H	Bro	21	M	1/16	1896	"	2002
	3							
	4							
	5							
	6							
	7							
	8							
	9							
	10							
	11							
	12							
	13							
	14							
	15							
	16							
	17							

ENROLLMENT
OF NOS. 1 and 2 HEREON
APPROVED BY THE SECRETARY
OF INTERIOR Aug 20 1904

TRIBAL ENROLLMENT OF PARENTS

Name of Father	Year	County	Name of Mother	Year	County
1 John T Boyd	Dead	non-citizen	Annie Boyd	Dead	Choctaw
2 " "	"	"	" "	"	"
3					
4					
5					

6 Nos 1 and 2 denied by Commission in 1896 Choctaw Case #265
7 Nos 1 and 2 admitted by U.S. Court Ardmore I.T. Dec 21 1897 Court Case #113
8 ~~Nos 1-2 admitted by Choctaw and Chickasaw Citizenship Court~~
9 Case #36T May 25, 1904
10 Nos 1-2 transferred from Choctaw Card #5141

9/23/98 Date of Application for Enrollment. Jul 29 1904

RESIDENCE: Chickasaw Nation COUNTY. **Choctaw Nation** **Choctaw Roll** *(Not Including Freedmen)* CARD NO.
POST OFFICE: Maxwell I.T. FIELD NO. **5784**

Dawes' Roll No.	NAME	Relationship to Person First Named	AGE	SEX	BLOOD	TRIBAL ENROLLMENT Year	County	No.
15557	1 Cotten, E.W.		36	M	1/16	1896	Chick Dist	3074
IW 1364	2 Cotton[sic], Minnie	Wife	31	F	I.W.	1896	" "	14439

ENROLLMENT OF NOS. 1 HEREON APPROVED BY THE SECRETARY OF INTERIOR AUG 20 1904

ENROLLMENT OF NOS. 2 HEREON APPROVED BY THE SECRETARY OF INTERIOR MAR 14 1905

TRIBAL ENROLLMENT OF PARENTS

Name of Father	Year	County	Name of Mother	Year	County
1 David B Cotten	Dead	noncitizen	Susan L Cotten	Dead	Choctaw roll
2 B. NeSmith		" "	Elizabeth J NeSmith	"	non citizen

No.2 on Choctaw 1896 Census roll as Minnie T. Cotton
No1 on Choctaw 1896 Census roll as E.M. Cotton
No.2 denied by Com in 1896 case #. in 96 Case #930
~~No1 denied by Com in 1896 case # in 96 Case #930~~
Nos 1&2 admitted by U.S. Court Southern District Case #90
No2 admitted as intermarried citizen of the Choctaw Nation
by Choctaw and Chickasaw Citizenship Court Case #103T
~~No1 admitted by Choctaw Chickasaw Citizenship Court~~
Case #103T June 30, 1904
Nos 1 and 2 originally listed on Choctaw card #D46, Sept 23, 1898
No1 transferred from Choctaw Card # D46 July 29, 1904
~~No2 transferred from Choctaw Card # D46 Dec. 24, 1904~~

transfer date to this card JUL 29 1904

Sept 23/98 Date of Application for Enrollment.

RESIDENCE: Chickasaw Nation COUNTY. **Choctaw Nation** **Choctaw Roll** *(Not Including Freedmen)* CARD NO.
POST OFFICE: Comanche, I.T. FIELD NO. 5785

Dawes' Roll No.	NAME	Relationship to Person First Named	AGE	SEX	BLOOD	TRIBAL ENROLLMENT Year	County	No.
IW959	1 Johnson, G.W.	First Named	52	M	I.W.			

ENROLLMENT
OF NOS. 1 HEREON
APPROVED BY THE SECRETARY
OF INTERIOR AUG 20 1904

TRIBAL ENROLLMENT OF PARENTS

Name of Father	Year	County	Name of Mother	Year	County
1 Pleas Johnson	Dead	noncitizen	Nancy Johnson	Dead	noncitizen

No1 admitted by Commission in 1896 Choctaw case #1046

No1 admitted by U.S. Court South McAlester I.T. October 8, 1897 Court Case No 222

No1 admitted by Choctaw Chickasaw Citizenship Court Case #129T.
June 27, 1904

~~No1 transferred from Choctaw Card #5272~~
For child of No.1 see NB (March 3, 1905) #1483

~~10/17/98~~ **Date of Application for Enrollment.**

~~Date of transfer~~ to this card
JUL 29 1904

Choctaw By Blood Enrollment Cards 1898-1914

RESIDENCE: Sugar Loaf COUNTY. **Choctaw Nation** **Choctaw Roll** *(Not Including Freedmen)* CARD NO.
POST OFFICE: Minco Okla FIELD NO. 5786

Dawes' Roll No.	NAME	Relationship to Person First Named	AGE	SEX	BLOOD	TRIBAL ENROLLMENT Year	County	No.
15620	1 Satterfield, Drusilla	First Named	39	F	1/4	1896	Sugar Loaf	11225
15621	2 " James	Son	19	M	1/8	1896	" "	11226
15622	3 " Idella	Dau	15	F	1/8	1896	" "	11228
15623	4 " Bennie	Son	11	M	1/8	1896	" "	11229
15624	5 " Ida	Dau	8	F	1/8	1896	" "	11230
15625	6 " Walter	son	6	M	1/8	1896	" "	11231
15930	7 " Rufus	"	4	M	1/8	1896	" "	11232

ENROLLMENT OF NOS. 1,2,3,4,5 and 6 HEREON APPROVED BY THE SECRETARY OF INTERIOR Sep 22 1904

ENROLLMENT OF NOS. Seven HEREON APPROVED BY THE SECRETARY OF INTERIOR Aug 23 1905

TRIBAL ENROLLMENT OF PARENTS

Name of Father	Year	County	Name of Mother	Year	County
1 Snider	Dead	non-citizen	Orpie[sic] Snider	Dead	Blue
2 Robt Satterfield	1896	" "	No.1		
3 "	1896	" "	No.1		
4 "	1896	" "	No.1		
5 "	1896	" "	No.1		
6 "	1896	" "	No.1		
7 "	1896	" "	No.1		

No3 on 1896 Choctaw Census roll as Della Satterfeild[sic]
No4 " 1896 " " " " Benny "
~~No7 denied by Dawes Commission in 1896. Choctaw case #1062. No appeal.~~
~~All transferred from Choctaw Card # D 220.~~

Date of Application for Enrollment.
~~6/8/99~~

~~Listed on this card Aug. 3, 1904~~

P.O. Minco I.T. 11/21/05

Choctaw By Blood Enrollment Cards 1898-1914

RESIDENCE: COUNTY. **Choctaw Nation** **Choctaw Roll** *(Not Including Freedmen)* CARD NO.
POST OFFICE: Cleora, I.T. FIELD NO. 5787

Dawes' Roll No.	NAME	Relationship to Person First Named	AGE	SEX	BLOOD	TRIBAL ENROLLMENT Year	County	No.
15626	1 Krebs, Edna L		24	F	1/8	1896	Tobucksy	7495
15627	2 Dobbs, Pushmataha	So	3	M	1/16			

ENROLLMENT OF NOS. 1 and 2 HEREON APPROVED BY THE SECRETARY OF INTERIOR SEP 22 1904

TRIBAL ENROLLMENT OF PARENTS

Name of Father	Year	County	Name of Mother	Year	County
1 Edmond F Krebs	Dead	Gaines	Theresa C Krebs		Cherokee
2 D. A. Dobbs		noncitizen	No1		

No1 on 1896 Choctaw roll as Laura Krebs

Nos 1 and 2 transferred from Choctaw Card D513
See decision of July 19, 1904
For child of No1 see NB (Mar 3 '05) #434

Oct 11/99 Date of Application for Enrollment.

Date of Transfer to this Card. AUG 4 1904

RESIDENCE: COUNTY. **Choctaw Nation** Choctaw [redacted] CARD NO.

POST OFFICE: Tecumseh, Oklahoma (Not Including Fre[redacted] FIELD NO. 5788

Dawes' Roll No.	NAME	Relationship to Person First Named	AGE	SEX	BLOOD	TRIBA[redacted]LLMENT Year	County	No.
~~DP~~	~~Allred, John Lewis~~	~~Named~~	~~35~~	~~M~~	~~I.W.~~			

REFUSED

DECISION RENDERED OCT 31 1905

COPY OF DECISION FORWARDED ATTORNEYS FOR CHOCTAW AND CHICKASAW NATIONS. OCT 31 1905

COPY OF DECISION FORWARDED ATTORNEY FOR APPLICANT. OCT 31 1905

COPY OF DECISION FORWARDED APPLICANT OCT 31 1905

RECORD FORWARDED DEPARTMENT. OCT 31 1905

TRIBAL ENROLLMENT OF PARENTS

Name of Father	Year	County	Name of Mother	Year	County
~~A. L. Allred~~			~~Mary Allred~~	~~Dead~~	

ACTION APPROVED BY SECRETARY OF INTERIOR. MAR 22 1906

NOTICE OF DEPARTMENTAL ACTION FORWARDED ATTORNEYS FOR CHOCTAW AND CHICKASAW NATIONS. APR -7 1906

No1 was admitted as an intermarried citizen by Dawes Commission in 1896 Choctaw case #376 no appeal

Marriage license and certificate with Choctaw 1896 citizenship case #376

Aug 9, 1906 Motion forwarded Department asking action on former motion

Jan 16/07 Motion denied by Dept

Notify [illegible] Weise Atty Ardmore I.T. of Dept action.

NOTICE OF DEPARTMENTAL ACTION MAILED APPLICANT. APR -7 1906

NOTICE OF DEPARTMENTAL ACTION FORWARDED ATTORNEY FOR APPLICANT. APR -7 1906

~~Date of transfer~~ to this card AUG 9 1904

Choctaw By Blood Enrollment Cards 1898-1914

RESIDENCE: COUNTY. **Choctaw Nation** **Choctaw Roll** *(Not Including Freedmen)* CARD NO.
POST OFFICE: FIELD NO. 5789

Dawes' Roll No.	NAME	Relationship to Person First Named	AGE	SEX	BLOOD	TRIBAL ENROLLMENT Year	County	No.
	1 Seale, E. C.	First Named			I.W.	1896	Atoka	15063
	2 " Fannie W	Wife				"	"	11679
	3 " Raymond	son				"	"	11680
	4 " Fred	son				"	"	11681
DP	5 " Mary	dau				"	"	11682
	6 " Callie	dau				"	"	11683
	7 " Edna	dau				"	"	11684
	8 " Robert	son				"	"	11685
	9 " Anna M	dau						

ACTION APPROVED BY SECRETARY OF INTERIOR. MAR 2- 1907

NOTICE OF DEPARTMENTAL ACTION MAILED APPLICANT. APR 11 1907

NOTICE OF DEPARTMENTAL ACTION FORWARDED ATTORNEY FOR APPLICANT. APR 11 1907

NOTICE OF DEPARTMENTAL ACTION FORWARDED ATTORNEYS FOR CHOCTAW AND CHICKASAW NATIONS. APR 11 1907

TRIBAL ENROLLMENT OF PARENTS

Name of Father	Year	County	Name of Mother	Year	County
1					
2					
3					
4					
5					
6					
7					
8					
9					
10					
11					

REFUSED FEB 14 1907

RECORD FORWARDED DEPARTMENT. FEB 14 1907

12 said to be residents of Texas

No.8 on 1896 Choctaw census roll as Robt. E. Seale

13 Nos 1 to 9 incl. admitted by Dawes Commission in 1896 Choctaw case #831; no appeal.

14 No1 on 1896 Choctaw census roll as E. C. Seal

~~No3 " " " " " " W.A. Seale~~

15 No4 " " " " " " Fred E Seale

16 No6 " " " " " " Callie H Seale

17 No7 " " " " " " Edna W Seale

~~Date of transfer~~ to this card Aug. 30, 1904

RESIDENCE: Choctaw Nation ~~COUNTY.~~ **Choctaw Nation** Choctaw Roll (Not Including Freedmen) CARD NO.
POST OFFICE: G~~l~~errett[sic] Ind Ter FIELD NO. 5790

Dawes' Roll No.	NAME	Relationship to Person First Named	AGE	SEX	BLOOD	TRIBAL ENROLLMENT Year	County	No.
IW 1048	1 Ramseyer, Grotleib[sic]		58	M	I.W.			
	2							
	3							
	4							
	5							
	6							
	7							
	8							
	9							
	10							
	11							
	12							
	13							
	14							
	15							
	16							
	17							

ENROLLMENT OF NOS. 1 HEREON APPROVED BY THE SECRETARY OF INTERIOR OCT 21 1904

TRIBAL ENROLLMENT OF PARENTS

	Name of Father	Year	County	Name of Mother	Year	County
1	John Ramseyer	Dead	non-citz	Margaret Ramseyer	Dead	non-citz

Choctaw wife died Married subsequently to a white woman.
No1 admitted by the Commission in 1896, as an intermarried ~~citizen. Choctaw citizenship case No 1108. No appeal~~
~~No1 transferred from Choctaw Card # D66. See~~ decision of August 31, 1904
For children of No1 see NB (Apr 26 '06) #1258

Date of Application for Enrollment.

Date of application for enrollment: Oct 11/98

~~transfer to this card: Sept 15, 1904~~

RESIDENCE: Chickasaw Nation ~~COUNTY.~~ **Choctaw Nation** **Choctaw Roll** *(Not Including Freedmen)* CARD NO.
POST OFFICE: Chickasha I.T. FIELD NO. 5791

Dawes' Roll No.	NAME	Relationship to Person First Named	AGE	SEX	BLOOD	TRIBAL ENROLLMENT Year	County	No.
IW 1049	1 Rayel, Robert W		44	M	I.W.			

ENROLLMENT
OF NOS. 1 HEREON
APPROVED BY THE SECRETARY
OF INTERIOR OCT 21 1904

TRIBAL ENROLLMENT OF PARENTS

Name of Father	Year	County	Name of Mother	Year	County
1 W^m W Rayel		non-citz	Sarah A Rayel		non-citz

Married in 1883 to Elsie Carpenter a Choctaw Indian woman under Choctaw law. Lived with her six months. Claims she abandoned him. She died in 1884.
Married in 1889 to Ellen Duncan a white woman
~~Admitted by the Commission in 1896 as an intermarried citizen in~~
Choctaw citizenship case No 646.
No1 transferred from Choctaw Card # D 106. See decision of August 31, 1904.

~~Oct 22/98~~ **Date of Application for Enrollment.**

~~Date of transfer~~ to this card
Sept 15, 1904

RESIDENCE: COUNTY. **Choctaw Nation** **Choctaw Roll** *(Not Including Freedmen)* CARD NO.

POST OFFICE: Forrest City, Ark FIELD NO. 5792

Dawes' Roll No.	NAME	Relationship to Person First Named	AGE	SEX	BLOOD	TRIBAL ENROLLMENT Year	County	No.
IW 1050	1 Folsom, Etta J		25	F	I.W.			
15632	2 " Myrta Lee	Dau	3	F	3/8			
	3							
	4							
	5							
	6							
	7							
	8							
	9							
	10							
	11							
	12							
	13							
	14							
	15							
	16							
	17							

ENROLLMENT OF NOS. 1 HEREON APPROVED BY THE SECRETARY OF INTERIOR Oct 21 1904

ENROLLMENT OF NOS. 2 HEREON APPROVED BY THE SECRETARY OF INTERIOR Oct 21 1904

TRIBAL ENROLLMENT OF PARENTS

Name of Father	Year	County	Name of Mother	Year	County
1 W.D. Gorman	Dead	non citz	Mary Gorman	1896	Non Citz
2 Benjamin F Folsom			No1		
3					
4					
5					

6 No1 was married to Benjamin Folsom Jany 16, 1899. They are now separated
7 Nos 1 and 2 transferred from Choctaw Card # D 259. See decision
8 of August 31, 1904.

~~6/20/99~~ Date of Application for Enrollment.

~~Date of transfer~~ to this card Sept. 15, 1904

Choctaw By Blood Enrollment Cards 1898-1914

RESIDENCE: Choctaw Nation ~~COUNTY.~~ **Choctaw Nation** **Choctaw Roll** *(Not Including Freedmen)*
POST OFFICE: Sans Bois, I.T.

Dawes' Roll No.	NAME	Relationship to Person First Named	AGE	SEX	BLOOD	TRIBAL ENROLLMENT Year	County	No.
IW 1051	1 Brinkley, Sarah E		29	F	I.W.			
	2							
	3							
	4							
	5							
	6							
	7							
	8							
	9							
	10							
	11							
	12							
	13							
	14							
	15							
	16							
	17							

ENROLLMENT
OF NOS. 1 HEREON
APPROVED BY THE SECRETARY
OF INTERIOR OCT 21 1904

TRIBAL ENROLLMENT OF PARENTS

	Name of Father	Year	County	Name of Mother	Year	County
1	Jno Drake	dead	non-citz	Nancy Drake	Dead	non-citz
2						
3						
4						
5						

Married Jany 15 1887 to Douglas Cooper a Choctaw Indian. After his death she married William Wilson white man from whom she was divorced and subsequently married William Brinkley a white man.
No1 transferred from Choctaw Card # D 505. See decision of August 31, 1904.

Sept 15/99 Date of Application for Enrollment.

Date of transfer to this card Sept 15, 1904

RESIDENCE: Chickasaw Nation ~~COUNTY.~~
POST OFFICE: Ardmore I.T.

Choctaw Nation

Choctaw Roll *(Not Including Freedmen)*

CARD NO.
FIELD NO. 5794

Dawes' Roll No.	NAME	Relationship to Person First Named	AGE	SEX	BLOOD	TRIBAL ENROLLMENT Year	County	No.
IW 1052	1 McLaughlin, Ezekiel C	First Named	64	M	I.W.	1896	Chick Dist	14886

ENROLLMENT
OF NOS. 1 HEREON
APPROVED BY THE SECRETARY
OF INTERIOR OCT 21 1904

TRIBAL ENROLLMENT OF PARENTS

Name of Father	Year	County	Name of Mother	Year	County
1 E.B. McLaughlin	Dead	Cherokee	Polly McLaughlin	Dead	Cherokee

No1 on 1896 Choctaw census roll as an intermarried citizen page 396 #14886

No1 married Susan Harkins a Choctaw woman with whom he lived until her death. He then ~~married Ellen Harkins a Choctaw woman who died in 1896.~~

~~was readmitted to Cherokee citizenship by an Act of Cherokee Council approved Nov 15 1894~~

Ellen McLaughlin, second wife of No.1 on 1896 roll Chick Dist. No. 9477

~~No1 transferred from Choctaw Card # D 720. See decision of August 31, 1904.~~

~~May 16.02~~ Date of Application for Enrollment.

~~Date of transfer~~ to this card
Sept 16 1904

RESIDENCE: Jackson COUNTY. **Choctaw Nation** Choctaw Roll (Not Including Freedmen) CARD NO. [redacted]
POST OFFICE: Mayhew, I.T. FIELD NO. 5795

Dawes' Roll No.	NAME	Relationship to Person First Named	AGE	SEX	BLOOD	TRIBAL ENROLLMENT Year	County	No.
IW 1053	1 Duncan, Gavin D		29	M	IW	1896	Jackson	14474
	2							
	3							
	4							
	5							
	6							
	7							
	8							
	9							
	10							
	11							
	12							
	13							
	14							
	15							
	16							
	17							

ENROLLMENT
OF NOS. 1 HEREON
APPROVED BY THE SECRETARY
OF INTERIOR OCT 21 1904

TRIBAL ENROLLMENT OF PARENTS

Name of Father	Year	County	Name of Mother	Year	County
1 John Duncan		non-citz	Mary Duncan		non-citz
2					
3					
4					
5					

6 No1 on 1896 roll as J.D. Duncan
7 No1 family on card #3657
No1 admitted by Dawes Commission in 1896 as an
8 intermarried citizen, Choctaw case #341. No appeal.
9 Divorced from Annie B. Duncan, Choc card 3659
10 Transferred from Choctaw Card # D 343. See decision of Sept 8, 1904.

Date of Application for Enrollment. Aug 21/99

Date of transfer to this card Sept 24 1904

Choctaw By Blood Enrollment Cards 1898-1914

RESIDENCE: COUNTY. **Choctaw Nation** CARD NO.

POST OFFICE: Durwood, SI.T. FIELD NO. **5796**

Dawes' Roll No.	NAME	Relationship to Person First Named	AGE	SEX	BLOOD	TRIBAL ENROLLMENT Year	County	No.
IW 1150	1 Lindsey, Selden T		47	M	I.W.	1896	Chick. Dist	14795

ENROLLMENT OF NOS. 1 HEREON APPROVED BY THE SECRETARY OF INTERIOR NOV 16 1904

TRIBAL ENROLLMENT OF PARENTS

Name of Father	Year	County	Name of Mother	Year	County
1 B.B. Lindsey	Dead	non-citizen	Martha Lindsey		non-citizen

No1 restored to roll by Departmental authority of January 19, 1904

Enrollment of No.1 cancelled by decree of Department [illegible]

Husband of Nina Lindsey, Choctaw roll, card No. 224. Final roll #15361 app 5/9/04

~~For child of No1 see NB (Mar 3, 1905) card #548~~

No.1 transferred from Choctaw Card # D-67; See decision of Oct 15, 1904

May 4, 1909 Report to Department in letter of W.S. Field referred to this office by letter of March 25, 1909.

Date of Application for Enrollment.

Oct 5/98

on this card ~~Oct. 31, 1904~~

RESIDENCE: Chickasaw Nation
POST OFFICE: Lebanon, Ind. T

Choctaw

Dawes' Roll No.	NAME	Relationship to Person First Named			BLOOD	TRIBAL ENROLLMENT Year	County	No.
IW 1151	1 Scott, Chapling				I.W.			

ENROLLMENT
OF NOS. 1 HEREON
APPROVED BY THE SECRETARY
OF INTERIOR NOV 16 1904

TRIBAL ENROLLMENT OF PARENTS

Name of Father		County	Name of Mother	Year	County
1 Sparrow Sc		non-citizen	Elizabeth Scott		non-citizen

No.1 is the husband of Phoebe Ethel Scott on Choctaw card #339
No.1 transferred from Choctaw Card # D-578; See decision of Oct. 15, 1904.
For child of No1 see NB (March 3, 1905) #1161

June 20/1900 — Date of Application for Enrollment.

Date of transferr to this card
Oct. 31, 1904

RESIDENCE: Chickasaw
POST OFFICE: Purcell

Choctaw

Dawes' Roll No.	NAME	Relationship to Person First Named	AGE	SEX	BLOOD	Year	County	No.
IW 1152	1 Carpenter, Walter D		55	M	I.W.		Choctaw I.M. Roll Page 19	
	12 See petition #W 77							

ENROLLMENT
OF NOS. 1 HEREON
APPROVED BY THE SECRETARY
OF INTERIOR NOV 16 1904

Name of Father					
1 David Carpenter	dead	non-citizen	Emily Carpenter	dead	non-citizen

6 No.1 transferred from Choctaw Card # D-4; See decision of Oct. 15, 1904
7 For children of No1 see NB (Apr 26 '06) #1092

Sept 3/98 Date of Application for Enrollment.

Date of transfer to this card
Oct. 31, 19(

RESIDENCE: COUNTY. **Choctaw Nation** **Choctaw Roll** *(Not Including Freedmen)* CARD NO.
POST OFFICE: Valliant, I.T. FIELD NO. 5799

Dawes' Roll No.	NAME	Relationship to Person First Named	AGE	SEX	BLOOD	TRIBAL ENROLLMENT Year	County	No.
IW 1153	1 Hewett, William J	First Named	46	M	I.W.			
	2							
	3							
	4							
	5							
	6							
	7							
	8							
	9							
	10							
	11							
	12							
	13							
	14							
	15							
	16							
	17							

ENROLLMENT
OF NOS. 1 HEREON
APPROVED BY THE SECRETARY
OF INTERIOR NOV 16 1904

TRIBAL ENROLLMENT OF PARENTS

Name of Father	Year	County	Name of Mother	Year	County
1 Robert Y. Hewitt	1896	non-citizen	Sarah Hewett	1896	non-citizen
2					
3					
4					
5					
6					
7					
8					
9					
10					
11					
12					
13					
14					
15					
16					
17					

Admitted as intermarried citizen by Dawes Commission as
J. W. Hewitt #$1369. Married white woman in 1898.
No.1 transferred from Choctaw Card # D-167: See decision of Oct. 15, 1904.

5/16/99 **Date of Application for Enrollment.**

Transfer date to this card
Oct. 31, 1904

Choctaw By Blood Enrollment Cards 1898-1914

RESIDENCE: COUNTY. **Choctaw Nation** **Choctaw Roll** *(Not Including Freedmen)* CARD NO.
POST OFFICE: Lexington, O.T. FIELD NO. 5800

Dawes' Roll No.	NAME	Relationship to Person First Named	AGE	SEX	BLOOD	TRIBAL ENROLLMENT Year	County	No.
IW 1154	1 Mc Fadden, Mary E	First Named	41	F	I.W.			
	2							
	3							
	4							
	5							
	6							
	7							
	8							
	9							
	10							
	11							
	12							
	13							
	14 ENROLLMENT							
	15 OF NOS. 1 HEREON							
	16 APPROVED BY THE SECRETARY OF INTERIOR Nov. 16, 1904							
	17		See petition No W 64					

TRIBAL ENROLLMENT OF PARENTS

Name of Father	Year	County	Name of Mother	Year	County
1 Jasper Yeargin	dead	Non-citizen	Mary Yeargin	dead	non-citizen
2					
3					
4					
5					
6 No.1 transferred from Choctaw Card # D-321: See decision of Oct 15, 1904.					
7					
8					
9					
10					
11					
12					
13				Date of Application for Enrollment	Aug. 15,1899
14			on Choc Card No. D-321 Age 37		
15					
16				Transferred to this card	
17					Oct. 31, 1904

RESIDENCE: Sans Bois COUNTY. **Choctaw Nation** **Choctaw Roll** *(Not Including Freedmen)* CARD NO.
POST OFFICE: Tamaha, I.T. FIELD NO. 5801

Dawes' Roll No.	NAME	Relationship to Person First Named	AGE	SEX	BLOOD	TRIBAL ENROLLMENT Year	County	No.
IW 1155	1 Robinson, Rosa	First Named	46	F	I.W.	1896	Sans Bois	14957
	2							
	3							
	4							
	5							
	6							
	7							
	8							
	9							
	10							
	11							
	12							
	13 See Petition W 90							
	14 ENROLLMENT							
	15 OF NOS. 1 HEREON							
	16 APPROVED BY THE SECRETARY OF INTERIOR NOV 16 1904							
	17							

TRIBAL ENROLLMENT OF PARENTS

Name of Father	Year	County	Name of Mother	Year	County
1 Luke Goodnight	dead	non-citizen	Jane Goodnight	dead	non-citizen
2					
3					
4					
5					
6 No.1 transferred from Choctaw Card # D-223: See decision of Oct. 15, 1904					
7 For child of No1 see NB (Apr 26-06) #1259					
8					
9					
10					
11					
12					
13					
14					
15					~~Date of transfer~~
16		~~6/12/99~~	Date of Application for Enrollment.		to this card
17					Oct 31, 1904

RESIDENCE: Jackson COUNTY. **Choctaw Nation** C[redacted] CARD NO.
POST OFFICE: Crowder, I.T. (Not Including Freedmen) FIELD NO. 5802

Dawes' Roll No.	NAME	Relationship to Person First Named	AGE	SEX	BLOOD	TRIBAL ENROLLMENT Year	County	No.
IW 1156	1 Bollinger, Ella	First Named	28	F	I.W.			

ENROLLMENT OF NOS. 1 HEREON APPROVED BY THE SECRETARY OF INTERIOR NOV 16 1904

TRIBAL ENROLLMENT OF PARENTS

Name of Father	Year	County	Name of Mother	Year	County
1 John Winn	dead	non-citizen	Nancy Winn	dead	non-citizen

No1 t[redacted]ed from Choctaw Card # D-390: See decision of Oct. 15, 1904.
~~For e[redacted] No1 see (Apr 26 '06) NB #1086~~

Aug 30/99 Date of Application for Enrollment.

Date of trans to this ca Oct 31,

RESIDENCE: Chickasaw Nation ~~COUNTY.~~ **Choctaw Nation** **Choctaw Roll** *(Not Including Freedmen)* CARD NO.
POST OFFICE: Madill, I.T. FIELD NO.

Dawes' Roll No.	NAME	Relationship to Person First Named	AGE	SEX	BLOOD	TRIBAL ENROLLMENT Year	County	No.
IW 1157	1 Pettyjohn Nannie		27	F	I.W.			
	2							
	3							
	4							
	5							
	6							
	7							
	8							
	9							
	10							
	11							
	12							
	13							
	14							
	15							
	16							
	17							

ENROLLMENT OF NOS. 1 HEREON APPROVED BY THE SECRETARY OF INTERIOR NOV 16 1904

TRIBAL ENROLLMENT OF PARENTS

Name of Father	Year	County	Name of Mother	Year	County
1 F.L. McShan		non-citizen	Mary E McShan		non-citizen
2					
3					
4					
5					
6 No.1 transferred from Choctaw Card # D-36 See decision of Oct. 15, 1904					
7 For children of No1 see NB (Apr 26-06) #1135					
8					
9					
10					
11					
12					
13					
14					
15					~~Date of transfer~~
16		~~Sept 16/98~~	**Date of Application for Enrollment.**		to this card
17					Oct 31, 1904

RESIDENCE: COUNTY. **Choctaw Nation** **Choctaw Roll** (*Not Including Freedmen*) CARD NO.

POST OFFICE: Grant, Ind. Ter. FIELD NO. 5804

Dawes' Roll No.	NAME	Relationship to Person First Named	AGE	SEX	BLOOD	TRIBAL ENROLLMENT Year	County	No.
IW 1158	1 Ervin, Ben F	First Named	41	M	I.W.	1896	Kiamitia Co.	14499

ENROLLMENT OF NOS. 1 HEREON APPROVED BY THE SECRETARY OF INTERIOR NOV 16 1904

TRIBAL ENROLLMENT OF PARENTS

Name of Father	Year	County	Name of Mother	Year	County
1 William Ervin	dead	non-citizen	Elizabeth Ervin		non citizen

See testimony in regard to marriage, separation and divorce from Choctaw wife.
Evidence of marriage of No.1 to Josephine Gardner filed Dec. 10, 1902.
No.1 transferred from Choctaw Card # D-563: See decision of Oct. 15, 1904.

March 6/1900 Date of Application for Enrollment.

Date of transfer to this card Oct 31, 1904

RESIDENCE: COUNTY. **Choctaw Nation** **Choctaw Roll** *(Not Including Freedmen)* CARD NO.
POST OFFICE: Ireton, Ind. Ter. FIELD NO. 5805

Dawes' Roll No.	NAME	Relationship to Person First Named	AGE	SEX	BLOOD	TRIBAL ENROLLMENT Year	County	No.
IW 1159	1 Ireton, Minnie Ann		21	F	I.W.			
	2							
	3							
	4							
	5							
	6							
	7							
	8							
	9							
	10							
	11							
	12							
	13							
	14							
	15							
	16							
	17							

ENROLLMENT
OF NOS. 1 HEREON
APPROVED BY THE SECRETARY
OF INTERIOR NOV 16 1904

TRIBAL ENROLLMENT OF PARENTS

Name of Father	Year	County	Name of Mother	Year	County
1 Samuel W. Johnson		non citizen	Susie E Johnson		non citizen
2					
3					
4					
5					

6 No.1 is the wife of David R. Ireton on Choctaw card #428.
7 No.1 transferred from Choctaw Card # D 627: See decision of Oct. 15, 1904.
8 For child of No1 see NB (March 3, 1905) #1159

Date of Application for Enrollment. April 6/01

Date of transfer to this card Oct 31, 1904

RESIDENCE: Choctaw Nation COUNTY. **Choctaw Nation** **Choctaw Roll** (Not Including Freedmen) CARD NO.
POST OFFICE: Durant, I.T. FIELD NO. 5806

Dawes' Roll No.	NAME	Relationship to Person First Named	AGE	SEX	BLOOD	TRIBAL ENROLLMENT Year	County	No.
IW 1160	1 Neukirchner, Clara		36	F	I.W.			
	2							
	3							
	4							
	5							
	6							
	7							
	8							
	9							
	10							
	11							
	12							
	13							
	14							
	15							
	16							
	17							

ENROLLMENT OF NOS. 1 HEREON APPROVED BY THE SECRETARY OF INTERIOR NOV 16 1904

TRIBAL ENROLLMENT OF PARENTS

	Name of Father	Year	County	Name of Mother	Year	County
1	Thompson Vaughn		non-citizen	Sissy Vaughn	dead	non-citizen

No.1 was married to John A. Durant, Oct. 15th, 1893 and lived with him until his death, Jan 26th, 1894 and subsequently on Dec. 20th, 1895 married H.A. Neukirchner, a non-citizen

See testimony of November 5th, 1900.

John Durant on 1893 pay roll, Blue County, page 28; #290

No.1 transferred from Choctaw Card # D 591: See decision of Oct. 15, 1904.

Date of transfer to this card Oct 31, 1904

Date of Application for Enrollment. Nov 5/1900

PO Pool, IT 2/18/05

RESIDENCE: COUNTY. **Choctaw Nation** **Choctaw Roll** (*Not Including Freedmen*) CARD NO.
POST OFFICE: Hugo, Ind. Ter. FIELD NO. 5807

Dawes' Roll No.	NAME	Relationship to Person First Named	AGE	SEX	BLOOD	TRIBAL ENROLLMENT Year	County	No.
IW 1161	1 Hynson, Noland		60	M	I.W.	1896	Kiamitia	14637

ENROLLMENT OF NOS. 1 HEREON APPROVED BY THE SECRETARY OF INTERIOR NOV 16 1904

TRIBAL ENROLLMENT OF PARENTS

Name of Father	Year	County	Name of Mother	Year	County
1 Henry Hynson	dead	non-citizen	Eliza A. Hynson	dead	non-citizen

Married to a Choctaw citizen in 1875. Separated and divorced about six years thereafter. Remarried and again divorced. Never married again. See evidence of himself and Mrs. Harriet Turnbull hereto attached.

~~No.1 transferred from Choctaw Card # D-153: See decision of Oct. 15, 1904~~

Children on card No. 1551.

~~5/10/99~~ Date of Application for Enrollment.

~~Date of transfer~~ to this card Oct 31, 1904

RESIDENCE: Chickasaw Nation COUNTY. **Choctaw Nation** Choctaw Roll (Not Including Freedmen) CARD [illegible]
POST OFFICE: Chickasha, I.T. FIELD NO. 5808

Dawes' Roll No.	NAME	Relationship to Person First Named	AGE	SEX	BLOOD	TRIBAL ENROLLMENT Year	County	No.
15695	1 Jones, Mary Ellen	First Named	22	F	1/16		Choctaw residing in Chickasaw Dist	C.C.R.#2 310
15696	2 " Mabel	Dau	7	"	1/32		" "	"
15697	3 " Henry Wilson	Son	5 1/2	M	1/32			
15698	4 " Ellen	Dau	3	F	1/32			
15699	5 " Liddy Josephine	"	1	"	1/32			
	6							
	7							
	8							
	9							
	10							
	11							
	12							
	13							
	14							
	15							
	16							
	17							

ENROLLMENT
OF NOS. 1,2,3,4 and 5 HEREON
APPROVED BY THE SECRETARY
OF INTERIOR DEC -2 1904

TRIBAL ENROLLMENT OF PARENTS

Name of Father	Year	County	Name of Mother	Year	County
1 Joseph Kirkendall (I.W.)		Choctaw residing in Chickasaw Dist	Jane Kirkendall		Choctaw residing in Chickasaw Dist
2 Jolly J. Jones		non-citizen	No.1		
3 " " "		" "	No.1		
4 " " "		" "	No.1		
5 " " "		" "	No.1		

6 No1 1896 Chickasaw Dist 7405 as May E. James
No2 1896 " " 7406 " Mabel "
7 ~~See card No. D-101 for parents of No.1~~
8 No.1 also on Choctaw Census Record No.1 Page 102
9 No.1 " " " " No.2 as Mary Ella James
No.4 born August 12, 1899: Enrolled Dec. 19/99
10 ~~No.5 " Sept. 22, 1901. " March 19, 1902~~
11 No.3 " June 26, 1897
12 Nos. 1 to 5 incl transferred from Choctaw Card # D-102, See decision of Oct. 15, 1904.
For child of No.1 see NB (March 3, 1905) #771
13
14
15 Date of transfer to this card
16
17 ~~Date of Application for Enrollment.~~ Oct 21/98 ~~Oct 31, 1904~~

RESIDENCE: COUNTY. **Choctaw Nation** **Choctaw Roll** *(Not Including Freedmen)* CARD No.
POST OFFICE: Dibble, I.T. FIELD No. 5809

Dawes' Roll No.	NAME	Relationship to Person First Named	AGE	SEX	BLOOD	TRIBAL ENROLLMENT Year	County	No.
IW 1162	1 Morse, James M		57	M	I.W.			
	2							
	3							
	4							
	5							
	6							
	7							
	8							
	9							
	10							
	11							
	12 See petition # W 75							
	13							
	14 ENROLLMENT							
	15 OF NOS. 1 HEREON							
	16 APPROVED BY THE SECRETARY OF INTERIOR NOV 16 1904							
	17							

TRIBAL ENROLLMENT OF PARENTS

Name of Father	Year	County	Name of Mother	Year	County
1 Joseph Morse	dead	non-citizen	Helen Morse	dead	non-citizen
2					
3					
4					
5					
6 Admitted by Dawes Com. Case No 363 and no appeal taken.					
7 No1 transferred from Choctaw Card # D-18; See decision of Oct. 15, 1904					
8					
9					
10					
11					
12					
13					
14					
15					Date of transfer
16			Date of Application		~~to this card~~
17			for Enrollment.	Sept 14/98	Oct 31, 1904

RESIDENCE: COUNTY. **Choctaw Nation** **Choctaw Roll** (Not Including Freedmen) CARD NO.

POST OFFICE: Healdton, I.T. FIELD NO. 5810

Dawes' Roll No.	NAME	Relationship to Person First Named	AGE	SEX	BLOOD	TRIBAL ENROLLMENT Year	County	No.
IW 1163	1 Rector, James H	First Named	55	M	I.W.		Choctaw residing in Chickasaw Dist	C.I. Roll 96
	2							
	3							
	4							
	5							
	6							
	7							
	8							
	9							
	10							
	11							
	12							
	13							
	14							
	15							
	16							
	17							

ENROLLMENT
~~OF NOS.~~ 1 ~~HEREON~~
APPROVED BY THE SECRETARY
OF INTERIOR NOV 16 1904

TRIBAL ENROLLMENT OF PARENTS

	Name of Father	Year	County	Name of Mother	Year	County
1	Enoch Rector	dead	non-citizen	Parthena Rector	dead	non-citizen
2						
3						
4						
5						

6 1896 Chickasaw Dist. 15011 as Jim H. Rector
7 On Choctaw roll as Jim H. Rector
Admitted by Dawes Com. Case No. 1118 and no appeal taken.
8 ~~No.1 transferred from Choctaw Card # D-83; See decision of Oct. 15, 1904~~
9 For children of No1 see NB (Apr 26'06) #1240

Date of Application for Enrollment. Oct 18/98

Date of transfer to this card ~~Oct 31, 1904~~

RESIDENCE: COUNTY. **Choctaw Nation** **Choctaw Roll** *(Not Including Freedmen)* CARD NO.
POST OFFICE: Stigler, Ind. Ter. FIELD NO. 5811

Dawes' Roll No.	NAME	Relationship to Person First Named	AGE	SEX	BLOOD	TRIBAL ENROLLMENT Year	County	No.
IW 1164	1 Evans, John		39	M	I.W.	1896	Chickasaw Dist	14505
	2							
	3							
	4							
	5							
	6							
	7							
	8							
	9							
	10							
	11							
	12							
	13							
	14							
	15							
	16							
	17							

ENROLLMENT OF NOS. 1 HEREON APPROVED BY THE SECRETARY OF INTERIOR NOV 16 1904

TRIBAL ENROLLMENT OF PARENTS

	Name of Father	Year	County	Name of Mother	Year	County
1	Sterling Evans	dead	non-citizen	Lotta Evans		non-citizen
2						
3						
4						
5						
6	No.1 transferred from Choctaw Card # D-487: See decision of Oct. 15, 1904					
7						
8						
9						
10						
11						
12						
13						
14						
15						
16						Da[illegible] to this card
17	PO Wallville IT 7/9/06			Date of Application for Enrollment. Sept 12/99		Oct 31, 1904

RESIDENCE: Chickasaw Nation COUNTY. **Choctaw Nation** **Choctaw Roll** (*Not Including Freedmen*) CARD NO.
POST OFFICE: Wheeler, Ind. Ter. FIELD NO. 5812

Dawes' Roll No.	NAME	Relationship to Person First Named	AGE	SEX	BLOOD	TRIBAL ENROLLMENT Year	County	No.
IW 1165	1 Wheeler, James S		52	M	I.W.			
IW 1166	2 " Lucretia N	Wife	44	F	I.W.			

ENROLLMENT
OF NOS. 1 and 2 HEREON
APPROVED BY THE SECRETARY
OF INTERIOR NOV 16 1904

TRIBAL ENROLLMENT OF PARENTS

Name of Father	Year	County	Name of Mother	Year	County
1 William Wheeler	dead	See testimony	Ruthie Wheeler	dead	See Choc R. 471
2 Samuel May	"	non-citizen	Nancy May	"	non-citizen

No.1 was refused by Commission at Atoka I.T. in Aug. 1899

No 1 and 2 transferred from Choctaw Card # D 582: See decision of Oct. 15, 1904.

Date of Application for Enrollment. July 16/1900

Date of transfer to this card Oct 31, 1904

RESIDENCE: COUNTY. **Choctaw Nation** **Choctaw Roll** *(Not Including Freedmen)* CARD NO.

POST OFFICE: Atoka, I.T. FIELD NO. 5813

Dawes' Roll No.	NAME	Relationship to Person First Named	AGE	SEX	BLOOD	TRIBAL ENROLLMENT Year	County	No.
IW 1167	1 Boykin, James	First Named	44	M	I.W.			
	2							
	3							
	4							
	5							
	6							
	7							
	8							
	9							
	10							
	11							
	12							
	13							
	14							
	15							
	16							
	17							

ENROLLMENT
OF NOS. 1 HEREON
APPROVED BY THE SECRETARY
OF INTERIOR NOV 16 1904

TRIBAL ENROLLMENT OF PARENTS

Name of Father	Year	County	Name of Mother	Year	County
1 Samuel Boykin		non-citizen	Elizabeth Boykin	dead	non-citizen
2					
3					
4					
5					
6 No.1 transferred from Choctaw Card # D-204: See decision of Oct. 15, 1904					
7					
8					
9					
10					
11					
12					
13					
14					
15					
16					
17					

Date of transfer to this card Oct 31, 1904

Date of Application for Enrollment. 3/17/02

RESIDENCE: Sugar Loaf COUNTY. **Choctaw Nation** **Choctaw Roll** *(Not Including Freedmen)* CARD NO.
POST OFFICE: Gilmore, I.T. FIELD NO. 5814

Dawes' Roll No.	NAME	Relationship to Person First Named	AGE	SEX	BLOOD	TRIBAL ENROLLMENT Year	County	No.
IW 1168	1 Griffith, Sarah C		42	F	I.W.			
	2							
	3							
	4							
	5							
	6							
	7							
	8							
	9							
	10							
	11							
	12							
	13							
	14							
	15							
	16							
	17 See Choctaw card R 395							

ENROLLMENT
OF NOS. 1 HEREON
~~APPROVED BY THE SECRETARY~~
OF INTERIOR NOV 16 1904

TRIBAL ENROLLMENT OF PARENTS

Name of Father	Year	County	Name of Mother	Year	County
1 Robert Mitchell	1896	non-citizen	Martha Mitchell	1896	non-citizen
2					
3					
4					
5					

6 No.1 transferred from Choctaw Card # D-213: See decision of Oct. 31, 1904
7 No.1 was rejected as a Choctaw by blood Oct. 10, 1899; See testimony with Choc. R-395
No.1 refused identification as a [illegible...] by the Commission
8 ~~on July 14, 1904. M.C.R. 5957 Record forwarded Department July 31, 1904 [Illergible...]~~
9
10 For children of No1 see NB (Apr 26-06) #1103

Date of transfer ~~to this card~~ Oct 31, 1904

Date of Application for Enrollment. ~~6/6/99~~

RESIDENCE: Chickasaw Nation COUNTY. **Choctaw Nation** **Choctaw Roll** (*Not Including Freedmen*) CARD NO.
POST OFFICE: Pauls Valley, I.T. FIELD NO. 5815

Dawes' Roll No.	NAME	Relationship to Person First Named	AGE	SEX	BLOOD	TRIBAL ENROLLMENT Year	County	No.
IW 1169	1 Whittle, Lillian Delories		19	F	I.W.			
	2							
	3							
	4							
	5							
	6							
	7							
	8							
	9							
	10							
	11							
	12							
	13							
	14							
	15							
	16							
	17							

ENROLLMENT OF NOS. 1 HEREON APPROVED BY THE SECRETARY OF INTERIOR Nov 16 1904

TRIBAL ENROLLMENT OF PARENTS

Name of Father	Year	County	Name of Mother	Year	County
1 Jas Woodard	dead	Non-citizen	Kate Woodard	Dead	Non-citizen

No1 transferred from Choctaw Card # D- 306: See decision of Oct. 15, 1904
No1 was married May 1899 to John Whittle Choc. Card #237
She is now divorced from him
~~Age given hereon as of September 25, 1902~~

Date of Application for Enrollment.
Aug 3/99
~~Date of transfer~~ to this card
Oct 31, 1904

RESIDENCE: Kinta COUNTY. **Choctaw Nation** **Choctaw Roll** *(Not Including Freedmen)* CARD NO.
POST OFFICE: Kinta, I.T. FIELD NO. 5816

Dawes' Roll No.	NAME	Relationship to Person First Named	AGE	SEX	BLOOD	TRIBAL ENROLLMENT Year	County	No.
IW 1170	1 Wren, Etha	First Named	54	F	I.W.	1896	Atoka	15191

ENROLLMENT OF NOS. 1 HEREON APPROVED BY THE SECRETARY OF INTERIOR Nov 16 1904

TRIBAL ENROLLMENT OF PARENTS

Name of Father	Year	County	Name of Mother	Year	County
1 Eli Tucker		Non-citizen	Martha Tucker		Non-citizen

Indian spouse thro' whom applicant claims is Jennette M[c]Daniels on Choc Card #245

No1 transferred from Choctaw Card # D- 439: See decision of Oct. 15, 1904

For children of No1 see NB (Apr 26'06) Card No 1302

Date of Application for Enrollment. 9/5/99

Date of transfer ~~to this card~~ Oct 31, 1904

RESIDENCE: COUNTY. **Choctaw Nation** **Choctaw Roll** (Not Including Freedmen) CARD NO.

POST OFFICE: Atoka, I.T. FIELD NO. 5817

Dawes' Roll No.	NAME	Relationship to Person First Named	AGE	SEX	BLOOD	TRIBAL ENROLLMENT Year	County	No.
IW 1171	1 Goodson, Rebecca		26	F	IW			
	2							
	3							
	4							
	5							
	6							
	7							
	8							
	9							
	10							
	11							
	12							
	13							
	14							
	15							
	16							
	17							

ENROLLMENT
OF NOS. 1 HEREON
APPROVED BY THE SECRETARY
OF INTERIOR Nov 16 1904

TRIBAL ENROLLMENT OF PARENTS

Name of Father	Year	County	Name of Mother	Year	County
1 Jas Buzbee		Non-citizen	Lucy Buzbee		Non-citizen

Husband "Louie Lawrence" 7-3969
Admitted by Dawes Com, Case No 1256 as Rebecca Lawrence
~~No.1 transferred from Choctaw Card # D- 412: See decision of Oct. 15, 1904~~

Date of Application for Enrollment. ~~Sept 2/99~~

~~Date of transfer~~ to this card
Oct 31, 1904

RESIDENCE: COUNTY. **Choctaw Nation** **Choctaw Roll** *(Not Including Freedmen)* CARD NO.
POST OFFICE: Antioch, I.T. FIELD NO. 5818

Dawes' Roll No.	NAME	Relationship to Person First Named	AGE	SEX	BLOOD	TRIBAL ENROLLMENT Year	County	No.
IW 1172	1 Worley, Jesse A		27	M	I.W.			
	2							
	3							
	4							
	5							
	6							
	7							
	8							
	9							
	10							
	11							
	12							
	13							
	14							
	15							
	16							
	17							

ENROLLMENT
OF NOS. 1 HEREON
APPROVED BY THE SECRETARY
OF INTERIOR Nov 16 1904

TRIBAL ENROLLMENT OF PARENTS

Name of Father	Year	County	Name of Mother	Year	County
1 John Worley		Non-citizen	Frances Worley		Non-citizen
2					
3					
4					
5					

6 ~~No.1 is husband of Annie Worley on Choctaw card #90~~
7 No1 transferred from Choctaw Card # D-531: See decision of Oct. 15, 1904

Date of Application for Enrollment. ~~Dec 4/99~~

~~Date of transfer~~ to this card Oct 31, 1904

RESIDENCE: COUNTY. **Choctaw Nation** **Choctaw Roll** *(Not Including Freedmen)* CARD NO.
POST OFFICE: Haileyville, I.T. FIELD NO. 5819

Dawes' Roll No.	NAME	Relationship to Person First Named	AGE	SEX	BLOOD	TRIBAL ENROLLMENT Year	County	No.
IW1173	1 Truitt, William M	First Named	30	M	I.W.			
	2							
	3							
	4							
	5							
	6							
	7							
	8							
	9							
	10							
	11							
	12							
	13							
	14							
	15							
	16							
	17							

ENROLLMENT
OF NOS. 1 HEREON
APPROVED BY THE SECRETARY
OF INTERIOR Nov 16 1904

TRIBAL ENROLLMENT OF PARENTS

Name of Father	Year	County	Name of Mother	Year	County
1 Lige Truitt	dead	non-citizen	Lizzie Truett[sic]		non-citizen
2					
3					
4					
5					

6 Is now the husband of Alice Truitt, on Choctaw care #3437.
7 Alice Truitt on final roll #9795: approved Feb. 4, 1903
No.1 transferred from Choctaw Card # D- 663: See decision of Oct. 15, 1904
8 For child of No.1 see NB (March 3, 1905) #805

Date of transfer to this card Oct 31, 1904

Date of Application for Enrollment. Oct 3/01

17 P.O. Wapanucka, I.T. 1/28/05

RESIDENCE: Cherokee Nation ~~COUNTY.~~ **Choctaw Nation** **Choctaw Roll** (Not Including Freedmen) CARD NO.
POST OFFICE: Muldrow, I.T. FIELD NO. 5820

Dawes' Roll No.	NAME	Relationship to Person First Named	AGE	SEX	BLOOD	TRIBAL ENROLLMENT Year	County	No.
15700	1 Jacobs, Isaac A	First Named	48	M	1/2	1893	Skullyville	259
	2							
	3							
	4							
	5							
	6							
	7							
	8							
	9							
	10							
	11							
	12							
	13							
	14							
	15							
	16							
	17							

ENROLLMENT
OF NOS. 1 HEREON
APPROVED BY THE SECRETARY
OF INTERIOR Dec. 2, 1904

TRIBAL ENROLLMENT OF PARENTS

Name of Father	Year	County	Name of Mother	Year	County
1 S. L. Levi	dead	Choctaw	Sealey Levi	dead	Choctaw
2					
3					
4					
5					

6 On 1893 Pay Roll Skullyville Co, Page 28, No 259
No.1 on 1896 Cherokee roll; page 1129; #3 Sequoyah District
7 ~~No.1 " 1880 " " " 705; #727 " "~~
8 ~~No.1 transferred 255: See decision of Oct. 15, 1904.~~
9 For child of No.1 see NB (Mar 3 '05) #544

Date of transfer ~~to this card~~ ~~Oct 31, 1904~~

Date of Application for Enrollment. 6/20/99

RESIDENCE: COUNTY. **Choctaw Nation** **Choctaw Ro[redacted]** (Not Including Freed[redacted]) [redacted]5821

POST OFFICE: Sterling, O.T.

Dawes' Roll No.	NAME	Relationship to Person First Named	AGE	SEX	BLOOD	TRIBAL ENROLLMENT Year	County	No.
IW 1174	1 Hale, Mary	First Named	27	F	I.W.			
	2							
	3							
	4							
	5							
	6							
	7							
	8							
	9							
	10							
	11							
	12							
	13							
	14							
	15							
	16							
	17							

ENROLLMENT
OF NOS. 1 HEREON
APPROVED BY THE SECRETARY
OF INTERIOR NOV 16 1904

TRIBAL ENROLLMENT OF PARENTS

Name of Father	Year	County	Name of Mother	Year	County
1 Jas Russell		non-citizen	Virginia Russell		non-citizen
2					
3					
4					
5					
6 No.1 transferred from Choctaw Card # D- 291: See decision of Oct. 15, 1904					
7					
8					
9					
10					
11					
12					
13					
14					
15					Date of transfer
16		Aug 2/99	Date of Application for Enrollment.		to this card
17					Oct 31, 1904

RESIDENCE: Skullyville COUNTY. **Choctaw Nation** **Choctaw Roll** *(Not Including Freedmen)* CARD NO.
POST OFFICE: Cameron, I.T. FIELD NO. 5822

Dawes' Roll No.	NAME	Relationship to Person First Named	AGE	SEX	BLOOD	TRIBAL ENROLLMENT Year	County	No.
IW 1175	1 Turner, George A		50	M	I.W.			

ENROLLMENT OF NOS. 1 HEREON APPROVED BY THE SECRETARY OF INTERIOR Nov 16 1904

TRIBAL ENROLLMENT OF PARENTS

Name of Father	Year	County	Name of Mother	Year	County
1 Louis W. Turner	dead	non-citizen	Caroline Turner	dead	non-citizen

No.1 admitted by Dawes Commission as intermarried citizen #292. no appeal
No.1 is the father of Jackson Turner on Choctaw card #4651
~~No.1 transferred from Choctaw Card # D- 219. See decision of Oct. 15, 1904~~
~~For children of No.1 see NB (Apr 26 '06) #1254~~

~~6/8/99~~ Date of Application for Enrollment.

~~Date of transfer~~ to this card Oct 31, 1904

RESIDENCE: Kiamitia COUNTY. **Choctaw Nation** Choctaw Roll (Not Including Freedmen) CARD NO.
POST OFFICE: Antlers, I.T. FIELD NO. 5823

Dawes' Roll No.	NAME	Relationship to Person First Named	AGE	SEX	BLOOD	TRIBAL ENROLLMENT Year	County	No.
15701	1 Edwards, Rufus M	First Named	34	M	1/2	1893	Kiamitia	115
15702	2 " Emma	sister	27	F	1/2	1893	"	197
15703	3 Long, Ida	"	23	"	1/2	1893	"	198
15704	4 Edwards, Kate	"	19	"	1/2	1893	"	199
15705	5 " Ada	"	17	"	1/2	1893	"	200
15706	6 Swink, Nannie	"	32	"	1/2	1896	Jacks Forks[sic]	11727
15707	7 " William E	nephew	7	M	1/4	1896	" "	11728
15708	8 Long, Charles Henry	child of No3	1	"	1/4			
15709	9 Swink, Ida May	child of No3	1	F	1/4			
15710	10 Long, Celeste	child of No3	3mo	"	1/4			
	11							
	12							
	13							
	14							
	15							
	16							
	17							

For child of No3 see NB (Mar 3'05) #435

ENROLLMENT OF NOS. 1,2,3,4,5,6,7,8,9,10 HEREON APPROVED BY THE SECRETARY OF INTERIOR Dec -2 1904

TRIBAL ENROLLMENT OF PARENTS

Name of Father	Year	County	Name of Mother	Year	County
1 Henry C. Edwards	dead		Lydia A. Edwards	dead	non-citizen
2 " " "	"		" " "	"	" "
3 " " "	"		" " "	"	" "
4 " " "	"		" " "	"	" "
5 " " "	"		" " "	"	" "
6 " " "	"		" " "	"	" "
7 William Swink	1896	white man			
8 W. B. Long		non-citizen	No.3		
9 William Swink	1896	white man	No.6		
10 W.B. Long		" "	No.3		

11 No.1 now husband of Bettie Nelson, Choc card #1179: Evidence of marriage filed Dec 10,1902
Husband of No.6 and father of No.7 on Choctaw card No. 1856
12 No.8 Enrolled June 11, 1901 For child of No.6 see NB (Apr 26-06) Card #778
13 No.9 " July 1, 1901 No.7 on 1896 roll as Wm E. Swink 303-11728
14 No.10 born Aug 31, 1902: enrolled Dec. 2, 1902 Date of Application for Enrollment. 5/18/99
15 No.3 is now wife of W B Long a non-citizen Evidence of marriage filed 6/11-1901
16 Nos 1 to 10 incl transferred from Choctaw Card #D-168: See decision of Oct. 15, 1904
Date of transfer to this card Oct 31, 1904
17 No7 P.O. Valliant, Okla 9/7/08

No3 P.O. Bokhoma, I.T. 2/25/04 No3 P.O. Idabel, I.T. 1/20/05

RESIDENCE:
POST OFFICE: Poteau, I.T.

ation **Choctaw Roll** *(Not Including Freedmen)* CARD NO. FIELD NO. 5824

Dawes' Roll No.	NAME	Relationship to Person First Named	AGE	SEX	BLOOD	TRIBAL ENROLLMENT Year	County	No.
IW 1176	1 Dukes, Eva		24	F	I.W.	1896	Wade	14467
16118	2 " James Bohanan	Son	1	M	7/16			

ENROLLMENT OF NOS. 2 HEREON APPROVED BY THE SECRETARY OF INTERIOR Feb 21 1907

ENROLLMENT OF NOS. 1 HEREON APPROVED BY THE SECRETARY OF INTERIOR Nov. 16, 1904

TRIBAL ENROLLMENT OF PARENTS

Name of Father	Year	County	Name of Mother	Year	County
1 James Maxey	dead	non-citizen	Ellen Maxey	dead	non-citizen
2 James Bohanan			No.1		

On 1896 roll as Avey Dukes
No.1 transferred from Choctaw Card # D-221: see decision of Oct. 15, 1904
No.2 " " " " D-221: " " " Jan 21, 1907

Date of Application for Enrollment. 6/12/99

Date of transfer to this card Oct 31, 1904

RESIDENCE: Skullyville COUNTY. **Choctaw Nation** **Choctaw Roll** *(Not Including Freedmen)* CARD NO. FIELD NO. 5825

POST OFFICE: Tucker, I.T.

Dawes' Roll No.	NAME	Relationship to Person First Named	AGE	SEX	BLOOD	TRIBAL ENROLLMENT Year	County	No.
IW 1177	1 Nichols, James H	Named	50	M	I.W.	1896	Sans Bois	14897

ENROLLMENT OF NOS. 1 HEREON APPROVED BY THE SECRETARY OF INTERIOR NOV 16 1904

TRIBAL ENROLLMENT OF PARENTS

Name of Father	Year	County	Name of Mother	Year	County
1 Wiley Nichols	dead	non-citizen	Margaret Nichols	dead	non-citizen

Admitted by Dawes Commission as an Intermarried Citizen, Case No. 1145, a J. H. Nichols. No appeal.

~~On 1896 roll as Henry Nichols.~~

No.1 transferred from Choctaw Card # D- 243: See decision of Oct. 15, 1904

~~Date of Application~~ for Enrollment.	~~Date of transfer~~ to this card
6/15/99	Oct 31, 1904

Quinton, I.T. COUNTY. **Choctaw Nation** Choctaw Roll (Not Including Freedmen) CARD NO. FIELD NO. 5826

Dawes' Roll No.	NAME	Relationship to Person First Named	AGE	SEX	BLOOD	TRIBAL ENROLLMENT Year	County	No.
IW 1178	1 Herron, John L		50	M	I.W.			
	2							
	3							
	4							
	5							
	6							
	7							
	8							
	9							
	10							
	11							
	12							
	13							
	14							
	15							
	16							
	17							

ENROLLMENT OF NOS. 1 HEREON APPROVED BY THE SECRETARY OF INTERIOR NOV 16 1904

TRIBAL ENROLLMENT OF PARENTS

Name of Father	Year	County	Name of Mother	Year	County
1 Jos. Herron		non-citizen	Elizabeth Herron		non-citizen
2					
3					
4					
5					
6 No.1 transferred from Choctaw Card # D- 506: See decision of Oct. 15, 1904					
7					
8					
9					
10					
11					
12					
13					
14					
15			~~Date of Application~~ for Enrollment.		~~Date of transfer~~ to this card
16					
17			Sept 15/99		Oct 31, 1904

RESIDENCE: COUNTY. **Choctaw Nation** **Choctaw Roll** *(Not Including Freedmen)* CARD NO.
POST OFFICE: Alma, I.T. FIELD NO. [redacted]

Dawes' Roll No.	NAME	Relationship to Person First Named	AGE	SEX	BLOOD	TRIBAL ENROLLMENT Year	County	No.
IW 1179	1 Woosley, Mattie		34	F	I.W.			
	2							
	3							
	4							
	5							
	6							
	7							
	8							
	9							
	10							
	11							
	12							
	13							
	14							
	15							
	16							
	17							

ENROLLMENT
OF NOS. 1 HEREON
APPROVED BY THE SECRETARY
OF INTERIOR NOV 16 1904

TRIBAL ENROLLMENT OF PARENTS

	Name of Father	Year	County	Name of Mother	Year	County
1	Sam Jones	dead	non-citizen	Sarah Jones		non-citizen
2						
3						
4						
5						

6 Admitted by Dawes Commission Case No 1083 as Mattie Durant. No appeal.
7 As ti remarriage see her testimony
8 No.1 transferred from Choctaw Card # D- 337: See decision of Oct. 15, 1904.

Date of Application for Enrollment.	Date of transfer to this card
Aug 18/99	Oct 31, 1904

Choctaw By Blood Enrollment Cards 1898-1914

RESIDENCE: COUNTY. **Choctaw Nation** **Choctaw Roll** *(Not Including Freedmen)* CARD NO.
POST OFFICE: Wade, I.T. FIELD NO. 5828

Dawes' Roll No.	NAME	Relationship to Person First Named	AGE	SEX	BLOOD	TRIBAL ENROLLMENT Year	County	No.
IW 1180	1 Turner, Sarah E		35	F	I.W.	1896	Blue	14331

ENROLLMENT OF NOS. 1 HEREON APPROVED BY THE SECRETARY OF INTERIOR NOV 16 1904

TRIBAL ENROLLMENT OF PARENTS

Name of Father	Year	County	Name of Mother	Year	County
1 J. P. Atkinson		non-citizen	Dorcas Atkinson		non-citizen

No.1 admitted by Dawes Commission No. 602 as Sarah Bohanan. No appeal.
No.1 on 1896 roll as Sarah Bohanan. As to residence see her testimony.
No.1 transferred from Choctaw Card # D- 334: See decision of Oct. 15, 1904

Date of Application for Enrollment. 8/17/99

Date of transfer to this card Oct 31, 1904

RESIDENCE: Sans Bois COUNTY. **Choctaw Nation** Choctaw Roll (Not Including Freedmen) CARD NO.
POST OFFICE: Ironbridge, I.T. FIELD NO. 5829

Dawes' Roll No.	NAME	Relationship to Person First Named	AGE	SEX	BLOOD	TRIBAL ENROLLMENT Year	County	No.
IW 1181	1 Barnett, Thomas M	First Named	38	M	I.W.	1896	Sans Bois	14284

ENROLLMENT OF NOS. 1 HEREON APPROVED BY THE SECRETARY OF INTERIOR NOV 16 1904

TRIBAL ENROLLMENT OF PARENTS

Name of Father	Year	County	Name of Mother	Year	County
1 Thomas M Barnett	dead	non-citizen	Nancy Barnett	1896	non-citizen

On 1896 roll as Thomas Barnett.
Wife obtained divorce and he marries non-citizen white woman.
See testimony of himself and Keziah Davis.
~~No.1 transferred from Choctaw Card # D- 236; see decision of Oct. 15, 1904~~

Date of Application for Enrollment. 5/12/99

~~Date of transfer~~ to this card Oct 31, 1904

RESIDENCE: COUNTY. **Choctaw Nation** **Choctaw Roll** *(Not Including Freedmen)* CARD NO.
POST OFFICE: Spiro, I.T. FIELD NO. 5830

Dawes' Roll No.	NAME	Relationship to Person First Named	AGE	SEX	BLOOD	TRIBAL ENROLLMENT Year	County	No.
IW 1182	1 Collins, Miles S		70	M	I.W.	1896	Skullyville	14382
	2							
	3							
	4							
	5							
	6							
	7							
	8							
	9							
	10							
	11							
	12							
	13							
	14							
	15							
	16							
	17							

ENROLLMENT OF NOS. 1 HEREON APPROVED BY THE SECRETARY OF INTERIOR NOV 16 1904

TRIBAL ENROLLMENT OF PARENTS

Name of Father	Year	County	Name of Mother	Year	County
1 Jno. S. Collins	dead	non-citizen	Minerva Collins	dead	non-citizen
2					
3					
4					
5					

Married Mary Daniels, a Choctaw citizen on February 1869. After she died he married a white non-citizen. See his testimony and that of Thos. D. Ainsworth.
No.1 transferred from Choctaw Card # D- 251; See decision of Oct. 15, 1904.
For child of No.1 see NB (Apr 26 '06) No 1093

Date of Application for Enrollment. 6/16/99

Date of transfer to this card Oct 31, 1904

Choctaw By Blood Enrollment Cards 1898-1914

RESIDENCE: Blue COUNTY. **Choctaw Nation** **Choctaw Roll** *(Not Including Freedmen)* CARD NO.
POST OFFICE: Durant, I.T. FIELD NO. 5831

Dawes' Roll No.	NAME	Relationship to Person First Named	AGE	SEX	BLOOD	TRIBAL ENROLLMENT Year	County	No.
IW 1183	1 Henderson, Lula		26	F	I.W.			
	2							
	3							
	4							
	5							
	6							
	7							
	8							
	9							
	10							
	11							
	12							
	13							
	14							
	15							
	16							
	17							

ENROLLMENT
OF NOS. 1 HEREON
APPROVED BY THE SECRETARY
OF INTERIOR NOV 16 1904

TRIBAL ENROLLMENT OF PARENTS

	Name of Father	Year	County	Name of Mother	Year	County
1	J.B. Brown		non-citizen	Tennie Brown		non-citz
2						
3						
4						
5						

6 Admitted by Dawes Commission as Mrs. Lula Carrens, Case No. 747 No appeal
7 As to separation from Choctaw husband and remarriage to U.S. Citizen
see her testimony.
8 ~~No.1 transferred from Choctaw Card # D- 326, See decision of Oct. 15, 1904.~~

Date of Application for Enrollment.	Date of transfer to this card
Aug 16/99	Oct 31, 1904

RESIDENCE: COUNTY. **Choctaw Nation** **Choctaw Roll** (Not Including Freedmen) CARD NO.
POST OFFICE: Linn, I.T. FIELD NO. 5832

Dawes' Roll No.	NAME	Relationship to Person First Named	AGE	SEX	BLOOD	TRIBAL ENROLLMENT Year	County	No.
IW 1184	1 Thompson, Mary Jane		41	F	I.W.			

ENROLLMENT OF NOS 1 HEREON APPROVED BY THE SECRETARY OF INTERIOR NOV 16 1904

TRIBAL ENROLLMENT OF PARENTS

Name of Father	Year	County	Name of Mother	Year	County
1 Abe Adcock	dead	non-citizen	Amanda Adcock	dead	non-citizen

6 First married to John Moore, a Choctaw, May 1, 1879. He died.
7 Married " N. Thompson a white man, Sept. 17, 1889.

8 ~~No.1 transferred from Choctaw Card # D- 68; See decision of Oct. 15, 1904~~
9 For child of No1 see NB (Apr 26-06) #1251

Date of Application for Enrollment.
Oct 12/98

Oct 31, 1904

RESIDENCE: COUNTY. **Choctaw Nation** Choctaw Roll (*Not Including Freedmen*) CARD NO.
POST OFFICE: Sutter, I.T. FIELD NO. 5833

Dawes' Roll No.	NAME	Relationship to Person First Named	AGE	SEX	BLOOD	TRIBAL ENROLLMENT Year	County	No.
IW 1185	1 Monks, John W.	First Named	36	M	I.W.			
	2							
	3							
	4							
	5							
	6							
	7							
	8							
	9							
	10							
	11							
	12							
	13							
	14							
	15							
	16							
	17							

ENROLLMENT OF NOS. 1 HEREON APPROVED BY THE SECRETARY OF INTERIOR NOV 16 1904

TRIBAL ENROLLMENT OF PARENTS

Name of Father	Year	County	Name of Mother	Year	County
1 F. M. Monks	1896	Non-citizen	Lu[illegible] Monks	1896	non-citizen
2					
3					
4					
5					

6 Admitted by Dawes Com. as an Intermarried Citizen Case No 368, as
7 John M. Monks. Separated and wife obtained a divorce, he then married
a white woman. These facts were not stated in application to Dawes Com. No appeal.
8 ~~No.1 transferred from Choctaw Card # D-208; see decision of Oct. 15, 1904~~
9 For children of No1 see NB (Apr 26 '06) #1151.

Date of Application for Enrollment.	Date of transfer to this card
6/6/99	Oct 31, 1904

RESIDENCE: Kiamitia COUNTY. **Choctaw Nation** Choctaw Roll (Not Including Freedmen) CARD NO.
POST OFFICE: Antlers, I.T. FIELD NO. 5834

Dawes' Roll No.	NAME	Relationship to Person First Named	AGE	SEX	BLOOD	TRIBAL ENROLLMENT Year	County	No.
IW 1186	1 Hagerman, Charles		67	M	I.W.			

ENROLLMENT
OF NOS. 1 HEREON
APPROVED BY THE SECRETARY
OF INTERIOR Nov 16 1904

TRIBAL ENROLLMENT OF PARENTS

Name of Father	Year	County	Name of Mother	Year	County
1 Wm Hagerman	dead	non-citizen	Mary Hagerman	dead	non-citizen

Admitted by Dawes Commission as an Intermarried Citizen Case No 1355, no appeal.
Married a Choctaw, was divorced from her on account of adultery on her part. She afterwards died and in September 1897 he married a ~~white woman, a citizen of the U.S. under U.S. Law.~~
No.1 transferred from Choctaw Card # D- 536; see decision of Oct. 15, 1904

Date of Application for Enrollment. Dec 5/99

Date of transfer to this card Oct 31, 1904

RESIDENCE: Atoka COUNTY. **Choctaw Nation** **Choctaw Roll** (*Not Including Freedmen*) CARD NO.
POST OFFICE: Atoka, Ind. Ter. FIELD NO. 5835

Dawes' Roll No.		NAME	Relationship to Person First Named	AGE	SEX	BLOOD	TRIBAL ENROLLMENT Year	County	No.
IW 1187	1	Messick, Arthur C.		42	M	I.W.			
	2								
	3								
	4								
	5								
	6								
	7								
	8								
	9								
	10								
	11								
	12								
	13								
	14								
	15								
	16								
	17								

ENROLLMENT
OF NOS. 1 HEREON
APPROVED BY THE SECRETARY
OF INTERIOR Nov 16 1904

TRIBAL ENROLLMENT OF PARENTS

	Name of Father	Year	County	Name of Mother	Year	County
1	Saml. Messick			Kate Messick		U.S. Cit.
2						
3						
4						
5						

Admitted by the Dawes Commission Case #1325 as A.C. Messick. No appeal.
as to marriage & separation see statement of A. Telle.
No.1 transferred from Choctaw Card # D- 471; see decision of Oct. 15, 1904

Date of Application for Enrollment. Sept 8/99

Date of transfer to this card Oct 31, 1904

RESIDENCE: COUNTY. **Choctaw Nation** **Choctaw Roll** *(Not Including Freedmen)* CARD NO.

POST OFFICE: Antlers, I.T. FIELD NO. 5836

Dawes' Roll No.	NAME	Relationship to Person First Named	AGE	SEX	BLOOD	TRIBAL ENROLLMENT Year	County	No.
IW 1188	1 Fronterhouse, John		47	M	I.W.	1896	Atoka	14543
	2							
	3							
	4							
	5							
	6							
	7							
	8							
	9							
	10							
	11							
	12							
	13							
	14							
	15							
	16							
	17							

ENROLLMENT OF NOS. 1 HEREON APPROVED BY THE SECRETARY OF INTERIOR NOV 16 1904

TRIBAL ENROLLMENT OF PARENTS

Name of Father	Year	County	Name of Mother	Year	County
1 Jno. Fronterhouse	dead	non-citizen	Lucinda Fronterhouse		non-citizen
2					
3					
4					
5					
6 as to marriage, see testimony of himself and that of William T. Clay					
7 Second wife on card No. 4441.					
8 No.1 transferred from Choctaw Card # D- 415; See decision of Oct. 15, 1904					
9					
10					
11					
12					
13					
14					
15			Date of Application for Enrollment.		Date of transfer to this card
16					
17			Sept 2/99		Oct 31, 1904

RESIDENCE: Tobucksy COUNTY. **Choctaw Nation** **Choctaw Roll** *(Not Including Freedmen)* CARD NO.
POST OFFICE: Canadian, I.T. FIELD NO. 5837

Dawes' Roll No.	NAME	Relationship to Person First Named	AGE	SEX	BLOOD	TRIBAL ENROLLMENT Year	County	No.
IW 1189	1 Pitts, Alice	First Named	45	F	I.W.			
	2							
	3							
	4							
	5							
	6							
	7							
	8							
	9							
	10							
	11							
	12							
	13							
	14							
	15							
	16							
	17							

ENROLLMENT OF NOS. 1 HEREON APPROVED BY THE SECRETARY OF INTERIOR NOV 16 1904

TRIBAL ENROLLMENT OF PARENTS

Name of Father	Year	County	Name of Mother	Year	County
1 Jno. M. McDougal		U.S. Cit	Harriet E. McDougal		U.S. Cit
2					
3					
4					
5					
6 As to marriage see her testimony.					
7 Certificate of license filed.					
8 No.1 transferred from Choctaw Card # D- 500; See decision of Oct. 15, 1904					
9					
10					
11					
12					
13					
14					
15			**Date of Application for Enrollment.**		Date of transfer to this card
16					
17			Sept 14/99		Oct 31, 1904

RESIDENCE: COUNTY. **Choctaw Nation** **Choctaw Roll** (Not Including Freedmen) CARD NO.
POST OFFICE: Caney, I.T. FIELD NO. 5838

Dawes' Roll No.	NAME	Relationship to Person First Named	AGE	SEX	BLOOD	TRIBAL ENROLLMENT Year	County	No.
IW 1190	1 Young, Mary A		23	F	I.W.			
	2							
	3							
	4							
	5							
	6							
	7							
	8							
	9							
	10							
	11							
	12							
	13							
	14							
	15							
	16							
	17							

ENROLLMENT
OF NOS. 1 HEREON
APPROVED BY THE SECRETARY
OF INTERIOR NOV 16 1904

TRIBAL ENROLLMENT OF PARENTS

Name of Father	Year	County	Name of Mother	Year	County
1 Henry Dollarhide		non-citizen	Alfie E Dollarhide		non-citizen
2					
3					
4					
5					
6 As to marriage and separation see her testimony.					
7 No.1 transferred from Choctaw Card # D- 882. See decision of Oct. 15, 1904					
8					
9					
10					
11					
12					
13					
14					
15			Date of Application for Enrollment.		Date of transfer to this card
16					
17			Aug 28/99		Oct 31, 1904

RESIDENCE: COUNTY. **Choctaw Nation** **Choctaw Roll** *(Not Including Freedmen)* CARD NO.
POST OFFICE: Massey, I.T. FIELD NO. 5839

Dawes' Roll No.	NAME	Relationship to Person First Named	AGE	SEX	BLOOD	TRIBAL ENROLLMENT Year	County	No.
IW 1191	1 Banks, Albert	First Named	36	M	I.W.	1896	Gaines	14299
	2							
	3							
	4							
	5							
	6							
	7							
	8							
	9							
	10							
	11							
	12							
	13							
	14							
	15							
	16							
	17							

ENROLLMENT OF NOS. 1 HEREON APPROVED BY THE SECRETARY OF INTERIOR NOV 16 1904

TRIBAL ENROLLMENT OF PARENTS

Name of Father	Year	County	Name of Mother	Year	County
1 Presley Banks	dead	non-citizen	Mary E Banks		non-citizen

6 On 1896 roll as Albert Bank.
7 As to marriage to Choctaw and afterwards to white woman see his testimony
Evidence of marriage to be supplied - Filed Oct 31/99
8 ~~No.1 transferred from Choctaw Card # D- 426; See decision of Oct. 15, 1904~~
9 For child of No1 see NB (Apr 26-06) #1088

Date of Application for Enrollment.	Date of transfer to this card
9/4/99	Oct 31, 1904

RESIDENCE: COUNTY. **Choctaw Nation** **Choctaw Roll** *(Not Including Freedmen)* CARD NO.
POST OFFICE: Ryan, I.T. FIELD NO. 5840

Dawes' Roll No.	NAME	Relationship to Person First Named	AGE	SEX	BLOOD	TRIBAL ENROLLMENT Year	County	No.
IW 1192	1 Spain, Maggie		18	F	I.W.			
	2							
	3							
	4							
	5							
	6							
	7							
	8							
	9							
	10							
	11							
	12							
	13							
	14							
	15							
	16							
	17							

ENROLLMENT
OF NOS. 1 HEREON
APPROVED BY THE SECRETARY
OF INTERIOR NOV 16 1904

TRIBAL ENROLLMENT OF PARENTS

	Name of Father	Year	County	Name of Mother	Year	County
1	John Stilwell	dead	non-citizen	Mattie Stilwell		claim Choctaw
2						
3						
4						
5						

No.1 is the wife of David B. Spain, deceased, on Choctaw card #119

No.1 and David B Spain were married April 15th, 1900 under a U.S. license, and lived together until the death of David B Spain, June 15, 1900.

No.1 transferred from Choctaw Card # D- 680; See decision of Oct. 15, 1904

Date of Application for Enrollment.	Date of transfer to this card
Nov 14/01	Oct 31, 1904

RESIDENCE: COUNTY. **Choctaw Nation** **Choctaw Roll** *(Not Including Freedmen)* CARD NO.
POST OFFICE: Purcell, I.T. 5841

Dawes' Roll No.		NAME	Relationship to Person First Named	AGE	SEX	BLOOD	TRIBAL ENROLLMENT Year	County	No.
IW 1197	1	Marcum, Henry W		30	M	I.W.			
15711	2	" Cordelia	Wife	27	F	1/16	1896	Chick. Dist.	8897
15712	3	" Jesse	Son	10	M	1/32	1896	Chick. Dist.	8900
15713	4	" Claudie	"	7	"	1/32	1896	Chick. Dist.	8901
15714	5	" Clarence	"	4	"	1/32			
15715	6	" Lulu	Dau	1	F	1/32			

ENROLLMENT OF NOS. 2,3,4,5 and 6 HEREON APPROVED BY THE SECRETARY OF INTERIOR DEC -2 1904

ENROLLMENT OF NOS. 1 HEREON APPROVED BY THE SECRETARY OF INTERIOR NOV 16 1904

TRIBAL ENROLLMENT OF PARENTS

	Name of Father	Year	County	Name of Mother	Year	County
1	Phillip Marcum		non citizen	Haley Marcum	dead	non citizen
2	Reuben Beal		Choctaw	Mary Jane Beal		" "
3	No.1			No.2		
4	No.1			No.2		
5	No.1			No.2		
6	No.1			No.2		

Marriage license and certificate filed June 4, 1900.
No.5 born Feb. 18, 1898; proof of birth filed April 1, 1903
No.6 " May 27, 1901; Evidence of birth filed Oct. 28, 1901.
~~Nos. 1 to 6 incl. transferred from Choctaw Card # D- 568; See decision of Oct. 15, 1904~~
For child of Nos 1 and 2 see NB (Mar 3 '05) #436

Date of Application for Enrollment. 6/4/1900

Date of transfer to this card Oct 31, 1904

RESIDENCE: Choctaw Nation COUNTY. **Choctaw Nation** **Choctaw Roll** *(Not Including Freedmen)* CARD NO.
POST OFFICE: Caddo, Ind. Ter. FIELD NO. 5842

Dawes' Roll No.	NAME	Relationship to Person First Named	AGE	SEX	BLOOD	TRIBAL ENROLLMENT Year	County	No.
15716	1 Beal, George		22	M	1/16	1896	Blue	1566
15717	2 " Millie Levana	Dau	2	F	1/32			
IW 1484	3 " Ada	Wife	22	F	I.W.			

ENROLLMENT
OF NOS. Three HEREON
APPROVED BY THE SECRETARY
OF INTERIOR Aug 22, 1905

ENROLLMENT
OF NOS. 1 and 2 HEREON
APPROVED BY THE SECRETARY
OF INTERIOR Dec 2, 1904

TRIBAL ENROLLMENT OF PARENTS

Name of Father	Year	County	Name of Mother	Year	County
1 Reuben Beal	1896	Blue	Mary Beal		non-citizen
No1			Ada Beal		" "
3 Frank Wingate		non citizen	Mahala Wingate		non citizen

No.1 on 1893 leased district pay roll Blue Co page 5, No. 55
No.1 Son of Reuben Beal who was admitted by act of Choctaw Council No.2 approved Oct. 25, 1890. No.1 was living at the time, but his name does not appear therein.
Evidence of marriage of parents of No.2 filed May 16, 1902
No.2 born Nov. 13, 1900; enrolled May 16, 1902
No.1 also on 1896 Choctaw census page 39 #1566 as George Beals[sic].
Nos 1 and 2 transferred from Choctaw Card # D- 719; See decision of Oct. 15, 1904
No.3 placed on this card June 22, 1905 in accordance with decision of the Commission of that date holding application was made within time limited by act of Congress approved July 1, 1902 (32 Stat. 641) See decision of Commission of June 22, 1905 enrolling No.3
For child of Nos 1&3 see NB (March 3-1900) #703

Date of Application for Enrollment. May 16/02

P.O. Silo IT 11/11/04

Date of transfer to this card Oct 31, 1904

RESIDENCE: Indian Territory COUNTY. **Choctaw Nation** Choctaw Roll (Not Including Freedmen) CARD NO.
POST OFFICE: Durant I.T. FIELD NO. 5843

Dawes' Roll No.		NAME	Relationship to Person First Named	AGE	SEX	BLOOD	TRIBAL ENROLLMENT Year	County	No.
15718	1	Beal, William Albert	First Named	28	M	1/16	1896	Blue	1564
15719	2	" Samantha	Dau	9	F	1/32	"	"	1574
15720	3	" Bulah	"	4	"	1/32			
15721	4	" William D	Son	2	M	1/32			
IW 1538	5	" Sallie Cora	Wife	21	F	I.W.			
	6								
	7								
	8	No5 Granted							
	9	Nov. 14, 1905							
	10	ENROLLMENT OF NOS. 5 HEREON APPROVED BY THE SECRETARY OF INTERIOR Mar 14, 1906							
	11								
	12	ENROLLMENT OF NOS. 1,2,3 and 4 HEREON APPROVED BY THE SECRETARY OF INTERIOR Dec 2, 1904							
	13								
	14								
	15								
	16								
	17								

TRIBAL ENROLLMENT OF PARENTS

	Name of Father	Year	County	Name of Mother	Year	County
1	Reuben Beal		Choctaw	Mary Beal		non citizen
2	No.1			Sallie Beal		" "
3	No.1			" "		" "
4	No.1			" "		" "
5						

6 No.1 is the son of Reuben Beal who was admitted to citizenship in the Choctaw Nation by
7 Choctaw council, October 24, 1890.
Nos 1 and 2 also drew leased district payment in 1893
8 ~~No1 also on 1893 leased district pay roll Blue Co page 661 as Albert Beals~~
9 No2 " " 1893 " " " " " " " 662 " Samantha Beals
10 No3 born Nov. 3, 1898; proof of birth filed June 22, 1904.
No4 affidavit to birth filed Sept 23, 1901.
11 ~~Nos 1 to 4 incl. transferred from Choctaw Card # R-18; see decision of Oct. 15, 1904~~
12 No5 placed on this card September 28th 1905 in accordance with order of the Commission to the
13 Five Civilized Tribes of that date holding application was made with time prescribed by act of
14 Congress approved July 1, 1902 (32 Stat 641)
15 For child of Nos 1 and 5 see NB (April 26 1906) #74
16 " " " " " " " " " " (March 3 1905) #1325

Date of transfer ~~to this card~~ Oct 31, 1904

17 No5 PO Silo IT 10/30/05

Date of Application for Enrollment Aug 14/99

RESIDENCE: COUNTY. **Choctaw Nation** **Choctaw Roll** *(Not Including Freedmen)* CARD NO.
POST OFFICE: Silo, I.T. FIELD NO. 5844

Dawes' Roll No.		NAME	Relationship to Person First Named	AGE	SEX	BLOOD	TRIBAL ENROLLMENT Year	County	No.
15722	1	Dills, Rosa		20	F	1/16	1896	Blue	1567
15723	2	" Nora M	Dau	5	"	1/32			
15724	3	" Lether[sic] Lee	"	2	"	1/32			
	4								
	5								
	6								
	7								
	8								
	9								
	10								
	11								
	12								
	13								
	14								
	15								
	16								
	17								

ENROLLMENT OF NOS. 1,2, and 3 HEREON APPROVED BY THE SECRETARY OF INTERIOR Dec 2, 1904

TRIBAL ENROLLMENT OF PARENTS

	Name of Father	Year	County	Name of Mother	Year	County
1	Reuben Beal	1896	Blue	Mary Beal		non-citizen
2	E.G. Dills		non-citizen	No.1		
3	" " "		" "	No.1		
4						
5						

6 No 1 also on 1893 leased district payroll, Blue Co, page 6 #59 as Rosey Beals
7 No.2 born Oct 8, 1897, proof of birth filed June 22, 1904.
Evidence of marriage filed June 22, 1904
8 ~~No.3 affidavit of birth filed Sept 22, 1901~~
9 ~~Nos 1 to 3 incl transferred from Choctaw Card #R-75: see decision of Oct. 15, 1904~~
10 For child of No1 see NB (Apr 26, 1906) Card No, 94
11 " " " " " " (March 3, 1905) " " 1097

	Date of Application for Enrollment.	~~Date of transfer~~ to this card
17 P.O. Durant I.T. 4/17/05	Aug 14/99	Oct 31, 1904

RESIDENCE: COUNTY. **Choctaw Nation** Choctaw Roll (Not Including Freedmen) CARD NO.
POST OFFICE: Silo, I.T. FIELD NO. 5845

Dawes' Roll No.	NAME	Relationship to Person First Named	AGE	SEX	BLOOD	TRIBAL ENROLLMENT Year	County	No.
15725	1 Beal, Reuben Jr	First Named	24	M	1/16	1896	Blue	1565
IW 1198	2 McCurry, Eliza	Wife	24	F	I.W.			
15726	3 Beal, Cora	Dau	5	"	1/32			
15727	4 " Benj. Lee	Son	4	M	1/32			
IW 1433	5 " Mosie	Wife	17	F	I.W.			

ENROLLMENT OF NOS. 5 HEREON APPROVED BY THE SECRETARY OF INTERIOR June 12, 1905

ENROLLMENT OF NOS. 1,3 and 4 HEREON APPROVED BY THE SECRETARY OF INTERIOR Dec 2, 1904

~~ENROLLMENT~~ OF NOS. 2 HEREON APPROVED BY THE SECRETARY ~~OF INTERIOR~~ Nov 16 1904

For children of No2 see NB (Apr 26-06) #1123

TRIBAL ENROLLMENT OF PARENTS

Name of Father	Year	County	Name of Mother	Year	County
1 Reuben Beal		Choctaw	Mary Beal		non-citizen
2 Moses G. Gardner		non citizen	Martha A Gardner		non citizen
3 No.1			No.2		
4 No.1			Mosie Beal		
5 Benjamin Gardner			Mary Gardner		Deceased

For child of Nos 1&5 see N.B. (March 3, 1905) #1529
~~For child of Nos 1&5 see N.B. (Apr 26-06) card #320~~
~~Reuben Beal Jr is on Choctaw Roll of 1896~~
son of Reuben Beal whose name is mentioned in act of Council #12, approved Oct 25 1890
Bill of divorce between Nos 1 and 2 filed Dec. 24, 1902
~~No3 born June 28, 1897; proof of birth filed June 17, 1904~~
~~Evidence of marriage between Nos 1&2 filed June 17, 1904~~
No1 also on 1893 leased district pay roll Blue Co page 5 #54 as Reuben Beals
Nos 1 to 4 incl transferred from Choctaw Card #R-19; see decision of Oct. 15, 1904
No5 placed hereon in accordance with order of the Commission of March 23, 1905 holding that
~~application was made for her enrollment within the time provided by the act of Congress~~
approved July 1, 1902 (32 Stat 641)
No1 P.O. Silo I.T. 2/6/05
P.O. Lehigh I.T. 6/15/04

Transfer Date Oct 31, 1904

Date of Application for Enrollment. Aug 14/99

RESIDENCE: Blue COUNTY. **Choctaw Nation** Choctaw Roll (Not Including Freedmen) CARD NO.
POST OFFICE: Durant I.T. FIELD NO. 5846

Dawes' Roll No.	NAME	Relationship to Person First Named	AGE	SEX	BLOOD	TRIBAL ENROLLMENT Year	County	No.
15728	1 Beal, Arthur	First Named	17	M	1/16	1896	Blue	1568
15729	2 " Johnnie	Bro	15	M	1/16	1896	"	1569

ENROLLMENT OF NOS. 1 and 2 HEREON APPROVED BY THE SECRETARY OF INTERIOR Dec 2, 1904

TRIBAL ENROLLMENT OF PARENTS

Name of Father	Year	County	Name of Mother	Year	County
1 Reuben Beal	1896	Blue	Mary Beal		non-citizen
2 " "			" "		" "

Father of these children admitted by Act of Choctaw Council No. 12, approved Oct. 25, 1890. Father enrolled on Choctaw #3367
No.1 also on 1893 Leased District pay roll Blue Co page 5 #56 as Author[sic] Beals
~~No.2 " " 1893 " " " " " " " 5 #57 " Johney[sic] Beals~~
~~Nos 1 and 2 transferred from Choctaw Card #R 384; See decision of Oct. 15, 1904~~
For child of No.1 see N.B. (Apr 26, 1906) Card No. 172

P.O. Silo I.T. 11/7/04

Date of Application for Enrollment. Aug 17/99

~~Date of transfer~~ to this card Oct 31, 1904

Choctaw By Blood Enrollment Cards 1898-1914

RESIDENCE: Blue County ~~COUNTY.~~ **Choctaw Nation** Choctaw Roll (Not Including Freedmen) CARD NO.
POST OFFICE: Albany, I.T. FIELD NO. 5847

Dawes' Roll No.	NAME	Relationship to Person First Named	AGE	SEX	BLOOD	TRIBAL ENROLLMENT Year	County	No.
15730	1 Beal, John Piler		17	M	1/16	1896	Blue	1625
15731	2 " Pony	Bro	15	"	1/16	1896	"	1626
15732	3 " Roy May	Sister	13	F	1/16	1896	"	1627

ENROLLMENT OF NOS. 1,2, and 3 HEREON APPROVED BY THE SECRETARY OF INTERIOR Dec. 2, 1904

TRIBAL ENROLLMENT OF PARENTS

Name of Father	Year	County	Name of Mother	Year	County
1 Pinkney Beal	1896	Blue	Ailsey Beal		non citizen
2 " "			" "		" "
3 " "			" "		" "

Father of these children admitted by act of Choctaw Council No.12 approved Oct. 25, 1890. Father enrolled on Choc. 3489

~~No1 also on 1893 leased district pay roll Blue Co page 14 #151 as John Beals~~

~~No2 " " 1893 " " " " " " " 14 #152 " Poney Beals~~

No3 " " 1893 " " " " " " " 14 #154 " Ray Beals

Nos 1 to 3 incl transferred from Choctaw Card #R.385; See decision of Oct. 15, 1904

~~Date of Application~~ for Enrollment.

Date of application for enrollment Aug. 17, 1899

" " transfer to this card Oct 31, 1904

RESIDENCE: Chickasaw Nation COUNTY. **Choctaw Nation** C[illegible]
POST OFFICE: Silo, I.T. (Not Including Freedmen) FIELD NO. [illegible]

Dawes' Roll No.	NAME	Relationship to Person First Named	AGE	SEX	BLOOD	TRIBAL ENROLLMENT Year	County	No.
15733	1 Moore, Ada Bell		18	F	1/16	1896	Blue	1541
15734	2 Beal, Annie	Sister	16	"	1/16	1896	"	1542
15735	3 Moore, Roy L.	Son	9mo	M	1/32			

ENROLLMENT OF NOS. 1,2 and 3 HEREON APPROVED BY THE SECRETARY OF INTERIOR DEC -2 1904

TRIBAL ENROLLMENT OF PARENTS

	Name of Father	Year	County	Name of Mother	Year	County
1	William C. Beal	1896	Blue	Donnie Beal		non-citizen
2	" " "			" "		" "
3	F. B. Moore			No.1		

No1 is now the wife of F.B. Moore a non-citizen white man; May 16, 1902
No.3 was born Jan. 11, 1902: Enrolled May 16, 1902
~~Evidence of marriage between Nos and F.B. Moore[sic] filed May 16, 1902~~
~~Nos 1 and 2 Father was admitted by Act of Council No 12, Approved Oct 25, 1890~~
Enrolled on Choctaw 3498
No1 on 1893 leased district pay roll Blue Co page 7 #76 as Ada Beals
~~No2 " 1893 " " " " " " " 7 #77 " Annie Beals~~
~~Nos 1 to 3 incl transferred from Choctaw Card #R-389; see decision of Oct. 15, 1904~~
For child of No.2 see NB (Apr 26, 1906) Card No. 168
" " " " 1 " " (March 3, 1905) " " 740
P.O. Dibble I.T. 3/12/06

Date of transfer to this card Oct 31, 1904

Aug 16/99 Date of Application for Enrollment.

RESIDENCE: Blue COUNTY. **Choctaw Nation** **Choctaw Roll** *(Not Including Freedmen)* CARD NO.
POST OFFICE: Albany, I.T. FIELD NO. 5849

Dawes' Roll No.	NAME	Relationship to Person First Named	AGE	SEX	BLOOD	TRIBAL ENROLLMENT Year	County	No.
15736	1 Beal, William T	Named	13	M	1/16	1896	Blue	1546
	2							
	3							
	4							
	5							
	6							
	7							
	8							
	9							
	10							
	11							
	12							
	13							
	14							
	15							
	16							
	17							

ENROLLMENT
OF NOS. 1 HEREON
APPROVED BY THE SECRETARY
OF INTERIOR DEC -2 1904

TRIBAL ENROLLMENT OF PARENTS

Name of Father	Year	County	Name of Mother	Year	County
1 Andrew P. Beal	1896	Blue	Broun Beal		non-citizen
2					
3					
4					
5					

6 Father of this child enrolled on Dawes Com card 3560
7 " admitted by Act of Council No.12 approved Oct. 25, 1890
No.1 on 1893 leased district pay roll Blue Co. page 14 #158 as W.T. Beals
8 ~~No.1 transferred from Choctaw Card # R-386; See decision of Oct. 15, 1904.~~

Date of transfer to this card Oct 31, 1904

Date of Application for Enrollment. Aug 17/99

RESIDENCE:
POST OFFICE: Maxwell, I.T. **Choctaw Nation** 850

Dawes' Roll No.	NAME	Relation to Person First Named		SEX	BLOOD	TRIBAL ENROLLMENT Year	County	No.
15737	1 Meek, Jacob		60	M	1/4			
15738	2 " James H							
15739	3 " Calvin W							
IW 1434	4 " Ada							
	5							
	6							
	7							
	8							
	9							
	10							
	11							
	12							
	13							
	14							
	15							
	16							
	17							

ENROLLMENT OF NOS. 4 HEREON APPROVED BY THE SECRETARY OF INTERIOR JUN 12 1905

ENROLLMENT OF NOS. 1 2 and 3 HEREON APPROVED BY THE SECRETARY OF INTERIOR DEC -2 1904

Name of Father			Name of Mother			
1 Simion[sic] Meek	dead	non-citizen	Laura Meek			
2 No.1			Sarah E Meek		"	"
3 No.1			Eliza A Meek		"	"
4 L. D. Meek		non citz	Eliza J Meek		"	"

6 Nos 1-2-3 were admitted by the Dawes Commission Dec. 2, 1896, Case #373

7 Appealed U.S. Court, Central District Ind. Ter. Appeal dismissed. Sept. 3rd 1897: Court Case #189

8 ~~See evidence attached May 24/99~~

9 No.2 is the husband of Ada Meek Choctaw card #D-691 Dec. 4, 1901.

10 Nos 1-2-3 transferred from Choctaw Card #5320; See decision of Oct. 15, 1904

11 No.4 originally listed for enrollment on Choctaw card #D-691 - Dec. 4, 1901: ~~transferred to this card May 15, 1905. See decision of Feb. 7, 1905~~

Date of transfer to this card: Oct 31, 1904

17 ~~PO Farris IT 6/13/05~~

PO Cornish IT 6/13/05

Date of Application for Enrollment. 9/15/98

RESIDENCE: Chickasaw Nation COUNTY. **Choctaw Nation** **Choctaw Roll** (*Not Including Freedmen*) CARD NO.
POST OFFICE: Chickasha, Ind. Ter. FIELD NO. 5851

Dawes' Roll No.	NAME	Relationship to Person First Named	AGE	SEX	BLOOD	TRIBAL ENROLLMENT Year	County	No.
15740	1 Edgar, Rhoda M		21	F	1/32	1896	Chickasaw Dist	7665
15741	2 " Earnest	Son	5	M	1/64			
15742	3 " Sarah Ettie	Dau	1	F	1/64			

ENROLLMENT OF NOS. 1, 2 and 3 HEREON APPROVED BY THE SECRETARY OF INTERIOR DEC -2 1904

TRIBAL ENROLLMENT OF PARENTS

	Name of Father	Year	County	Name of Mother	Year	County
1	Jos. Kirkendall (I.W.)		Choctaw residing ~~in Chickasaw Dist~~	Sarah Jane Kirkendall		Choctaw residing ~~in Chickasaw Dist~~
2	Paul Edgar		non-citizen	No.1		
3	" "		" "	No.1		

No.1 on 1893 leased district pay roll Chick. Dist page 34 #330 as Rhoda M Kuykendall[sic]
No.1 " 1896 Chickasaw Dist 7665 as Rhoda M Kirkingdall[sic]
Parents of No.1 (Card 5736) claim to have been admitted by Act of Council Nov. 5, 1
~~No.1 not named in said act.~~
No.2 born Sept. 18, 1897
For Act of No. 5, 1888 see Ephraim Foster card #5713
No.3 born Aug. 16, 1901; enrolled March 13, 1902
~~Nos 1-2-3 transferred from Choctaw Card # D- 107: See decision of Oct. 15, 1904~~
For child of No.1 see NB (Apr 26, 1906) Card No. 92

PO Tuttle IT 5/5/06

Date of Application for Enrollment. Oct 22/98

Date of transfer to this card Oct 31, 1904

Choctaw By Blood Enrollment Cards 1898-1914

RESIDENCE: COUNTY. [redacted] n **Choctaw Roll** *(Not Including Freedmen)* CARD NO.

POST OFFICE: Hunton, I.T. FIELD NO. 5852

Dawes' Roll No.	NAME	Relationship to Person First Named	AGE	SEX	BLOOD	TRIBAL ENROLLMENT Year	County	No.
15743	1 Moran, James E	First Named	24	M	1/16			
15744	2 " [Maud Ola]	[redacted]au	3	F	1/32			
15745	3 " [Georgia Elnora]	"	11mo	F	1/32			
[redacted]	[Fannie]	[redacted]ife	27	"	I.W.			

ENROLLMENT OF NOS. 4 HEREON APPROVED BY THE SECRETARY OF INTERIOR NOV 26 1906

ENROLLMENT OF NOS. 1 2 and 3 HEREON APPROVED BY THE SECRETARY OF INTERIOR DEC -2 1904

TRIBAL ENROLLMENT OF PARENTS

	Name of Father	Year	County	Name of Mother	Year	County
1	Marmaduke Moran	C.C.R.#2 358	Choctaw residing ~~in Chickasaw Dist~~	Selina Moran	dead	non-citizen
2	No.1			Fannie Moran		" "
3	No.1			" "		" "
4	John Williams			Cynthia Williams		

~~No.1 is son of Marmaduke Y Moran on Choctaw card #43~~

No.1 transferred from Choctaw Card # D- 774; see decision of Oct. 15, 1904

No.1 is father of Nos 2 and 3 on Choctaw card #D-774

~~No.1 evidence of marriage to mother of Nos 2 and 3 filed Oct 27-1904~~

~~No.2 Born May 7 1899; proof of birth filed Oct. 27-1904~~

No.3 Born Sept 15, 1901; proof of birth filed Oct 27-1904

Nos 2 and 3 transferred from Choctaw Card # D- 774 10-[?]-04

~~No.4 placed on this card Aug. 17, 1906 under order of Commissioner to the Five Civilized Tribes of Aug. 8, 1906, holding that application was made for her enrollment within the time~~ limited by the provisions of the Act of Congress approved April 26, 1906

For child of Nos 1&4 see NB (March 3, 1905) card #5852

Aug 22/02 — Date of Application for Enrollment.

Date of transfer to this card: Oct 31, 1904

~~P.O. Comanche I.T. 11/13/05~~

Choctaw By Blood Enrollment Cards 1898-1914

RESIDENCE: Choctaw Nation ~~COUNTY~~. **Choctaw Na[redacted]** **Choctaw Roll** *(Not Including Freedmen)* CARD NO.
POST OFFICE: So - Mc Alester, I.T. FIELD NO. 5853

Dawes' Roll No.		NAME	Relationship to Person First Named	AGE	SEX	BLOOD	TRIBAL ENROLLMENT Year	County	Page ~~No.~~
IW 1199	1	Prola, John	First Named	36	M	I.W.	1897	Chick residing in Choctaw N. 1st Dist	82
	2								
	3								
	4								
	5								
	6								
	7								
	8								
	9								
	10								
	11								
	12								
	13								
	14	ENROLLMENT							
	15	OF NOS. 1 HEREON							
	16	APPROVED BY THE SECRETARY OF INTERIOR NOV 16 1904							
	17								

TRIBAL ENROLLMENT OF PARENTS

	Name of Father	Year	County	Name of Mother	Year	County
1	Peter Prola		non-citizen	Clara Prola		non-citizen
2						
3						
4						
5						

6 No.1 admitted by Dawes Commission as an intermarried citizen of the Choctaw
7 Nation Dec. 6/99 Case #610. No appeal.
No.1 on Chickasaw roll as "John Proler"
8 No.1 transferred from Chickasaw Card # 180 OCT 30 1904

Date of Application for Enrollment. Sept 5/98

RESIDENCE: Chickasaw Nation COUNTY. **Choctaw Nation** Choctaw Roll (Not Including Freedmen) CARD NO.
POST OFFICE: Duncan, I.T. FIELD NO. 5854

Dawes' Roll No.	NAME	Relationship to Person First Named	AGE	SEX	BLOOD	TRIBAL ENROLLMENT Year	County	No.
IW 1228	1 Tucker, Nancy		46	F	IW			
	2							
	3							
	4							
	5							
	6							
	7							
	8							
	9							
	10							
	11 ENROLLMENT							
	12 OF NOS. I HEREON APPROVED BY THE SECRETARY							
	13 OF INTERIOR DEC 13 1904							
	14							
	15							
	16							
	17 See Petition No 1046							

TRIBAL ENROLLMENT OF PARENTS

Name of Father	Year	County	Name of Mother	Year	County
1 Bannister Stone	Dead	Non-citizen	Katie Stone		noncitizen
2					
3					
4					
5					
6 No1 admitted by Commission in 1896 Choctaw case #298. Admitted					
7 by U.S. Court, South McAlester, I.T. Jan. 18, 1898. Court Case No 237.					
8					
9					
10 No1 transferred from Choctaw Card #5273					
11					
12					
13					
14					
15			Date of Application for Enrollment.		Date of transfer
16					to this card
17			10/17/98		NOV 3- 1904

RESIDENCE: COUNTY. **Choctaw Nation** **Choctaw Roll** *(Not Including Freedmen)* CARD NO.

POST OFFICE: Pauls Valley, I.T. FIELD NO. 5855

Dawes' Roll No.	NAME	Relationship to Person First Named	AGE	SEX	BLOOD	TRIBAL ENROLLMENT Year	County	No.
IW 1229	1 Loyd, John J.		35	M	I.W.			

ENROLLMENT
OF NOS. 1 HEREON
APPROVED BY THE SECRETARY
OF INTERIOR DEC 13 1904

TRIBAL ENROLLMENT OF PARENTS

Name of Father	Year	County	Name of Mother	Year	County
1 John Loyd	1896	Non Citz	Mary Loyd	dead	Non Citz

No.1 formerly husband of Elsa Loyd (nee Elsa, Asa or Isabel Frazier)
1893 Pay Roll, Cedar County, page 45, No. 477, now deceased. Also, formerly husband
of Sarah Loyd on card #989, final roll No. 2604.
No.1 was first married to Elsey Frazier License in name of
Elsey Frazier. Proof shows Asa Frazier. Claimed that Isabelle Frazier found on
page 45 No. 477, Cedar Co. 1893 Payroll; 15 years old, is the same person.
No.1 transferred from Choctaw Card # D- 131; See decision of Nov. 10, 1904.
No.1 originally listed for enrollment on Choctaw card #D- 131 April 28 '99.

Date of Application for Enrollment. April 28/99

Date of transfer to this card Nov. 26, 1904

RESIDENCE: COUNTY. **Choctaw Nation** **Choctaw Roll** *(Not Including Freedmen)* CARD NO.
POST OFFICE: Hugo, Ind. Ter. FIELD NO. 5856

Dawes' Roll No.	NAME	Relationship to Person First Named	AGE	SEX	BLOOD	TRIBAL ENROLLMENT Year	County	No.
IW 1230	1 Norris, Sallie		43	F	I.W.	1896	Kiamitia	14902
	2							
	3							
	4							
	5							
	6							
	7							
	8							
	9							
	10							
	11							
	12							
	13							
	14							
	15							
	16							
	17							

ENROLLMENT
OF NOS. 1 HEREON
APPROVED BY THE SECRETARY
OF INTERIOR DEC 13 1904

TRIBAL ENROLLMENT OF PARENTS

	Name of Father	Year	County	Name of Mother	Year	County
1	R. S. Rollins	dead	Non Citz	Tennie Rollins	dead	Non Citz

No.1 transferred from Choctaw Card # D-157; See decision of Nov. 10, 1904
No.1 originally listed for enrollment on Choctaw card #D- 157 May 11 or 12, 1899
No.1 formerly wife of Andrew Jackson Norris, 1896 Choctaw census roll, Towson Co. No 9664 (as Tone Norris) and who died in about the year 1900.

Date of Application for Enrollment.	Date of transfer to this card
5/11/99	Nov. 26, 1904

RESIDENCE: COUNTY. **Choctaw Nation** Choctaw Roll (*Not Including Freedmen*) CARD NO.

POST OFFICE: Antlers, I.T. FIELD NO. 5857

Dawes' Roll No.	NAME	Relationship to Person First Named	AGE	SEX	BLOOD	TRIBAL ENROLLMENT Year	County	No.
15755	1 Edwards, Thomas B		27	M	1/2	1893	Kiamitia	201
IW 1462	2 " Minnie	Wife	30	F	IW	1896	"	14495
15878	3 " Emma	Dau	5	F	1/4			
15994	4 " Mary L	"	1	F	1/4			

ENROLLMENT OF NOS. 3 HEREON APPROVED BY THE SECRETARY OF INTERIOR JUN 12 1905

ENROLLMENT OF NOS. 1 HEREON APPROVED BY THE SECRETARY OF INTERIOR DEC 15 1904

ENROLLMENT OF NOS. 2 HEREON APPROVED BY THE SECRETARY OF INTERIOR JUN 12 1905

ENROLLMENT OF NOS. 4 HEREON APPROVED BY THE SECRETARY OF INTERIOR JUN 16 1906

TRIBAL ENROLLMENT OF PARENTS

	Name of Father	Year	County	Name of Mother	Year	County
1	H.C. Edwards	1896	Choc Roll	Lydie Edwards	dead	Non Citz
2	Irull[sic] Dyson	Dead	Noncitizen	Mary Dyson	"	" "
3	No 1			No.2		
4	No.1			No2		

6 ~~No.1 on 1893 Pay roll as Ben Edwards, Page 23, No. 201, Kiamitia Co.~~

7 No2 was admitted by Dawes Commission in 1896 Choctaw case #1170. No appeal

No3 born August 17, 1897. Proof of birth filed February 17, 1905

8 ~~No3 transferred from Choctaw Card # D-170 February 20, 1905~~

10 No.1 transferred from Choctaw Card # D-170; See decision of Nov. 9, 1904

No.1 originally listed for enrollment on Choctaw card #D-170 5/18/99

11 ~~No2 transferred from Choctaw Card # D-170 February 20, 1905. See~~

12 ~~decision of February 3, 1905~~

13 No.4 was born Nov. 5, 1901; application received March 4, 1905

14 under Act of Congress approved March 3, 1905

Date of Application for Enrollment 5/1

Nov.

Date o

to th

17 ~~PO Valliant I.T. 2/24/05~~

[Illegible] I.T.

RESIDENCE: COUNTY. **Choctaw Nation** **Choctaw Roll** *(Not Including Freedmen)* CARD NO.
POST OFFICE: Lutie, I.T. FIELD NO. 5858

Dawes' Roll No.	NAME	Relationship to Person First Named	AGE	SEX	BLOOD	TRIBAL ENROLLMENT Year	County	No.
15756	1 Lomer, Mary		76	F	1/2	1896	Gaines	7833
	2							
	3							
	4							
	5							
	6							
	7							
	8							
	9							
	10							
	11							
	12							
	13							
	14							
	15							
	16							
	17							

ENROLLMENT
OF NOS. 1 HEREON
APPROVED BY THE SECRETARY
OF INTERIOR DEC 15 1904

TRIBAL ENROLLMENT OF PARENTS

	Name of Father	Year	County	Name of Mother	Year	County
1	Jeremiah Ward	dead	Non Citz	Katie Ward	dead	Choctaw
2						
3						
4						
5						

6 See her testimony
7 No.1 on 1893 Pay Roll Gaines County, page 35, No. 322 as Mary Loman.
No.1 on 1885 Census " " " No. 467 as Mary Loman.
8 No.1 transferred from Choctaw Card # D- 271; see decision of Nov. 3, 1904
9 No.1 originally listed for enrollment on Choctaw card #D-271 Aug 1/99
10 No.1 on 1896 Census roll as Mary Lomer.

Date of Application for Enrollment. Aug 1/99

Date of transfer to this card Nov. 26, 1904

RESIDENCE: Tobucksy COUNTY. **Choctaw Nation** **Choctaw Roll** *(Not Including Freedmen)*

POST OFFICE: M^c^Alester, I.T.

Dawes' Roll No.	NAME	Relationship to Person First Named	AGE	SEX	BLOOD	TRIBAL ENROLLMENT Year	County	No.
IW 1231	1 McCay, Sarah E	Named	40	F	I.W.			
	2							
	3							
	4							
	5							
	6							
	7							
	8							
	9							
	10							
	11							
	12							
	13							
	14							
	15							
	16							
	17							

ENROLLMENT
OF NOS. 1 HEREON
APPROVED BY THE SECRETARY
OF INTERIOR DEC 13 1904

TRIBAL ENROLLMENT OF PARENTS

	Name of Father	Year	County	Name of M
1	Taggert	dead	Non Citz	Sarah Taggert
2				
3				
4				

No.1 formerly wife of Osborne Pusley a recognized Choctaw by blood who died in 1886 or 1887 the name of whose daughter (Elmira Mitchell) by said marriage is No. 14943 on final Choctaw roll.

~~Certificate of marriage between Osborne Pusley and Sallie, his wife, July 28/73 filed herewith.~~

As to intermarriage and re-marriage, see testimony of her husband Alfred M^c^Cay.

~~Evidence of divorce between No.1 and her Choctaw husband Osborne Pusley, received and filed Nov. 5, 1902.~~

No.1 transferred from Choctaw Card # D-292: See decision of Nov. 3, 1904

~~No.1 originally listed for enrollment on Choctaw card #D- 292.~~

Sept 3/99
Date of Application for Enrollment.

~~Nov. 26, 1904~~
transfer date

RESIDENCE:
POST OFFICE: Roena, I.T.

Choctaw Nation — **Choctaw Roll** (Not Including Freedmen) — CARD NO. 5860

Dawes' Roll No.	NAME	Relationship to Person First Named	AGE	SEX	BLOOD	TRIBAL ENROLLMENT Year	County	No.
IW 1232	1 Askew, Maxie		21	F	I.W.			
	2							
	3							
	4							
	5							
	6							
	7							
	8							
	9							
	10							
	11							
	12							
	13							
	14							
	15							
	16							
	17							

ENROLLMENT
OF NOS. 1 HEREON
APPROVED BY THE SECRETARY
OF INTERIOR DEC 13 1904

TRIBAL ENROLLMENT OF PARENTS

Name of Father	Year	County	Name of Mother	Year	County
1 Dave Witter		Non Citz	Annie Witter	Dead	Non Citz

6 ~~Daniel B. Askew husband of No.1 on final roll, No. 14272~~
7 As to marriage see testimony of Daniel B. Askew, husband, on care #343
8 No.1 transferred from Choctaw Card # D-451: See decision of Nov. 9, 1904
~~No.1 originally listed for enrollment on Choctaw card #D-451 9/7/99~~

Date of Application for Enrollment. 9/7/99

Date of transfer to this card Nov. 26, 1904

RESIDENCE: COUNTY. **Choctaw Nation** Choctaw Roll (Not Including Freedme[n])

POST OFFICE: Colbert, I.T.

Dawes' Roll No.	NAME	Relationship to Person First Named	AGE	SEX	BLOOD	TRIBAL ENROLLMENT Year	County	No.
IW1233	1 Askew, Arkansas		23	F	I.W.			

ENROLLMENT OF NOS. 1 HEREON APPROVED BY THE SECRETARY OF INTERIOR DEC 13 1904

TRIBAL ENROLLMENT OF PARENTS

Name of Father	Year	County	Name of Mother	Year	County
1 R. W. Voss		No[n Citizen]			

6 No.1 is wife of Oscar Askew on Choctaw card 343, final roll #14274

7 As to marriage see testimony of husband Oscar Askew

No.1 originally listed for enrollment on Choctaw card #D-452 9/7/99

8 Transferred to this card Nov. 26, 1904; see decision of Nov. 3, 1904

10 For child of No1 see NB (Apr 26/06) Card #337

Date of Application for Enrollment.	Date of transfer to this card
9/7/99	Nov. 26, 1904

RESIDENCE: COUNTY. **Choctaw Nation** **Choctaw Roll** *(Not Including Freedmen)* CARD NO.
POST OFFICE: Bache, I.T. FIELD NO. 5862

Dawes' Roll No.	NAME	Relationship to Person First Named	AGE	SEX	BLOOD	TRIBAL ENROLLMENT Year	County	No.
IW 1234	1 Brashears, Martha H		42	F	I.W.			
	2							
	3							
	4							
	5							
	6							
	7							
	8							
	9							
	10							
	11							
	12							
	13							
	14							
	15							
	16							
	17							

ENROLLMENT OF NOS. 1 HEREON APPROVED BY THE SECRETARY OF INTERIOR DEC 13 1904

TRIBAL ENROLLMENT OF PARENTS

Name of Father	Year	County	Name of Mother	Year	County
1 Wm Grissom		Non-Cit	Mary Grissom		U.S. Cit
2					
3					
4					
5					

~~Former husband, Albert Brashears (deceased) who is identified~~ upon the 1885 Choctaw Census Roll, Atoka County, #824.
No.1 originally listed for enrollment on Choctaw card #D-453 Sept 8/99 ~~and transferred to this card Nov. 26, 1904. See decision of Nov. 9, 1904~~

Date of Application for Enrollment. Sept 8/99

~~Date of transfer~~ N[redacted]4

RESIDENCE: COUNTY. **Choctaw Nation** **Choctaw Roll** (Not Including Freedmen) CARD No.
POST OFFICE: Wapanucka, I.T. FIELD No.

Dawes' Roll No.		NAME	Relationship to Person First Named	AGE	SEX	BLOOD	TRIBAL ENROLLMENT Year	County	No.
IW 4235	1	Taliaferro, John D.		26	M	I.W.			
	2								
	3								
	4								
	5								
	6								
	7								
	8								
	9								
	10								
	11								
	12								
	13								
	14								
	15								
	16								
	17								

ENROLLMENT
OF NOS. 1 HEREON
APPROVED BY THE SECRETARY
OF INTERIOR DEC 13 1904

TRIBAL ENROLLMENT OF PARENTS

	Name of Father	Year	County	Name of Mother	Year	County
1	Sam Taliaferro		non Citz	Eliza Taliaferro		non Citz
2						
3						
4						
5						

6 Nora Taliaferro on final Choctaw roll No. 15382
7 License issued by County Judge Tishomingo Co. Sept 2-99
Married Sept 10-99
8 ~~License to be recorded and returned~~
9 ~~See enrollment of wife, Nora Dibble, Choctaw card #408.~~
10 Evidence of marriage filed this day May 9, 1901
11 No.1 originally listed for enrollment on Choctaw card #D-481-9/11/99 and transferred to this card Nov. 26, 1904; see decision of Nov. 9, 1904
12 ~~For child of No.1 see N.B. (April 26, 1906) Card No. 137~~
13 " " " " " " (March 3, 1905) " " 684

Date of Application for Enrollment.	Date of transfer to this card
9/11/99	Nov. 26, 1904

Choctaw By Blood Enrollment Cards 1898-1914

RESIDENCE:
POST OFFICE: Pine,

Dawes' Roll No.	NAME	Relationship to Person First Named	AGE	SEX	BLOOD	TRIBAL ENROLLMENT Year	County	No.
IW 1236	1 Hancock, Henry		40	M	I.W.			

ENROLLMENT
OF NOS. 1 HEREON
APPROVED BY THE SECRETARY
OF INTERIOR DEC 13 1904

TRIBAL ENROLLMENT OF PARENTS

Name of Father	Year	County	Name of Mother	Year	County
1 Lige Hancock	dead	Non Citz	Frances Hancock	dead	Non Citz

As to marriage see his testimony
Married a Choctaw, lived with her until she died, since married a white woman
Testimony or Don J. Folsom who issued license to be supplied
~~Heard at Atoka, IT Aug 20th, 1901~~

No.1 originally listed for enrollment on Choctaw card #D- 538 Dec 7/99
transferred to this card Nov. 26, 1904. See decision of Nov. 3, 1904
~~No.1 formerly husband of Minirva[sic] Hancock (nee Shults) 1893 pay roll~~
~~Atoka Co page 49 No. 528 and who died about 1892.~~
For children of No1 see NB (Apr 26 '06) No 1116

Date of Application for Enrollment. Dec. 7/99

Date of transfer to this card Nov. 26, 1904

Choctaw By Blood Enrollment Cards 1898-1914

RESIDENCE: COUNTY. **Choctaw Nation** **Choctaw Roll** *(Not Including Freedmen)* CARD NO.
POST OFFICE: Hart, I.T. FIELD NO. 5865

Dawes' Roll No.	NAME	Relationship to Person First Named	AGE	SEX	BLOOD	TRIBAL ENROLLMENT Year	County	No.
IW 1237	1 Rogers, Lizzie		47	F	I.W.			
	2							
	3							
	4							
	5							
	6							
	7							
	8 [The majority of information on this card is completely illegible]							
	9							
	10							
	11							
	12							
	13							
	14							
	15							
	16							
	17							

TRIBAL ENROLLMENT OF PARENTS

Name of Father	Year	County	Name of Mother	Year	County
1 Bill Jones	dead	Non-citizen	Nancy Jones	dead	Cherokee
2					
3					
4					
5					
6 No.1 formerly wife of Alfred Victor, Choctaw [remainder illegible]					
7 No.1 claims [remainder illegible]					
8					
9					
10					
11 No.1 is now the wife of J.F. Rogers [remainder illegible]					
12					
13					
14					
15					
16					
17					

RESIDENCE: Choctaw Nation COUNTY. **Choctaw Nation** **Choctaw Roll** (*Not Including Freedmen*) CARD NO.
POST OFFICE: Coalgate, Ind. Ter. FIELD NO. 5866

[redacted]		NAME	Relationship to Person First Named	AGE	SEX	BLOOD	TRIBAL ENROLLMENT Year	County	No.
15757	1	Marshall, William Henry		30	M	1/4	1896	Atoka	8816
IW 1240	2	" Annie Palmer	Wife	22	F	I.W.			
15758	3	" William Henry Jr	Son	2	M	1/8			
	4								
	5								
	6								
	7								
	8								
	9								
	10								
	11								
	12								
	13								
	14								
	15								
	16								
	17								

ENROLLMENT
OF NOS. 1 and 3 HEREON
APPROVED BY THE SECRETARY
OF INTERIOR DEC 15 1904

ENROLLMENT
OF NOS. 2 HEREON
APPROVED BY THE SECRETARY
OF INTERIOR DEC 13 1904

TRIBAL ENROLLMENT OF PARENTS

	Name of Father	Year	County	Name of Mother	Year	County
1	Henry Marshall	1896	Atoka	Nancy Marshall		non citz
2	John Palmer		non citz	Winnie Palmer	dead	"
3	No.1			No.2		
4						
5						

6 No.1 on 1893 Pay Roll, Atoka County, page 74 No. 771
7 No.1 is the son of Henry Marshall on Choctaw care #4401
admitted by act of Choctaw Council approved November 4, 1886.
8 No.1 was not included in the act admitting his father.
9 Affidavit as to age of No2 and names of her parents, Filed Feb. 7, 1901
10 Certificate of marriage received and filed March 14, 1903.
No.3 born May 17, 1900; proof of birth filed Oct. 5, 1903.
11 Nos 1-2-3 originally listed for enrollment on Choctaw card #D- 598 Dec. 10, 1900;
12 transferred to this card Nov. 26, 1904. See decision of Nov. 3, 1904
13 For child of Nos 1 and 2 see NB (March 3, 1905) #1256

Date of Application for Enrollment. Dec. 10,1900

Date of transfer to this card Nov. 26, 1904

RESIDENCE: COUNTY. **Choctaw Nation** **Choctaw Roll** *(Not Including Freedmen)*

POST OFFICE: Hartshorne, I.T.

Dawes' Roll No.	NAME	Relationship to Person First Named	AGE	SEX	BLOOD	TRIBAL ENROLLMENT Year	County	No.
IW 1241	1 Baker, Mollie	First Named	31	F	I.W.			
15759	2 " Ella	Dau	4	F	1/2			
	3							
	4							
	5							
	6							
	7							
	8							
	9							
	10							
	11							
	12							
	13							
	14							
	15							
	16							
	17							

ENROLLMENT OF NOS. 2 HEREON APPROVED BY THE SECRETARY OF INTERIOR DEC 15 1904

ENROLLMENT OF NOS. 1 HEREON APPROVED BY THE SECRETARY OF INTERIOR DEC 13 1904

TRIBAL ENROLLMENT OF PARENTS

Name of Father	Year	County	Name of Mother	Year	County
1 Jim Tubbs	dead	non citizen	Scott Tubbs		non-citizen
2 Billy Baker	"	Choctaw	No.1		
3					
4					
5					

6 Billy Baker former husband of No.1 on 1896 Choctaw census roll Sugar Loaf Co No. 768
7 No.1 claims as an intermarried citizen by reason of her marriage
8 Sept 21st 1895 to Billy Baker, a full blood Choctaw Indian, with whom she lived until his death June 8, 1898
9 No.2 claims to be the child of Billy Baker
10 As to Cherokee blood of applicants and former marriage and divorce
11 of Billy Baker, see testimony of Aug. 24th, 1901.
Nos. 1 and 2 originally listed for enrollment on Choctaw card #D- 656 Aug 24, 1901:
12 transferred to this card Nov. 26, 1904. See decision of Nov. 9, 1904

Date of transfer to this card Nov. 26, 1904

Date of Application for Enrollment. Aug 24/01

Choctaw By Blood Enrollment Cards 1898-1914

RESIDENCE: COUNTY. **Choctaw Nation** **Choctaw Roll** *(Not Including Freedmen)* CARD NO.
POST OFFICE: Cumberland, I.T. FIELD NO.

Dawes' Roll No.	NAME	Relationship to Person First Named	AGE	SEX	BLOOD	TRIBAL ENROLLMENT Year	County
IW 1238	1 Dillard, Alpha Vituria		19	F	I.W.		
	2						
	3						
	4						
	5						
	6						
	7						
	8						
	9						
	10						
	11						
	12						
	13						
	14						
	15						
	16						
	17						

ENROLLMENT
OF NOS. 1 HEREON
APPROVED BY THE SECRETARY
OF INTERIOR DEC 13 1904

TRIBAL ENROLLMENT OF PARENTS

Name of Father	Year	County	Name of Mother	Year	County
1 Dabney Barnes		non-citizen	Mollie Barnes		non-citizen
2					
3					
4					
5					

6 ~~No.1 is the wife of Lee Hamilton Dillard on Choc. card #268, final roll #569~~
7 Married Feb. 10, 1901. See evidence of marriage filed Aug. 29, 1902.
8 No.1 originally listed for enrollment on Choctaw card #D- 780 Aug. 29, 1902
transferred to this card Nov. 26, 1904 See decision of Nov. 9, 1904

Date of Application for Enrollment. Aug 29/02

Date of transfer to this card Nov. 26, 1904

Choctaw By Blood Enrollment Cards 1898-1914

RESIDENCE: Chickasaw Nation COUNTY. **Choctaw Nation** **Choctaw Roll** *(Not Including Freedmen)*
POST OFFICE: McGee, Ind. Ter. FIELD NO. 5869

Dawes' Roll No.	NAME	Relationship to Person First Named	AGE	SEX	BLOOD	TRIBAL ENROLLMENT Year	County	No.
IW 1239	1 Hibdon, Emma Lively		19	F	I.W.			
	2							
	3							
	4							
	5							
	6							
	7							
	8							
	9							
	10							
	11							
	12							
	13							
	14							
	15							
	16							
	17							

ENROLLMENT
OF NOS. 1 HEREON
APPROVED BY THE SECRETARY
OF INTERIOR DEC 13 1904

TRIBAL ENROLLMENT OF PARENTS

	Name of Father	Year	County	Name of Mother	Year	County
1	Wash Lively		non-citizen	Frances Lively		non-citizen

6 Claims rights as an intermarried citizen by reason of her marriage
7 in Aug 1901 to Henry Hibdon Choctaw card #90, final roll #170
Evidence of marriage filed Oct 21, 1902.
8 No.1 originally listed for enrollment on Choctaw card #D- 815 Oct. 21, 1902;
9 transferred to this card Nov. 26, 1904 See decision of Nov. 9, 1904

11 For child of No.1 see NB (Apr 26-06) Card #388
" " " " " " " (Mar 3-05) " # 28

Date of transfer to this card Nov. 26, 1904

Date of Application for Enrollment. Oct 21/02

17 PO Byars IT 12/14/04

RESIDENCE: Tobucksy COUNTY. **Choctaw Nation** **Choctaw Roll** (Not Including Freedmen) CARD NO. FIELD NO. 5870
POST OFFICE: Carbon, I.T.

Dawes' Roll No.		NAME	Relationship to Person First Named	AGE	SEX	BLOOD	TRIBAL ENROLLMENT Year	County	No.
IW 1268	1	Phebus, Margaret	First Named	35	F	I.W.			
	2								
	3								
	4								
	5								
	6								
	7								
	8								
	9								
	10								
	11								
	12								
	13								
	14								
	15								
	16								
	17								

ENROLLMENT
OF NOS. 1 HEREON
APPROVED BY THE SECRETARY
OF INTERIOR DEC 30 1904

TRIBAL ENROLLMENT OF PARENTS

	Name of Father	Year	County	Name of Mother	Year	County
1	Wiley Garvin	D'd	non-citizen	Liddy Garvin		Gaines
2						
3						
4						
5						

6 No.1 admitted in '96 Case #988
7 No.1 admitted by U.S. Court at So. McAlester Aug. 25/97
8 Case #187 as Margaret Welch. See her testimony as
to her residence and the birth of her child as to her
9 parents see her testimony and that of Wiley Garvin
10 No.1 is now the wife of W. M. Phebus, a non citizen 12/24/02
11 Sallie Welch, daughter of No.1 is on Choctaw R #426
No.1 transferred from Choctaw Card # D- 4650 12/5/04

Date of transfer to this card 12/5/04

Date of Application for Enrollment. 9/6/99

RESIDENCE: Choctaw Nation ~~COUNTY.~~ **Choctaw Nation** **Choctaw Roll** *(Not Including Freedmen)* CAR[redacted]
POST OFFICE: Antlers, I.T. FIELD NO. 5871

Dawes' Roll No.	NAME	Relationship to Person First Named	AGE	SEX	BLOOD	TRIBAL ENROLLMENT Year	County	No.
IW 1269	1 Hamilton, Laura		35	F	I.W.	1885	Blue	740

ENROLLMENT OF NOS. 1 HEREON APPROVED BY THE SECRETARY OF INTERIOR DEC 30 1904

TRIBAL ENROLLMENT OF PARENTS

Name of Father	Year	County	Name of Mother	Year	County
1 Jesse Boyd	dead	non citizen	Elizabeth Brown		non citizen

~~No.1 is identified upon the 1885 Choctaw Census Roll, Blue Co., No 740~~
(as Laura Durand)
No.1 was formerly wife of Pike Durant, a Choctaw by blood, who is on Choctaw ~~Roll, No. 13853 as Albert P. Durant.~~
~~No.1 is now the wife of Lafe Hamilton, a noncitizen white man..~~
No.1 originally listed for enrollment Oct 12/98 on Chickasaw card #D-161; transferred to this card Dec. 15, 1904. See decision of Nov. 9, 1904.
~~For children of No1 see NB (Apr 26-06) #1122~~

Date of Application for Enrollment. Oct 12/98

Date of transfer to this card 12/15/04

Choctaw By Blood Enrollment Cards 1898-1914

RESIDENCE: Skullyville COUNTY. **Choctaw Nation** **Choctaw Roll** *(Not Including Freedmen)* FIELD NO.

POST OFFICE: Cameron, I.T.

Dawes' Roll No.	NAME	Relationship to Person First Named	AGE	SEX	BLOOD	TRIBAL ENROLLMENT Year	County	No.
IW 1270	1 Wade, Margaret	First Named	66	F	I.W.	1896	Skullyville	15144
	2							
	3							
	4							
	5							
	6							
	7							
	8							
	9							
	10							
	11							
	12							
	13							
	14							
	15							
	16							
	17							

ENROLLMENT
OF NOS. 1 HEREON
APPROVED BY THE SECRETARY
OF INTERIOR Dec 30 1904

TRIBAL ENROLLMENT OF PARENTS

	Name of Father	Year	County	Name of Mother	Year	County
1	Aaron Brooks	dead	non citz	Martha Brooks	1896	Non Citz

After the death of her Choctaw husband Cunningham Wade, No.1 married James Haggard, a white man. Cunningham Wade died in 1878

No.1 originally listed for enrollment June 5/99 on Choctaw card #D-200; transferred to this card Dec. 15,1904, See decision of Nov. 28, 1904

Date of Application for Enrollment June 5/99

Date of transfer to this card 12/15/04

RESIDENCE: Atoka COUNTY. **Choctaw Nation** Choctaw Rol
POST OFFICE: Atoka, I.T. (Not Including Freedmen) FIELD NO. 5873

Dawes' Roll No.	NAME	Relationship to Person First Named	AGE	SEX	BLOOD	TRIBAL ENROLLMENT Year	County	No.
IW 1271	1 Jones, Laura A	First Named	54	F	I.W.	1896	Atoka	7280
	2							
	3							
	4							
	5							
	6							
	7							
	8							
	9							
	10							
	11							
	12							
	13							
	14							
	15							
	16							
	17							

ENROLLMENT
OF NOS. 1 HEREON
APPROVED BY THE SECRETARY
OF INTERIOR DEC 30 1904

TRIBAL ENROLLMENT OF PARENTS

Name of Father	Year	County	Name of Mother	Year	County
1 Yancey Atchison	dead	Non Citz	Jane Atchison	dead	Non Citz
2					
3					
4					
5					

6 ~~On 1896 roll as Lucy Ann Jones.~~
7 Husband of No.1, Noel Jones, on Choctaw card #4080, No. 11412 on Choctaw roll.
As to marriage and separation see her testimony
8 ~~No.1 originally listed for enrollment Sept 2/99 on Choctaw card #D- 41 ;~~
9 ~~transferred to this card Dec. 15,1904 See decision of Nov. 28, 1904~~

Date of Application for Enrollment.	~~Date of transfer~~ to this card
Sept 2/99	12/15/04

RESIDENCE: Chickasaw Nation COUNTY. **Choctaw Nation** **Choctaw Roll** *(Not Including Freedmen)* CARD No.
POST OFFICE: Marlow, Ind. Ter

Dawes' Roll No.	NAME	Relationship to Person First Named	AGE	SEX	BLOOD	TRIBAL ENROLLMENT Year	County	No.
IW 1272	1 Burkes, Alice V.R		40	F	I.W.			
	2							
	3							
	4							
	5							
	6							
	7							
	8							
	9							
	10							
	11							
	12							
	13							
	14							
	15							
	16							
	17							

ENROLLMENT
OF NOS. 1 HEREON
APPROVED BY THE SECRETARY
OF INTERIOR DEC 30 1904

TRIBAL ENROLLMENT OF PARENTS

Name of Father	Year	County	Name of Mother	Year	County
1 J. D. Echols	dead	non citizen	Tabitha C. Calhoun	dead	non citizen
2					
3					
4					
5					

No.1 claims as an intermarried citizen by reason of her marriage
to John G. Burkes on Choctaw card #77, Choctaw roll No. 14173.
No.1 originally listed for enrollment Oct 15, 1902 on Choctaw card #D-812;
transferred to this card Dec. 15,1904 See decision of Nov. 28, 1904

Date of Application for Enrollment. Oct 15/02

Date of transfer to this card 12/15/04

RESIDENCE: COUNTY. **Choctaw Nation** **Choctaw Roll** *(Not Including Freedmen)* CARD NO.
POST OFFICE: Sulphur, I.T. FIELD NO. 5875

Dawes' Roll No.		NAME	Relationship to Person First Named	AGE	SEX	BLOOD	TRIBAL ENROLLMENT Year	County	No.
273	1	M^c^Gee, Nannie		28	F	I.W.			
	2								
	3								
	4								
	5								
	6								
	7								
	8								
	9								
	10								
	11								
	12								
	13								
	14								
	15								
	16								
	17								

ENROLLMENT OF NOS. 1 HEREON APPROVED BY THE SECRETARY OF INTERIOR DEC 30 1904

TRIBAL ENROLLMENT OF PARENTS

	Name of Father	Year	County	Name of Mother	Year	County
1	Ben Duncan		non-citizen	Elizabeth Duncan		non-citizen

Formerly wife of Andrew Collins on Choctaw card #2732, Choctaw roll #7972
After separation and divorce she married Arch M^c^Gee on Chickasaw card #736 Chickasaw roll #2176 (as Archie M^c^Gee)
~~No.1 originally listed for enrollment Nov. 7, 1902 on Choctaw card #D-822: transferred to this card Dec. 15,1904 See decision of Nov. 26, 1904~~

Date of Application for Enrollment. 11/7/02

Date of transfer to this card 12/15/04

[illegible]octaw Nation
Garvin, I.T.

COUNTY. **Choctaw Nation**

Choctaw Roll
(Not Including Freedmen)

Dawes' Roll No.		NAME	Relationship to Person First Named	AGE	SEX	BLOOD	TRIBAL ENROLLMENT Year	County	No.
IW 1274	1	Williams, Rocey Lee		20	F	I.W.			
	2								
	3								
	4								
	5								
	6								
	7								
	8								
	9								
	10								
	11								
	12								
	13								
	14								
	15								
	16								
	17								

ENROLLMENT
OF NOS. 1 HEREON
APPROVED BY THE SECRETARY
OF INTERIOR DEC 30 1904

TRIBAL ENROLLME[illegible]

	Name of Father	Year	County	[illegible]		[illegible]nty
1	Alvus Pigg		non citizen	E[illegible]	[illegible]	[illegible]-citizen
2						
3						
4						
5						

6 No.1 is separated from her husband, Abner Williams, on Choctaw card
7 #534 Choctaw roll #1137
8 No.1 originally listed for enrollment Nov. 26, 1902 on Choctaw card #D- 843
transferred to this card Dec. 15,1904 See decision of Nov. 28, 1904

Date of Application for Enrollment. 11/26/02

Date of transfer to this card 12/15/04

RESIDENCE: Chicka[redacted]
POST OFFICE: Box #314, Ada, Ind. Ter.

Choctaw Nation — Choctaw Roll (Not Including Freedmen) — CARD NO. / FIELD NO. 5877

Dawes' Roll No.		NAME	Relationship to Person First Named	AGE	SEX	BLOOD	TRIBAL ENROLLMENT Year	County	No.
15771	1	Stewart, John B	First Named	40	M	1/4	1893	Atoka	960
15772	2	" John D	son	7	M	1/8			
15773	3	" Stella May	dau	6	F	1/8			
15774	4	" George E	son	3	M	1/8			
15775	5	" Wynona Elizabeth	dau	2	F	1/8			
15776	6	" Knox	son	1	M	1/8			
IW 1539	7	" Sarah I.	Wife	28	F	I.W.			

ENROLLMENT OF NOS. 7 HEREON APPROVED BY THE SECRETARY OF INTERIOR Mar 14, 1906

ENROLLMENT OF NOS. 1,2,3,4,5 and 6 HEREON APPROVED BY THE SECRETARY OF INTERIOR Dec 28 1904

[redacted]NTS

	Name of Father	Year	County	Name of Mother	Year	County
1	John Stewart	IW	Atoka	Nancy J Stewart	dead	Choc. roll
2	No.1			Sarah I Stewart		Court citizen
3	No.1			" "		" "
4	No.1			" "		" "
5	No.1			" "		" "
6	No.1			" "		" "
7	George King			Elizabeth King		non citz

No.1 admitted by decision of U.S. Indian Agent (Union Agency) Oct. 12, 1889 which action was approved by the Secretary of Interior Nov. 19, 1889

Nos 1 to 6 incl enrolled by decision of Commission to Five Civilized Tribes of July 20, 1903: ~~which decision was approved by the Secretary of the Interior Dec. 1, 1904 (I.T.D.2996-1904)~~

Nos 1,2,3 and 4 transferred from Choctaw Card # D-1 and Nos 5 and 6 transferred from Choctaw Card #15, Dec. 9, 1904.

No7 transferred to this card from Choctaw D-977, November 27, 1905 see ~~decision of November 11, 1904.~~

Ages given hereon as of September 25, 1902.

Date of Application for Enrollment. Sep. 2/98

Date of Transfer ~~to this Card~~ Dec. -9 1904

Choctaw By Blood Enrollment Cards 1898-1914

RESIDENCE: Chic

POST OFFICE: Purdy, Ind. Ter.

Choctaw Nation

Choctaw Roll *(Not Including Freedmen)*

CARD N

FIELD NO. [illegible]

Dawes' Roll No.	NAME	Relationship to Person First Named	AGE	SEX	BLOOD	TRIBAL ENROLLMENT Year	County	No.
IW 1365	1 Thompson, Mary Ann		44	F	I.W.			
	16 See Petition No W 44							

ENROLLMENT OF NOS. 1 HEREON APPROVED BY THE SECRETARY OF INTERIOR MAR 13 1905

				Year	County
1 Henry Meyers	dead	Non citizen	Elizabeth Meyers		Non citizen

Husband of No.1 is No.1 on Choctaw card #R-301

No.1 admitted by Commission in 1896, case #274

~~No.1 admitted by United States Court, Central District, August 2, 1898 in citizenship case #227~~

No.1 admitted as a citizen by [remainder illegible]

~~No.1 transferred from Choctaw Card # 5031, December 24, 1904~~

Date of Application for Enrollment. 9/8/99

Date of transfer to this card DEC 24 1904

Choctaw By Blood Enrollment Cards 1898-1914

RESIDENCE: Chickasaw Nation ~~COUNTY~~.
POST OFFICE: Lone Grove, Ind Ter

Choctaw Nation

Choctaw Roll *(Not Including Freedmen)*

CARD NO.
FIELD NO.

Dawes' Roll No.		NAME	Relationship to Person First Named	AGE	SEX	BLOOD	TRIBAL ENROLLMENT Year	County	No.
IW 1366	1	Nelson, Lula		35	F	I.W.			
	2								
	3								
	4								
	5								
	6								
	7								
	8								
	9								
	10								
	11								
	12								
	13								
	14								
	15								
	16								
	17								

ENROLLMENT
OF NOS. 1 HEREON
APPROVED BY THE SECRETARY
OF INTERIOR MAR 14 1905

TRIBAL ENROLLMENT OF PARENTS

	Name of Father	Year	County	Name of Mother	Year	County
1	Geo. W. Morse		non-citizen	Elizabeth Morse		non-citizen
2						
3						
4						

~~Admitted by Dawes Com 1896, Case No. 408 and no appeal taken.~~
Married in Texas under U.S. law to A. P. Harkins, a Choctaw Indian,
Nov. 20, 1895, After his death she married George C. Nelson, a white man,
in Dec, 1896,
~~No.1 originally listed for enrollment on Choctaw card D-30 Sept 22/98~~
transferred to this card Feb. 1, 1905. See decision of Jan. 16, 1905.
Albert P. Harkins, former husband of No.1 1893 Blue No 536
He died in January, 1896

Date of Application for Enrollment. Sept 22/98

Date of transfer to this card Feb. 1, 1905

DENCE: Chickasaw Nation ~~COUNTY.~~ **Cl[redacted] Nation** **Choctaw Roll** *(Not Including Freedmen)* CARD NO. FIELD NO. 5880

OFFICE: Ninnekah, I.T.

ves' No.		NAME	Relationship to Person First Named	AGE	SEX	BLOOD	TRIBAL ENROLLMENT Year	County	No.
367	1	Stephens, Charlotte		32	F	I.W.			
	2								
	3								
	4								
	5								
	6								
	7								
	8								
	9								
	10	ENROLLMENT							
	11	OF NOS. 1 HEREON							
	12	APPROVED BY THE SECRETARY OF INTERIOR MAR 14 1905							
	13								
	14								
	15								
	16								
	17	See Petition No W 86-87							

TRIBAL ENROLLMENT OF PARENTS

	Name of Father	Year	County	Name of Mother	Year	County
1	Tom Mason		non citizen	Sarah Mason		non citizen
2						
3						
4						
5						
6	~~Married first to John Freeney, a Choctaw, in 1891. He died in 1894.~~					
7	" next " Dave Stephens, a white man, in 1896.					
8	John Freeney on 1893 Pay Roll, Blue Co, page 40, No. 423					
	~~No.1 originally listed for enrollment on Choctaw card #D- 82 Oct. 17/98~~					
9	~~transferred to this card Feb. 1, 1905. See decision of Jan. 16, 1905.~~					
10	For children of No.1 see NB (Apr 26-06) #1248					
11						
12						
13						
14						
15						
16						~~Date of transfer~~ to this card
17			Date of Application for Enrollment.	Oct 17/98		Feb. 1, 1905

RESIDENCE: State of Texas ~~COUNTY.~~ **Choctaw Nation** Choctaw Roll (Not Including Freedmen) CARD NO.
POST OFFICE: Checotah, Texas FIELD NO. 5881

Dawes' Roll No.	NAME	Relationship to Person First Named	AGE	SEX	BLOOD	TRIBAL ENROLLMENT Year	County	No.
15814	1 Davis, Albert		28	M	Full	1896	Kiamitia	3460

ENROLLMENT
OF NOS. 1 HEREON
APPROVED BY THE SECRETARY
OF INTERIOR MAR 15 1905

~~Send all letters to No.1 to Hugo, I.T.~~
Care of National Real Estate Co. 10/22/04

TRIBAL ENROLLMENT OF PARENTS

Name of Father	Year	County	Name of Mother	Year	County
1 Geo Davis	dead	Jacks Fork	Elsie	dead	Jacks Fork

Also on 1893 Pay roll as an orphan Page 124 No,
Has lived in Texas since 1879

Date of Application for Enrollment.

No.1 originally listed for enrollment on Choctaw card #D- 171 5/18/99;
transferred to this card Jan. 28, 1905. See decision of Jan. 12, 1905

Date of transfer to this card
Jan. 28, 1905

RESIDENCE: Wade COUNTY. **Choctaw N**[redacted] CARD NO.
POST OFFICE: Talihina, I.T. FIELD NO. 5882

Dawes' Roll No.	NAME	Relationship to Person First Named	AGE	SEX	BLOOD	TRIBAL ENROLLMENT Year	County	No.
15815	1 Woods, Minnie		12	F	1/2	1896	Wade	13072

ENROLLMENT
~~OF NOS.~~ 1 ~~HEREON~~
APPROVED BY THE SECRETARY
OF INTERIOR MAR 15 1905

TRIBAL ENROLLMENT OF PARENTS

Name of Father	Year	County	Name of Mother	Year	County
1 William Woods	dead	Wade	Winnie Woods	1896	Non Citz

~~No.1 Illegitimate child~~
No.1 is identified upon the 1893 Pay Roll, Wade County page 36, No. 300
No.1 originally listed for enrollment on Choctaw card #D-183 5/29/99
~~transferred to this card Jan. 28, 1905. See decision of Jan. 12, 1905~~

Date of Application for Enrollment.	~~Date of transfer~~ to this card
5/29/99	Jan. 28, 1905

RESIDENCE: Sugar Loaf COUNTY. **Choctaw Nation** Choctaw Roll (Not Including Freedmen) CARD NO.
POST OFFICE: Poteau, I.T. FIELD NO. 5883

Dawes' Roll No.	NAME	Relationship to Person First Named	AGE	SEX	BLOOD	TRIBAL ENROLLMENT Year	County	No.
IW 1368	1 Welch, Leamon		25	F	I.W.	1896	Sugar Loaf	15159

ENROLLMENT OF NOS. 1 HEREON APPROVED BY THE SECRETARY OF INTERIOR Mar 14, 1905

TRIBAL ENROLLMENT OF PARENTS

Name of Father	Year	County	Name of Mother	Year	County
1 James Fry	1896	Non Citz	Fannie Fry	1896	Non Citz

No.1 husband Ed. E. Walker, the son of Geo. W. Walker is on 1890 Creek roll as Eddie Walker.
No.1 formerly the wife of E. E. Walker a recognized and enrolled citizen by blood of the Choctaw Nation who is identified upon the 1893 Pay Roll Skullyville Co. page 70, No. 682, as Edward E. Walker. After the death of E. E. Walker in 1896, No.1 married William Welch, a white man
No.1 originally listed for enrollment on Choctaw card #D-215 6/7/99 transferred to this card Jan. 30, 1905. See decision of Jan. 14, 1905

Date of Application for Enrollment.	Date of transfer to this card
6/7/99	Jan. 30, 1905

Choctaw By Blood Enrollment Cards 1898-1914

RESIDENCE: Sans Bois
POST OFFICE: Stigler, I.T.

Roll (…edmen) CARD NO.
FIELD NO. 5884

Dawes' Roll No.	NAME					TRIBAL ENROLLMENT Year	County	No.
IW 1369	1 Wilson, William W					…85	Sans Bois	8…
	2							
	3							
	4							
	5							
	6							
	7							
	8							
	9							
	10							
	11							
	12							
	13							
	14							
	15							
	16							
	17							

ENROLLMENT
OF NOS. 1 HEREON
APPROVED BY THE SECRETARY
OF INTERIOR MAR 14 1905

TRIBAL ENROLLMENT OF PARENTS

		County	Name of Mother	Year	County
1		…n citz	Frances Wilson	dead	non citz

No.1 on 1885 Choctaw Census Roll Sans Bois Co. #813 as Wm Wilson

No.1 formerly the husband of Nancy Wilson (nee Anderson) a recognized and enrolled citizen by blood of the Choctaw Nation whose name appears upon the 1885 Choc. Census Roll, Sans Bois Co. #814. They lived together about three weeks when they separated. Soon after Nancy Wilson died No.1 then married a white woman.

No.1 originally listed for enrollment on Choctaw card #D-254. 6/20/99 transferred to this card Jan. 28, 1905 See decision of Jan. 12, 1905.

Date of Application for Enrollment. 6/20/99

Date of Transfer to this Card Jan. 28, 1905

[RESI]DENCE: | COUNTY. | **Choctaw Nation** | **Choctaw Roll** (*Not Including Freedmen*) | CARD NO.
[POS]T OFFICE: Ada, I.T. | | | | FIELD NO. 5885

[Da]wes' No.	NAME	Relationship to Person First Named	AGE	SEX	BLOOD	TRIBAL ENROLLMENT Year	County	No.
[1]370	1 Thompson, Mary		36	F	I.W.	1885	Blue	1433
	2							
	3							
	4							
	5							
	6							
	7							
	8							
	9							
	10							
	11							
	12							
	13							
	14							
	15							
	16							
	17							

ENROLLMENT
~~OF NOS.~~ 1 ~~HEREON~~
APPROVED BY THE SECRETARY
OF INTERIOR MAR 14 1905

TRIBAL ENROLLMENT OF PARENTS

	Name of Father	Year	County	Name of Mother	Year	County
1	Jas. Crump		Non Citz	Caroline Crump	dead	non citz
2						
3						
4						
5						

No.1 formerly the wife of Israel Folsom Robinson, a recognized and enrolled citizen by blood of the Choctaw Nation, who is identified upon the 1885 ~~Choc. Census Roll, Blue Co. #1432 as G.F. Robinson. He died April 25, 1886~~
~~In 1889 No.1 married John Hickox, and on Sept. 2, 1902 married R.S. Thompson,~~ both being white men.
No.1 on 1885 Choc. Census Roll, Blue Co. #1433 as Minnie B. Robinson
~~No.1 originally listed for enrollment on Choctaw card #D- 318 Aug. 14/99~~
~~transferred to this card Dec. 31, 1904. See decision of Dec. 15, 1904~~

Date of Application for Enrollment.	Date of transfer to this card
Aug 14/99	Dec. 31, 1904

RESIDENCE: COUNTY. **Choctaw Nation** Choctaw Roll (Not Including Freedmen) CARD NO.
POST OFFICE: Stringtown, I.T. FIELD NO. 5886

Dawes' Roll No.	NAME	Relationship to Person First Named	AGE	SEX	BLOOD	TRIBAL ENROLLMENT Year	County	No.
IW 1371	1 Henderson, George W.		37	M	I.W.			

ENROLLMENT
OF NOS. 1 HEREON
APPROVED BY THE SECRETARY
OF INTERIOR MAR 14 1905

TRIBAL ENROLLMENT OF PARENTS

Name of Father	Year	County	Name of Mother	Year	County
1 B.P. Henderson	1896	Non Citz	Nancy Henderson	1896	Non Citz

No.1 denied admission as a citizen by blood by Com. in 1896 case #425
No.1 admitted as a citizen by blood by U.S. Court, Central district Ind. Ter.
~~Jany. 18th, 1898; Court case #44, Nancy Henderson vs. Choctaw Nation.~~

On July 6, 1897, No.1 married Hattie Henderson (nee Hewett), a recognized and enrolled citizen by blood of the Choc. Nation who is identified upon the 1896 Choc. Census ~~Roll, Jacks Fork Co. #6096. Hattie Henderson died Jan. 31, 1900~~
~~Wife and daughter of No.1 on Choctaw card #1904: both are dead.~~
No.1 transferred from Choctaw Card # 1904 Jan. 25, 1905.
See decision of Jan. 9, 1905

P.O. Kiowa IT 3/8/05

Date of Application for Enrollment. 5/22/99

~~Date of transfer~~ to this card Jan. 25, 1905

SIDENCE: Blue COUNTY. **Choctaw Nation** **Choctaw Roll** (Not Including Freedmen) CARD NO. FIELD NO. 5887
ST OFFICE:

awes' oll No.	NAME	Relationship to Person First Named	AGE	SEX	BLOOD	TRIBAL ENROLLMENT Year	County	No.
1372	1 Kinghorn, Jennie		53	F	I.W.	1885	Blue	518
1663	2 " Thomas A	Hus	44	M	IW			

ENROLLMENT OF NOS. 2 HEREON APPROVED BY THE SECRETARY OF INTERIOR MAR 4- 1907

ENROLLMENT OF NOS. 1 HEREON APPROVED BY THE SECRETARY OF INTERIOR MAR 14 1905

GRANTED FEB 27 1907

TRIBAL ENROLLMENT OF PARENTS

Name of Father	Year	County	Name of Mother	Year	County
1 Moses Hildebrand		Cherokee	Don't know		Cherokee
2 Alex Kinghorn		Non Citz	Christina Kinghorn	Dead	Non Citz

In 1871 No.1 was married to Daniel Graves, a citizen by blood of the Choctaw Nation They lived together two years when he died. In 1873 No.1 was married to Alfred Wright a recognized and enrolled citizen by blood of the Choctaw Nation; identified on the 1885 Choc. Census Roll, Blue Co #517. They lived together about sixteen years when Alfred Wright died. In 1891 No1 married Thomas A Kinghorn, a white man.

No.1 appears on the 1885 Choc. Census Roll, Blue Co. #518 as Jane Wright.

No.1 originally listed for enrollment on Choctaw card #D- 324 Aug. 15/99; transferred to this card Feb. 1, 1905. See decision of Jan. 16, 1905

No.2 transferred from Choctaw Card # D- 324 Feby 27-1907 - See decision of same date.

Date of Application for Enrollment. 8/15/99

Feb. 1, 1905 Date of transfer to this card

RESIDENCE: COUNTY. **Choctaw Nation** **Choctaw Roll** (Not Including Freedmen) CARD NO.
POST OFFICE: Bokchito, I.T. FIELD NO. 5888

Dawes' Roll No.	NAME	Relationship to Person First Named	AGE	SEX	BLOOD	TRIBAL ENROLLMENT Year	County	No.
15816	1 Edens, Ari Anna F.		30	F	1/16	1896	Blue	3816
15817	2 Hammit, Wilkie	Son	11	M	1/32	1896	"	5867
15818	3 Edens, John J	Son	2	M	1/32			
15819	4 " Hester Lorine	Dau	1	F	1/32			

ENROLLMENT OF NOS. 1,2,3 and 4 HEREON APPROVED BY THE SECRETARY OF INTERIOR Mar 15 1905

TRIBAL ENROLLMENT OF PARENTS

Name of Father	Year	County	Name of Mother	Year	County
1 Charles Lewis		Non Citz	Lavinia S Senter nee Lewis		Blue
2 Chas. Hammit		" "	No.1		
3 C. W. Edens		" "	No.1		
4 " " "		" "	No.1		

~~No.1 on 1893 Pay Roll Blue County page 74 No 784 as Annie Lewis~~
No.2 " " " " " " " 74 " 785 " Wilky[sic] Harrit[sic]
No.2 " 1896 Roll as Wilkey[sic]Hammet[sic]
~~No.1 " 1896 roll as Arianna Edens was also admitted by Act of Choctaw Council No. 13 approved October 29/87 as Arianna Lewis.~~
No.3 enrolled July 16, 1900.
No4 born Oct 2, 1901; Proof of birth filed Nov. 9, 1901
~~Nos. 1 and 2 originally listed for enrollment on Choctaw card #D- 347 Aug 22/99~~
~~Nos 1-4 transferred to this card Jan. 18, 1905. See decision of Jan. 2, 1905~~

~~Date of Application for Enrollment.~~ Aug 22/99

Date of transfer to this card Jan. 18, 1905

RESIDENCE: Jacks Fork COUNTY. **Choctaw Nation** **Choctaw Roll** *(Not Including Freedmen)* CARD NO. [redacted]
POST OFFICE: Tushkahomma, I.T. FIELD NO. [redacted]

Dawes' Roll No.	NAME	Relationship to Person First Named	AGE	SEX	BLOOD	TRIBAL ENROLLMENT Year	County	No.
15820	1 Colbert, Margaret		45	F	Full	1885	Jacks Fork	471
	2							
	3							
	4							
	5							
	6							
	7							
	8							
	9							
	10							
	11							
	12							
	13							
	14							
	15							
	16							
	17							

ENROLLMENT
OF NOS. 1 HEREON
APPROVED BY THE SECRETARY
OF INTERIOR Mar 15 1905

TRIBAL ENROLLMENT OF PARENTS

Name of Father	Year	County	Name of Mother	Year	County
1 Billie William	dead	Jacks Fork	Susan William	dead	Nashoba
2					
3					
4					
5					

6 No.1 on 1885 Choctaw Census Roll, Jacks Fork County, Number 471, as
7 Margarett Colbert.
No.1 identified upon the 1893 Chickasaw Pay Roll (Maytubby Roll No2)
8 (her enrollment on said roll being indicated by the figure 2 [laces
9 after the name of her husband, James Colbert, on said roll)
10 Husband on Chickasaw Care #1707
No.1 originally listed for enrollment on Choctaw card #D- 174 5/22/99
11 transferred to this card Feb. 11, 1905. See decision of Jan. 26, 1905

Date of Application for Enrollment. 5/22/99

Date of transfer to this card Feb. 11, 1905

: Chickasaw Nation COUNTY. **Choctaw Nation** **Choctaw Roll** *(Not Including Freedmen)* CARD NO.
E: McGee, I.T. FIELD NO. 58

Dawes Roll No.	NAME	Relationship to Person First Named	AGE	SEX	BLOOD	TRIBAL ENROLLMENT Year	County	No.
15821	1 Orndorff, John	First Named	20	M	3/8	1896	Atoka	10015
	2							
	3							
	4							
	5							
	6							
	7							
	8							
	9							
	10							
	11							
	12							
	13							
	14							
	15							
	16							
	17							

ENROLLMENT
OF NOS. 1 HEREON
APPROVED BY THE SECRETARY
OF INTERIOR MAR 15 1905

TRIBAL ENROLLMENT OF PARENTS

Name of Father	Year	County	Name of Mother	Year	County
1 Ed Orndorff		non citz	Ellen Orndorff	dead	Choctaw
2					
3					
4					
5					

6 No.1 on 1893 Pay roll, page 125, No. 18, Kiamitia Co as John Arndorff[sic] Also
7 on 1896 roll Atoka Co, page 254 #10015, as John Ondaff[sic]
8 ~~No.1 originally listed for enrollment on Choctaw card #D-358 Aug. 24/99~~
9 ~~transferred to this card Jan. 23, 1905 See decision of Jan. 7, 1905~~
10 For child of No.1 see N.B. (Apr 26 '06) No. 786.

Date of Application for Enrollment. Aug 24/99

Date of transfer to this card Jan. 23, 1905

RESIDENCE: Atoka COUNTY. **Choctaw Nation** **Choctaw Roll** *(Not Including Freedmen)* CARD NO.
POST OFFICE: Atoka, I.T. FIELD NO. 5891

Dawes' Roll No.	NAME	Relationship to Person First Named	AGE	SEX	BLOOD	TRIBAL ENROLLMENT Year	County	No.
IW 1373	1 Hendrix, Myra	First Named	35	F	I.W.			
	2							
	3							
	4							
	5							
	6							
	7							
	8							
	9							
	10							
	11							
	12							
	13							
	14							
	15							
	16							
	17							

ENROLLMENT
OF NOS. 1 HEREON
APPROVED BY THE SECRETARY
OF INTERIOR MAR 14 1905

TRIBAL ENROLLMENT OF PARENTS

Name of Father	Year	County	Name of Mother	Year	County
1 K. Clayman	dead	Non Citz	Mary Clayman	dead	Non Citz
2					
3					
4					

In 1884 No.1 married Norris Nelson, a recognized and enrolled citizen by blood of the Choctaw Nation who is identified on 1885 Choc. roll, Atoka Co. #951. They lived together thirteen months when they separated and were divorced. On Dec. 23, 1891 No.1 married Albert Perkins, a recognized and enrolled citizen by blood of the Choctaw Nation, whose name appears as #124 on the lists made by this Commission. They lived together two months when they separated and were divorced.
No.1 then married Taylor Durant a recognized and enrolled citizen by blood of the Choc Nation, whose name appears as #11463 on the lists prepared by this Com. They lived together three months when they separated and were then divorced.
In 1897 No.1 married John Hendrix, a white man.
No.1 originally listed for enrollment on Choctaw card #D-408 Sept 1/99. ← Date of Application for Enrollment.
transferred to this card Jan. 28, 1905. See decision of Jan. 12, 1905

Jan. 28, 1905
Date of transfer to this card

RESIDENCE: Tobucksy COUNTY. **Choctaw Nation** **Choctaw Roll** *(Not Including Freedmen)*

POST OFFICE: M^c^Alester, I.T.

Dawes' Roll No.	NAME	Relationship to Person First Named	AGE	SEX	BLOOD	TRIBAL ENROLLMENT Year	County	No.
IW 1374	Edwards, Martha A	First Named	50	F	IW			
16211	Evans, Annie	dau	27	"	1/4	1885	Tobucksy	
16212	" Maria	Gr dau	7	"	1/8			

ENROLLMENT OF NOS. 2 and 3 HEREON APPROVED BY THE SECRETARY OF INTERIOR MAR 4 1907

ENROLLMENT OF NOS. 1 HEREON APPROVED BY THE SECRETARY OF INTERIOR MAR 14 1905

See Petition #W-65

TRIBAL ENROLLMENT OF PARENTS

Name of Father	Year	County	Name of Mother	Year	County
Ivey Stepp		non citizen	Frances E. Stepp		non cit
George W. Brashears			No.1		
Charley Evans		Non Citz	No.2		

On April 25, 1869 No.1 married Alex Burns, a citizen by blood of the Choc. Nation They lived together a year, when they separated and were divorced

~~On July 20, 1879 No.1 married William Stanton, a recognized and enrolled citizen~~ by blood of the Choc. Nation; identified on 1885 Choc. Roll, Tobucksy Co. #800

They lived together until the death of the said William Stanton, seven or eight years later. No.1 then married E. Edwards, a white man.

~~No.1 originally listed for enrollment on Choctaw card #D- 455 7-9-1899; transferred to~~ this card Feb. 1, 1905 See decision of Jan. 16, 1905

Nos 2&3 placed hereon under order of the Commission to the Five Civilized Tribes of Feby 20-1907 holding that application was made for their enrollment within the time ~~provided by the Act of Congress approved April 26' 1906~~

Irene Evans, child of Annie Evans, on card #23-1296.

7/9/88 Date of Application for Enrollment.

Feb. 1, 1905 Date of transfer ~~to this card~~

RESIDENCE: COUNTY. **Choctaw Nation** **Choctaw Roll** *(Not Including Freedmen)* CARD NO.
POST OFFICE: Dow, I.T. FIELD NO. 5893

Dawes' Roll No.	NAME	Relationship to Person First Named	AGE	SEX	BLOOD	TRIBAL ENROLLMENT Year	County	No.
IW 1375	1 Lemasters, Belle		25	F	I.W.			

ENROLLMENT
OF NOS. 1 HEREON
APPROVED BY THE SECRETARY
OF INTERIOR MAR 14 1905

TRIBAL ENROLLMENT OF PARENTS

Name of Father	Year	County	Name of Mother	Year	County
1 S. Smith	dead	Non Cit.	May Penfeild[sic]		U.S. Citizen

~~No.1 formerly the wife of Johnny Beams (now deceased), a recognized and~~ enrolled citizen by blood of the Choctaw Nation; identified upon the 1896 Choc Census Roll, Tobucksy Co. #874 as John Beams; they lived together ~~about three years when they separated and were divorced. In 1896 No.1 married Walter Lemasters, a white man~~

No.1 originally listed for enrollment on Choctaw card #D- 480 Sept 11th 1899 transferred to this card Jan. 30, 1905 See decision of Jan. 14, 1905

Date of Application for Enrollment.	Date of transfer to this card
Sept 1/99	Jan. 30, 1905

RESIDENCE: Tobucksy COUNTY. **Choctaw Nation** **Choctaw Roll** [redacted] No.
POST OFFICE: Krebs, I.T. *(Not Including Freedmen)* [redacted] No. 5894

Dawes' Roll No.	NAME	Relationship to Person First Named	AGE	SEX	BLOOD	TRIBAL ENROLLMENT Year	County	No.
IW 1376	1 Dunn, Rachel		28	F	I.W.			

ENROLLMENT
~~OF NOS.~~ 1 ~~HEREON~~
APPROVED BY THE SECRETARY
OF INTERIOR MAR 14 1905

TRIBAL ENROLLMENT OF PARENTS

Name of Father	Year	County	Name of Mother	Year	County
1 Ja[redacted]er	dead	Non Citz	Mary Creamer	dead	Non Citz

No.1 formerly the wife of Johnson Frazier, a recognized and enrolled citizen by blood of the Choctaw Nation whose name appears as #9424 on the lists prepared by this Commission. They lived together for one month when they separated ~~and were divorced. On May 16, 1893 No.1 married David M. Dunn a white man~~
No.1 originally listed for enrollment on Choctaw card #D- 527 Nov. 16/99.
transferred to this card Jan. 28, 1905 See decision of Jan. 12, 1905

Date of Application for Enrollment.	~~Date of transfer~~ to this card
Nov. 16/99	Jan. 28, 1905

RESIDENCE: Chickasaw Nation ~~COUNTY.~~ **Choctaw Nation** **Choctaw Roll** (*Not Including Freedmen*) CARD NO.
POST OFFICE: Oakman, I.T. FIELD NO. 589

Dawes' Roll No.	NAME	Relationship to Person First Named	AGE	SEX	BLOOD	TRIBAL ENROLLMENT Year	County	No.
IW 1377	1 West, Liddy		20	F	I.W.			
	2							
	3							
	4							
	5							
	6							
	7							
	8							
	9							
	10							
	11							
	12							
	13							
	14							
	15							
	16							
	17							

ENROLLMENT
~~OF NOS.~~ 1 ~~HEREON~~
APPROVED BY THE SECRETARY
OF INTERIOR MAR 14 1905

TRIBAL ENROLLMENT OF PARENTS

Name of Father	Year	County	Name of Mother	Year	County
1 John A. Morse		non citizen	Lodemia Morse	dead	non citizen

~~No.1 was married to Robert West, a recognized and enrolled citizen by blood of the Choctaw Nation, whose name appears as #39 upon the lists prepared by this Commission.~~
~~No.1 is the wife of Robert West on Choctaw #27~~
~~No.1 originally listed for enrollment on Choctaw card #D- 614 Feb. 6-1901~~
transferred to this card Jan. 30, 1905
For child of No.1 see NB (Apr 26, 1906) Card No. 54
" " " " " " (Mar 3-1905) " " 34

Date of Application for Enrollment.	Date of transfer to this card
Feb 6/01	Jan. 30, 1905

RESIDENCE: Chickasaw Nation ~~COUNTY.~~
POST OFFICE: Ardmore, Ind. Ter.

Choctaw Nation

Choctaw Roll (Not Including Freedmen)

CARD NO.
FIELD NO. 5896

Dawes' Roll No.	NAME	Relationship to Person First Named	AGE	SEX	BLOOD	TRIBAL ENROLLMENT Year	County	No.
IW 1378	1 Poland, Emer M. G.	First Named	24	F	IW			
	2							
	3							
	4							
	5							
	6							
	7							
	8							
	9							
	10							
	11							
	12							
	13							
	14							
	15							
	16							
	17							

ENROLLMENT OF NOS. HEREON APPROVED BY THE SECRETARY OF INTERIOR MAR 14 1905

TRIBAL ENROLLMENT OF PARENTS

Name of Father	Year	County	Name of Mother	Year	County
1 D. J. Grigsby		non citz	Lillie Grigsby		non citz
2					
3					
4					
5					

~~On October 4, 1900 No.1 was married to Robert P. Poland, a recognized~~ and enrolled citizen by blood of the Choctaw Nation, whose name appears as #411 upon the lists prepared by this Commission

~~Husband of No.1 is on Choctaw card #206~~

~~No.1 originally listed for enrollment on Choctaw card #D-626 March 21, 1901~~ transferred to this card Jan. 28, 1905 See decision of Jan. 12, 1905

Date of Application for Enrollment.	~~Date of transfer~~ to this card
March 21/01	Jan. 28, 1905

RESIDENCE: Choctaw Nation ~~COUNTY.~~ **Choctaw Nation** **Choctaw Roll** *(Not Including Freedmen)* CARD NO.
POST OFFICE: Blaine, Ind. Ter. FIELD NO. 5897

Dawes' Roll No.	NAME	Relationship to Person First Named	AGE	SEX	BLOOD	TRIBAL ENROLLMENT Year	County	No.
IW 1379	1 Isaac, Margaret		69	F	I.W.			
	2							
	3							
	4							
	5							
	6							
	7							
	8							
	9							
	10							
	11							
	12							
	13							
	14							
	15							
	16							
	17							

ENROLLMENT
~~OF NOS.~~ 1 ~~HEREON~~
APPROVED BY THE SECRETARY
OF INTERIOR MAR 14 1905

TRIBAL ENROLLMENT OF PARENTS

Name of Father	Year	County	Name of Mother	Year	County
1 William Keffer	dead	non citizen	Mahala Keffer	dead	non citizen
2					
3					
4					
5					

6 No.1 formerly the wife of James Isaac, a recognized citizen by blood
7 of the Choctaw Nation. They lived together until the death of James
Isaac about the year 1881; that thereafter No.1 was married to
8 Thomas Dickerson, a white man.
9 No.1 originally listed for enrollment on Choctaw card #D- 670 Oct. 28, 1901;
10 transferred to this card Jan. 30, 1905 See decision of Jan. 12, 1905

Date of Application for Enrollment.
~~Oct 2801~~

Date of transfer to this card Jan. 30, 1905

RESIDENCE: Chickasaw Nation COUNTY. **Choctaw Nation** **Choctaw Roll** *(Not Including Freedmen)* CARD NO.
POST OFFICE: Harrisburg, Ind. Ter. FIELD NO. 5898

Dawes' Roll No.	NAME	Relationship to Person First Named	AGE	SEX	BLOOD	TRIBAL ENROLLMENT Year	County	No.
IW 1380	1 Spain, Martha Elizabeth		14	F	I.W.			
	2							
	3							
	4							
	5							
	6							
	7							
	8							
	9							
	10							
	11							
	12							
	13							
	14							
	15							
	16							
	17							

ENROLLMENT
~~OF NOS.~~ 1 ~~HEREON~~
APPROVED BY THE SECRETARY
OF INTERIOR MAR 14 1905

TRIBAL ENROLLMENT OF PARENTS

Name of Father	Year	County	Name of Mother	Year	County
1 J. W. M^c^Henry		non-citizen	Cora M^c^Henry		non-citizen
2					
3					
4					

5 On September 18, 1902 No.1 was married to Jubilee Spain, a recognized
6 and enrolled citizen by blood of the Choctaw Nation, whose name
~~appears as #289 upon the lists prepared by this Commission~~
7 ~~Jubilee Spain, husband of No 1 is on Choctaw card #144~~
8 No.1 originally listed for enrollment on Choctaw card #D- 802 Sept 24, 1902;
9 transferred to this card Jan. 23, 1905 See decision of Jan. 7, 1905
~~Record as to enrollment of No.1 forwarded Department~~
10 ~~Record returned See opinion of Assistant Attorney General of [remainder illegible]~~
11 For child of No.1 see NB (Mar 3-1905) Card #78

Date of Application for Enrollment.
Sept 24/02

~~Date of transfer~~ to this card Jan. 29, 1905

RESIDENCE: Choctaw Nation COUNTY. **Choctaw Nation** **Choctaw Roll** *(Not Including Freedmen)* CARD NO.
POST OFFICE: Caddo, Ind. Ter. FIELD NO. 5899

Dawes' Roll No.	NAME	Relationship to Person First Named	AGE	SEX	BLOOD	TRIBAL ENROLLMENT Year	County	No.
IW 1381	1 Goforth, Mary A		48	F	I.W	1896	Jackson	14260

ENROLLMENT
~~OF NOS.~~ 1 ~~HEREON~~
APPROVED BY THE SECRETARY
OF INTERIOR MAR 14 1905

TRIBAL ENROLLMENT OF PARENTS

Name of Father	Year	County	Name of Mother	Year	County
1 Isaac Dick	dead	Cherokee	Susan Dick	dead	Cherokee

March 10 '03: elects to be enrolled as a Choctaw by intermarriage
No.1 on 1894 Cherokee strip payment roll. See Cherokee card #D-1308
On Feb. 29, 1869 No.1 married Joe Homer, a recognized citizen by blood of
~~the Choctaw Nation. They lived together till the death of Joe Homer, about 1883-84~~
In 1889 No.1 married Walter Attaway, a white man from whom she was
afterwards divorced. On July 11, 1900 No.1 married Solomon Goforth
a recognized and enrolled citizen by blood of the Chickasaw Nation, whose
~~name appears as #3185 upon the lists prepared by this Commission~~
No.1 on 1896 Choctaw Census Roll Jackson Co page 380 #14260, as Mary Attaway.
No.1 originally listed for enrollment on Choctaw card #D- 722 May 19, 1902
transferred to this card Jan. 28, 1905 See decision of Jan. 12, 1905
~~Solomon Goforth husband of No.1 is on Chickasaw card #1067~~

Date of Application for Enrollment. May 19/02

Jan. 28, 1905
Date of transfer to this card

RESIDENCE: Choctaw Nation ~~COUNTY~~. **Choctaw Nation** **Choctaw Roll** *(Not Including Freedmen)* CARD NO.
POST OFFICE: Poteau, Ind. Ter. FIELD NO. 5900

Dawes' Roll No.		NAME	Relationship to Person First Named	AGE	SEX	BLOOD	TRIBAL ENROLLMENT Year	County	No.
IW 1382	1	Perse, George R		55	M	I.W.			
	2								
	3								
	4								
	5								
	6								
	7								
	8								
	9								
	10								
	11								
	12								
	13								
	14								
	15								
	16								
	17	See Petition No W 55							

ENROLLMENT
~~OF NOS.~~ 1 ~~HEREON~~
APPROVED BY THE SECRETARY
OF INTERIOR Mar 14 1905

TRIBAL ENROLLMENT OF PARENTS

	Name of Father	Year	County	Name of Mother	Year	County
1	William R. Perse	dead	non citz	Rhoda Ann Perse	dead	non citz
2						
3						
4						
5						

~~About the year 1874 No.1 was married to Parmelia Morrison (formerly~~
Parmelia Folsom) a recognized citizen by blood of the Choctaw Nation.
They lived together about eight months when they separated. No.1
~~then married Delila E. Loggains, a non-citizen of the Choctaw Nation~~
~~Wife and two children on Choctaw Card D-731~~
No.1 originally listed for enrollment on Choctaw card #D- 731 May 27, 1902
transferred to this card Jan. 23, 1905 See decision of Jan. 7, 1905

Date of Application for Enrollment.	Date of transfer to this card
May 2/02	Jan. 23, 1905

RESIDENCE: Choctaw Nation ~~COUNTY.~~ **Choctaw Nation** **Choctaw Roll** *(Not Including Freedmen)* FIELD NO. 5901
POST OFFICE: Utica, Ind. Ter.

Dawes' Roll No.	NAME	Relationship to Person First Named	AGE	SEX	BLOOD	TRIBAL ENROLLMENT Year	County	No.
IW 1383	1 Carr, William Madison	First Named	27	M	IW			
	2							
	3							
	4							
	5							
	6							
	7							
	8							
	9							
	10							
	11							
	12							
	13							
	14							
	15							
	16							
	17							

ENROLLMENT
~~OF NOS.~~ 1 ~~HEREON~~
APPROVED BY THE SECRETARY
OF INTERIOR MAR 14 1905

TRIBAL ENROLLMENT OF PARENTS

Name of Father	Year	County	Name of Mother	Year	County
1 John Carr		non citizen	Lucinda Carr	dead	non citizen

On July 8, 1902 No.1 was married to Alma Carr (nee Whittle) a
recognized and enrolled citizen by blood of the Choctaw Nation
Alma Carr wife of No.1 is on Choctaw card #237; final roll #503
~~No.1 originally listed for enrollment on Choctaw card #D-766 July 29, 1902~~
~~transferred to this card Jan. 28, 1905 See decision of Jan. 12, 1905~~
Record as to enrollment of No.1 forwarded Department [remainder illegible]

Date of Application for Enrollment.	Date of transfer to this card
July 29/02	Jan. 28, 1905

RESIDENCE: Choctaw Nation ~~COUNTY.~~
POST OFFICE: Caddo, Ind. Ter

Choctaw Nation

Choctaw Roll *(Not Including Freedmen)*

CARD NO.
FIELD NO. **5902**

Dawes' Roll No.		NAME	Relationship to Person First Named	AGE	SEX	BLOOD	TRIBAL ENROLLMENT Year	County	No.
IW 1384	1	Allen, Charley	Named	28	M	I.W.			

ENROLLMENT
~~OF NOS.~~ 1 ~~HEREON~~
APPROVED BY THE SECRETARY
OF INTERIOR MAR 14 1905

TRIBAL ENROLLMENT OF PARENTS

	Name of Father	Year	County	Name of Mother	Year	County
1	Henderson Allen		non citizen	Cynthia Allen	dead	non-citizen

~~On July 13, 1902 No.1 was married to Cora Allen (nee Ward) a recognized~~
citizen by blood of the Choctaw Nation; on final roll (as Cora E. Allen)
#15057, Choctaw card #3935
~~No.1 originally listed for enrollment on Choctaw card #D- 769 Aug. 1, 1902-~~
~~transferred to this card Jan. 28, 1905 See decision of Jan. 12, 1905~~
Record as to enrollment of No.1 forwarded Department March 14, 1906
Record returned. See opinion of Assistant Attorney General of March [illegible] 1906

Date of Application for Enrollment.	~~Date of transfer~~ to this card
Aug 1/02	Jan. 28, 1905

RESIDENCE: Choctaw Nation ~~COUNTY.~~ **Choctaw Nation** Choctaw Roll *(Not Including Freedmen)* CARD NO.
POST OFFICE: Caddo, Ind. Ter. FIELD NO. 5903

Dawes' Roll No.		NAME	Relationship to Person First Named	AGE	SEX	BLOOD	TRIBAL ENROLLMENT Year	County	No.
IW1385	1	Nicholson, Omer R		23	M	IW			
	2								
	3								
	4								
	5								
	6								
	7								
	8								
	9								
	10								
	11								
	12								
	13								
	14								
	15								
	16								
	17								

ENROLLMENT
~~OF NOS.~~ 1 ~~HEREON~~
APPROVED BY THE SECRETARY
OF INTERIOR MAR 14 1905

TRIBAL ENROLLMENT OF PARENTS

	Name of Father	Year	County	Name of Mother	Year	County
1	W. C. Nicholson		non citizen	Mary J Nicholson		non citizen
2						
3						
4						
5						

~~On 17th of Sept 1902 No.1 was married to Mamie E. Nicholson, a recognized~~ citizen by blood of the Choctaw Nation; final roll #10399 Choctaw card #3678
No.1 originally listed for enrollment on Choctaw card #D- 793 Sep 19, 1902;
~~transferred to this card Jan. 28, 1905 See decision of Jan. 12, 1905~~
[Entry illegible...]

Date of Application for Enrollment. Sept 19/02

~~Date of transfer~~ to this card Jan. 28, 1905

RESIDENCE: COUNTY. **Choctaw Nation** [redacted] 904

POST OFFICE: Bokhoma, Ind. Ter.

Dawes' Roll No.		NAME	Relationship to Person First Named	AGE	SEX	BLOOD	TRIBAL ENROLLMENT Year	County	No.
IW 1386	1	Camden, A. B.		25	M	I.W.			
	2								
	3								
	4								
	5								
	6								
	7								
	8								
	9								
	10								
	11								
	12								
	13								
	14								
	15								
	16								
	17								

ENROLLMENT
~~OF NOS.~~ 1 ~~HEREON~~
APPROVED BY THE SECRETARY
OF INTERIOR MAR 14 1905

TRIBAL ENROLLMENT OF PARENTS

	Name of Father	Year	County	Name of Mother	Year	County
1	L. B. Camden		non citizen	Dorinda Camden		non citizen
2						
3						
4						

On Aug. 31, 1902 No.1 was married to Ida B. Camden (nee Harrison), a recognized citizen by blood of the Choctaw Nation; final roll #11526 Choctaw card #4112

~~No.1 made application for identification as a M[redacted] case refused by the Commission in M.C.R. case Nathaniel P. Gotcher, et al, M.C.R. #3666~~

No.1 originally listed for enrollment on Choctaw card #D- 803 Sept 23, 1902 ~~transferred to this card Jan. 29, 1905 See decision of Jan. 13, 1905~~

~~Record as to enrollment of No.1 forwarded Department Mch 14, 1906~~

Record returned. See opinion of Assistant Attorney General of March 15, 1906 in case of Omer R Nicholson

For child of No.1 see NB (March 3, 1905) #1096

Date of Application for Enrollment.	Date of transfer to this card
Sept 23/02	Jan. 29, 1905

RESIDENCE: COUNTY. **Choctaw Nation** Choctaw Roll (Not Including Freedmen) [redacted] 905

POST OFFICE: Harrisburg, Ind. Ter.

Dawes' Roll No.	NAME	Relationship to Person First Named	AGE	SEX	BLOOD	TRIBAL ENROLLMENT Year	County	No.
IW 1387	1 Spain, Minnie Lee		16	F	I.W.			
	2							
	3							
	4							
	5							
	6							
	7							
	8							
	9							
	10							
	11							
	12							
	13							
	14							
	15							
	16							
	17							

ENROLLMENT
~~OF NOS.~~ 1 ~~HEREON~~
APPROVED BY THE SECRETARY
OF INTERIOR MAR 14 1905

TRIBAL ENROLLMENT OF PARENTS

	Name of Father	Year	County	Name of Mother	Year	County
1	J.W. McHenry		non citizen	Cora McHenry		non citizen

On Aug. 12, 1902 No.1 was married to Sidney B. Spain, a recognized citizen by blood of the Choctaw Nation; Final roll No. 239 Choctaw care #119

No.1 originally listed for enrollment on Choctaw card #D- 804 Sep 24, 1902 transferred to this card Jan. 29, 1905 See decision of Jan. 13, 1905

~~Record as to enrollment of No.1 forwarded Department Mch 14, 1906~~

Record returned. See opinion of Assistant Attorney General of March 15, 1906 in case of Omer R Nicholson

For children of No1 see NB (Mar 3, 1905) #608 and (April 26, 1906) #1200.

Date of Application for Enrollment.	Date of transfer to this card
Sept 24/02	Jan. 29, 1905

RESIDENCE: Choctaw Nation ~~COUNTY.~~ **Choctaw Nation** Cl. oll (Not Including Freedmen) CARD No. 5906
POST OFFICE: Antlers, Ind. Ter.

Dawes' Roll No.	NAME	Relationship to Person First Named	AGE	SEX	BLOOD	TRIBAL ENROLLMENT Year	County	No.
IW 1388	1 Archer, Charles E.		32	M	I.W.			
	2							
	3							
	4							
	5							
	6							
	7							
	8							
	9							
	10							
	11							
	12							
	13							
	14							
	15							
	16							
	17							

ENROLLMENT
~~OF NOS.~~ 1 ~~HEREON~~
APPROVED BY THE SECRETARY
~~OF INTERIOR~~ MAR 14 1905

TRI

Name of Father	Year	County	
1 John M Archer		non citizen	Ja
2			
3			
4			
5			

On Sept 13, 1902 No.1 was married to Mary A Archer, a recognized and enrolled citizen by blood of the Choctaw Nation. Choc card #1735: final roll #4913

No.1 originally listed for enrollment on Choctaw card #D- 811 Sept. 29, 1902: transferred to this card Feb. 1, 1905 See decision of Jan. 16, 1905

Date of Application for Enrollment.	Date of transfer to this card
Sept 29/02	Feb. 1, 1905

RESIDENCE: Tobucksy COUNTY. **Choctaw Nation** **Choctaw Roll** (*Not Including Freedmen*) CARD NO.
POST OFFICE: McAlester, I.T. FIELD NO. 5

Dawes' Roll No.	NAME	Relationship to Person First Named	AGE	SEX	BLOOD	TRIBAL ENROLLMENT Year	County	No.
IW 1388	1 Jennings, Henry C	First Named	50	M	I.W.			
	2							
	3							
	4							
	5							
	6							
	7							
	8							
	9							
	10							
	11							
	12							
	13							
	14							
	15							
	16							
	17							

ENROLLMENT OF NOS. 1 HEREON APPROVED BY THE SECRETARY OF INTERIOR MAR 14 1905

TRIBAL ENROLLMENT OF PARENTS

Name of Father	Year	County	Name of Mother	Year	County
1 L. B. Jennings		non citz	Eliza Jennings		non citz
2					
3					
4					
5					

No.1 claims through marriage in 1892 with Mary E. Jennings, on Choctaw card #4728, final roll #15492 as Mary E. Boyd.
No.1 was admitted as an intermarried citizen of the Choctaw Nation by the Dawes Commission in 1896 and no appeal taken. 1896 Citizenship case #219.
No.1 originally listed for enrollment on Choctaw card #D- 813 Oct. 20, 1902 transferred to this card Feb. 1, 1905 See decision of Jan. 16, 1905

Date of Application for Enrollment.	Date of transfer to this card
Oct 20/02	Feb. 1, 1905

RESIDENCE: Choctaw Nation ~~COUNTY.~~ **Choctaw Nation** **Choctaw Roll** (Not Including Freedmen) CARD NO.
POST OFFICE: Valliant, I.T. FIELD NO. 5908

Dawes' Roll No.	NAME	Relationship to Person First Named	AGE	SEX	BLOOD	TRIBAL ENROLLMENT Year	County	No.
IW 1390	1 Folsom, Laura	First Named	19	F	I.W.			
	2							
	3							
	4							
	5							
	6							
	7							
	8							
	9							
	10							
	11							
	12							
	13							
	14							
	15							
	16							
	17							

ENROLLMENT
~~OF NOS.~~ 1 ~~HEREON~~
APPROVED BY THE SECRETARY
OF INTERIOR MAR 14 1905

TRIBAL ENROLLMENT OF PARENTS

Name of Father	Year	County	Name of Mother	Year	County
1 Jim Davis		non-citizen	Elizabeth Davis		non-citizen

~~No.1 was married to Robert Folsom a recognized and enrolled citizen~~
by blood of the Choctaw Nation, whose name appears on Choctaw card
#5430, final roll #13777 as Robert E. Folsom
~~No.1 originally listed for enrollment on Choctaw card #D- 852 Dec. 2, 1902;~~
~~transferred to this card Jan. 29, 1905 See decision of Jan. 13, 1905~~
For child of No.1 see N.B. (Apr 26, 1906) Card No. 69

Date of Application for Enrollment.	~~Date of transfer~~ to this card
Dec 2/02	Jan. 29, 1905

RESIDENCE: Choctaw Nation ~~COUNTY.~~ **Choctaw Nation** **Choctaw Roll** *(Not Including Freedmen)* CARD NO.
POST OFFICE: Antlers, Ind. Ter FIELD NO. 5909

Dawes' Roll No.	NAME	Relationship to Person First Named	AGE	SEX	BLOOD	TRIBAL ENROLLMENT Year	County	No.
IW 1391	1 Treep, Josephine	Named	29	F	I.W.			
	2							
	3							
	4							
	5							
	6							
	7							
	8							
	9							
	10							
	11							
	12							
	13							
	14							
	15							
	16							
	17							

ENROLLMENT
~~OF NOS.~~ 1 ~~HEREON~~
APPROVED BY THE SECRETARY
OF INTERIOR MAR 14 1905

TRIBAL ENROLLMENT OF PARENTS

Name of Father	Year	County	Name of Mother	Year	County
1 Joe Baker	dead	non-citizen	Lucina Baker	Dead	non-citizen
2					
3					
4					
5					

No.1 formerly the wife of David Campbell, a recognized and enrolled citizen by blood of the Choctaw Nation; identified on the 1896 Choctaw Roll, Cedar Co, page 58 #2407 and who died in 1898.
No.1 originally listed for enrollment on Choctaw card #D- 946 Dec. 5, 1902
Transferred to this card Jan. 29, 1905 See decision of Jan. 13, 1905

Date of Application for Enrollment.	Date of transfer to this card
Dec. 5/02	Jan. 29, 1905

RESIDENCE: Choctaw Nation COUNTY. **Choctaw Nation** **Choctaw Roll** *(Not Including Freedmen)* CARD NO.
POST OFFICE: Atoka, Ind. Ter. FIELD NO. 5910

Dawes' Roll No.		NAME	Relationship to Person First Named	AGE	SEX	BLOOD	TRIBAL ENROLLMENT Year	County	No.
IW 1392	1	McGahey, Minnie	Named	25	F	I.W.			
	2								
	3								
	4								
	5								
	6								
	7								
	8								
	9								
	10								
	11								
	12								
	13								
	14								
	15								
	16								
	17								

ENROLLMENT
OF NOS. 1 HEREON
APPROVED BY THE SECRETARY
OF INTERIOR MAR 14 1905

TRIBAL ENROLLMENT OF PARENTS

	Name of Father	Year	County	Name of Mother	Year	County
1	Joseph W. Neely		non citizen	Frances C. Neely		claims Choctaw
2						
3						
4						
5						

6 No.1 denied by Commission in '96 case 1144 as a citizen by blood
7 No.1 was admitted by U.S. Court, Central Dist, Court case #76 as a citizen by blood
8 No.1 was denied as a citizen by blood C.C.C.C. 79M
Husband of No.1, John H. McGahey, is on Choctaw card #1788, final roll #5070
9 No.12 originally listed for enrollment on Choctaw card #D- 983 Dec. 24, 1902;
10 transferred to this card Jan. 29, 1905 See decision of Jan. 13, 1905

Date of Application for Enrollment.	Transfer date
Dec. 24/02	Jan. 29, 1905

RESIDENCE: COUNTY. **Choctaw Nation** **Choctaw Roll** *(Not Including Freedmen)* CARD NO.
POST OFFICE: Blanco, I.T. FIELD NO. 5911

Dawes' Roll No.	NAME	Relationship to Person First Named	AGE	SEX	BLOOD	TRIBAL ENROLLMENT Year	County	No.
15879	1 James, Joseph		56	M	Full	1896	Gaines	6595

ENROLLMENT
OF NOS. 1 HEREON
APPROVED BY THE SECRETARY
OF INTERIOR JUN 12 1905

TRIBAL ENROLLMENT OF PARENTS

Name of Father	Year	County	Name of M[other]	Year	County
1 Nosaka	Dead	Choctaw	(Lashama) [Sooky James]		

See testimony of January 7, 12 and 14, 1905 and also testimony of No.1 of February 10, 1905.

No.1 transferred from Choctaw Card # D- 883 Originally listed on card D 883 December 24, 1902

No.1 is father of No.1 on Choctaw card #48667

Date of Application for Enrollment.	Transfer date
Dec 24/02	FEB 21 1905

RESIDENCE: COUNTY. **Choctaw Nation** **Choctaw Roll** *(Not Including Freedmen)* CARD NO.

[PO]ST OFFICE: Crowder, Ind. Ter. FIELD NO. 5912

[D]awes' [R]oll No.	NAME	Relationship to Person First Named	AGE	SEX	BLOOD	TRIBAL ENROLLMENT Year	County	No.
[1]463	1 Cockrum, Samantha		30	F	I.W.			

ENROLLMENT
~~OF NOS.~~ 1 ~~HEREON~~
APPROVED BY THE SECRETARY
OF INTERIOR Jun 12 1905

TRIBAL ENROLLMENT OF PARENTS

	Name of Father	Year	County	Name of Mother	Year	County
1	Samuel Van Brunt		non-citizen	Jane Stewart	Dead	non-citizen

~~No.1 placed hereon in accordance with order of the Commission~~
of March 23, 905 holding that application was made for her enrollment within the time provided by the act of July 1, 1902 (32 Stat. 641)

~~No.1 formerly wife of Calvin Howell, Choctaw roll No. 896 to whom she was married on Oct 27, 1888, and from whom she was divorced about nine years thereafter.~~

For children of No.1 see NB (Apr 26 '06) #1098.

Date of Application for Enrollment. July 1/02

Transfer date Mar 23, 1905

RESIDENCE: Chickasaw Nation COUNTY. **Choctaw Nation** Choctaw Roll (Not Including Freedmen) CARD NO.
POST OFFICE: Marlow, Ind. Ter FIELD NO. 5913

Dawes' Roll No.	NAME	Relationship to Person First Named	AGE	SEX	BLOOD	TRIBAL ENROLLMENT Year	County	No.
15995	1 Thompson, William C.	First Named	63	M	1/4	1896	Chick district	12521
IW 1564	2 " Sarah S	Wife	55	F	I.W.	1896	" "	15121
15996	3 Stubblefield, Sarah T	Grand niece	7	F	1/16			
15997	4 Thompson, William R.	nephew	19	M	1/8	1896	Chick district	12523

ENROLLMENT OF NOS. 2 HEREON APPROVED BY THE SECRETARY OF INTERIOR Aug 2 1906

ENROLLMENT OF NOS. 1, 3 and 4 HEREON APPROVED BY THE SECRETARY OF INTERIOR Jun 16 1906

No.4 P.O. Clinton, Okla

TRIBAL ENROLLMENT OF PARENTS

Name of Father	Year	County	Name of Mother	Year	County
1 Wm Thompson	dead	Choctaw	Elizabeth Thompson	dead	Choctaw
2 Thos. C. Estes	dead	non-citizen	Sarah S. Estes		non-citizen
3 Wm R. Stubblefield		" "	Terry Stubblefield		Choctaw
4 Arthur Thompson	dead	Choctaw	Elizabeth Thompson	dead	"

~~Nos 1 to 4 inclusive restored to roll by departmental authority of February 20, 1909 (File 5-51)~~

Nos 1,2,3 and 4 admitted as citizens of the Choctaw Nation by decree of Choctaw citizenship committee of October 8, 1896,

~~Nos 1,2,3 and 4 were refused identification as Mississippi Choctaw case of Wm C. Thompson et al (MC R#341) the decision refusing the applicants as Mississippi Choctaws was affirmed by~~ the Secretary of the Interior March 24th, 1905 but the Commission was directed to enroll Nos. 1,2,3 and 4 as citizens of the Choctaw Nation and their names were transferred to this card ~~April 5, 1905. See Mississippi Choctaw Case #341~~

~~March 15, 1906: Department after consideration of motion for review directed~~ enrollment of applicants.

June 19/1900
Date of Application for Enrollment.

Date of Transfer ~~to this card Oct.~~ Apr -5 1905

~~Enrollment of Nos 1 to 4 inclusive cancelled by order of Department of Feb. 23, 1907.~~

RESIDENCE: Chickasaw Nation COUNTY. **Choctaw Nation** Choctaw Roll (*Not Including Freedmen*) CARD NO.
POST OFFICE: Marlow, Ind. Ter. FIELD NO. 5914

Dawes' Roll No.		NAME	Relationship to Person First Named	AGE	SEX	BLOOD	TRIBAL ENROLLMENT Year	County	No.
15998	1	McNeese, Mary M		34	F	1/8	1896	Chick district	9535
15999	2	" " Harrold Graham	son	10	M	1/16	1896	" "	9534
	3								
	4								
	5								
	6								
	7								
	8	Child of no1 on NB (Apr 26-06) Card #288							
	9								
	10								
	11								
	12	ENROLLMENT							
	13	OF NOS. 1 and 2 HEREON							
	14	APPROVED BY THE SECRETARY OF INTERIOR Jun 16 1906							
	15								
	16								
	17								

TRIBAL ENROLLMENT OF PARENTS

	Name of Father	Year	County	Name of Mother	Year	County
1	Wm C Thompson	1896	Chick district	Sarah S Thompson		non-citizen
2	Wm G. McNeese		non-citizen	No.1		
3						
4						

5 Nos 1 and 2 restored to roll by departmental authority of February 20, 1909 (File 5-51)
6 No1 admitted as a citizen of the Choctaw Nation by decree of Choctaw citizenship committee of October 8, 1896.
7 Nos 1 and 2 were refused identification as Mississippi Choctaws by decision of
8 Commission of March 5, 1904 inconsolidated[sic] Mississippi Choctaw Case of Wm C. Thompson
9 et al (M.C.R. #341); the decision of the Commission refusing the applicants as Mississippi Choctaws was affirmed by the secretary[sic] of the Interior March 25th 1905, but the Commission
10 was directed to enroll nos 1 and 2 as citizens of the Choctaw Nation, and their names were
11 transferred to this card April 5, 1905
12 See Mississippi Choctaw case #517

Date of Application for Enrollment.	Transfer date
July 30, 1900	Apr -5 1905

17 Enrollment of Nos 1 and 2 cancelled by order of Department of Feb. 23, 1907.

RESIDENCE: Chickasaw Nation COUNTY. **Choctaw Nation** **Choctaw Roll** (Not Including Freedmen) CARD NO.
POST OFFICE: Marlow, Ind. Ter. FIELD NO. 5915

Dawes' Roll No.		NAME	Relationship to Person First Named	AGE	SEX	BLOOD	TRIBAL ENROLLMENT Year	County	No.
16000	1	Thompson, William C, Jr		27	M	1/8	1896	Chick District	12523
IW 1565	2	" Maud	Wife	24	F	I.W.			
	3								
	4								
	5								
	6								
	7								
	8								
	9								
	10								
	11								
	12								
	13								
	14								
	15								
	16								
	17								

ENROLLMENT OF NOS. 1 HEREON APPROVED BY THE SECRETARY OF INTERIOR Jun 16 1906

ENROLLMENT OF NOS. 2 HEREON APPROVED BY THE SECRETARY OF INTERIOR Aug 2 1906

TRIBAL ENROLLMENT OF PARENTS

	Name of Father	Year	County	Name of Mother	Year	County
1	Wm C. Thompson		Choctaw	Sarah S Thompson		Card #5913
2	J.D. Bateman		non-citizen	~~~~~ Bateman		non-citizen

~~Nos 1 and 2 restored to roll by Departmental authority of February 20, 1909 (File 5-51)~~

~~Enrollment of Nos 1 and 2 cancelled by order of Department of Feb. 23, 1907~~

No1 admitted as a citizen of the Choctaw Nation by decree of Choctaw citizenship committee of October 8, 1896.

~~Nos 1 and 2 were refused identification as Mississippi Choctaws by decision of~~ Commission of March 5, 1904 inconsolidated[sic] Mississippi Choctaw Case of Wm C. Thompson et al (M.C.R. #341); the decision of the Commission refusing the applicants as Mississippi Choctaws was affirmed by the Secretary of the Interior March 25th 1905, but the ~~Commission was directed to enroll Nos 1 and 2 as citizens of the Choctaw Nation, and their~~ names were transferred to this card April 7, 1905

See Mississippi Choctaw case #516

Child of nos 1&2 on NB (Apr 26 '06) Card #286

Date of Application for Enrollment.
~~June 19 1900~~

Transfer ~~date~~
~~Apr - 7 1905~~

RESIDENCE: Chickasaw Nation COUNTY.
POST OFFICE: Marlow, Ind. Ter.

Choctaw Nation

Choctaw Roll (Not Including Freedmen)

CARD NO.
FIELD NO. 5916

Dawes' Roll No.	NAME	Relationship to Person First Named	AGE	SEX	BLOOD	TRIBAL ENROLLMENT Year	County	No.
16001	1 Thompson, Arthur M	Named	33	M	1/8	1896	Chick district	12522
	2							
	3							
	4							
	5							
	6							
	7							
	8							
	9							
	10							
	11							
	12							
	13							
	14							
	15							
	16							
	17							

ENROLLMENT
~~OF NOS.~~ 1 ~~HEREON~~
APPROVED BY THE SECRETARY
OF INTERIOR Jun 16 1906

TRIBAL ENROLLMENT OF PARENTS

Name of Father	Year	County	Name of Mother	Year	County
1 Wm C. Thompson		Choctaw	Sarah S Thompson		Card #5913
2					
3					
4					

No.1 restored to roll by Departmental authority of February 20, 1909 (File 5-51)
~~Enrollment of No.1 cancelled by order of Department of Feb. 23, 1907.~~
~~No1 admitted as a citizen of the Choctaw Nation by decree of Choctaw citizenship committee of October 8, 1896.~~
No.1 was refused identification as Mississippi Choctaws by decision of Commission of March 5, 1904 inconsolidated[sic] Mississippi Choctaw Case of Wm C. ~~Thompson et al (M.C.R. #341), the decision refusing the applicant as a Mississippi Choctaw~~ was affirmed by the Secretary of the Interior March 25th 1905, but the Commission was directed to enroll No.1 as a citizen of the Choctaw Nation, and his name was transferred to this card April 7, 1905
~~See Mississippi Choctaw case #582~~

Date of Application for Enrollment.
Aug 13/1900

For date of application for enrollment see Miss. Choc. Card R582
Transferred to this card Apr -7 1905

RESIDENCE: Choctaw Nation COUNTY. **Choctaw Nation** Choctaw Roll (Not Including Freedmen) CARD NO.
POST OFFICE: Hoyt, Ind. Ter. FIELD NO. 5917

Dawes' Roll No.	NAME	Relationship to Person First Named	AGE	SEX	BLOOD	TRIBAL ENROLLMENT Year	County	No.
1464	1 Cummings, Henry A	First Named	40	M	I.W.	1885	Sans Bois	247
5880	2 Southard, Ida M	Dau	17	F	1/4	1893	Sans Bois	937
5881	3 " Engle	son of No2	1	M	1/8			

~~Nos 1, 2 and 3~~
Dismissed
Sep 23 1904

Oct. 19, 1904: Record forwarded Secty of Interior April 1, 1904; Secty of ~~Interior directs Commission to enroll~~ Nos 1,2 and 3.

ENROLLMENT OF NOS. 2 and 3 HEREON APPROVED BY THE SECRETARY OF INTERIOR Jun 12 1905

ENROLLMENT OF NOS. 1 HEREON APPROVED BY THE SECRETARY OF INTERIOR Jun 12 1905

TRIBAL ENROLLMENT OF PARENTS

Name of Father	Year	County	Name of Mother	Year	County
Jim Cummings	dead	non-citizen	Catherine Cummings	dead	non-citizen
No.1			Donia Cummings	dead	Sans Bois
N.T. Southard		non-citizen	No.2		

~~No.1 on 1885 Choctaw roll as Henry Cummings~~
No.2 on 1893 " " " Ida May Cummings
No.3 born May 31, 1902: Enrolled Oct 15, 1902
~~Nos. 1 and 2 admitted by Dawes Commission in 1896: Choctaw Case #963~~
~~Nos 1 and 2 admitted by U.S. Court Central District Aug 25th 1897: Court case No 176~~
No appeal to Choctaw and Chickasaw citizenship Court
Nos.[sic] 1 transferred from Choctaw Card # 2622 and Nos 2 and 3 from Choctaw card #4629 ~~to this card April 17, 1905.~~
~~For child of No.2 see N.B. (Apr 26, 1906) No. 549~~
" children of " 1 " " " " " " 1095

Date of Application for Enrollment. 6/14/99

~~Enrollment of No.1 cancelled by order of Department of February 28, 1907.~~
No.1 restored to roll by departmental authority of January 19, 1909 (File 5-51)
No.2 P.O. Quinton I.T. 11/9/05
~~Apr 17 1905~~

RESIDENCE: Eagle COUNTY. **Choctaw Nation** **Choctaw Roll** *(Not Including Freedmen)* CARD NO.
POST OFFICE: Eagletown, I.T. FIELD NO. 5918

Dawes' Roll No.		NAME	Relationship to Person First Named	AGE	SEX	BLOOD	TRIBAL ENROLLMENT Year	County	No.
15882	1	Thompson, Eddy A	First Named	21	M	1/2			
15883	2	" Callie	sister	18	F	1/2			
15884	3	" James L	Bro	16	M	1/2			
15885	4	" Viola	sister	14	F	1/2			
15886	5	" Albert	Bro	12	M	1/2			
15887	6	" Emma	sister	10	F	1/2			
	7	~~" Martha~~	~~Mother~~	~~45~~	~~F~~	~~I.W.~~			

ENROLLMENT OF NOS. 1,2,3,4,5 and 6 HEREON APPROVED BY THE SECRETARY OF INTERIOR Jun 12 1905

No7 Action approved by Secretary of Interior Mar 4 1907

Notice of departmental action mailed parties herein May 6, 1907

TRIBAL ENROLLMENT OF PARENTS

	Name of Father	Year	County	Name of Mother	Year	County
1	Robert Thompson	dead		Martha Thompson		non citz
2	" "	"		" "		" "
3	" "	"		" "		" "
4	" "	"		" "		" "
5	" "	"		" "		" "
6	" "	"		" "		" "
7		~~Dead~~	~~non citizen~~	~~Mary McKellar~~	~~Dead~~	" "

Robert Thompson the father of No.1 to 6 incl. was a recognized and enrolled citizen by blood of the Choctaw Nation, his name is on the 1893 Choc. Leased Dist. Payment Roll Eagle Co. Page 64, No 599; also upon the 1896 Choc. Census Roll, Eagle Co. Page 318 No. 12252

Nos 1 to 6 incl. originally listed for enrollment on Choctaw card #D- 118; transferred to this card May 15, 1905. See decision of April 28, 1905

No.7 placed hereon March 23, 1906 under order of Commission to Five Civilized Tribes of the date holding application was made for her enrollment within the time provided by act of Congress of July 1, 1902 (32 Stat 641)

No.7 REFUSED Feb 18 1907

April 24/99
Date of Application for Enrollment.

Date of Transf to this card May 15, 190

RESIDENCE: COUNTY. **Choctaw Nation** Choctaw Roll (*Not Including Freedmen*) CARD NO.
POST OFFICE: Garvin, I.T. FIELD NO. 5919

Dawes' Roll No.	NAME	Relationship to Person First Named	AGE	SEX	BLOOD	TRIBAL ENROLLMENT Year	County	No.
IW 1435	1 Haley, Nancy		85	F	I.W.			

ENROLLMENT
OF NOS. 1 HEREON
APPROVED BY THE SECRETARY
OF INTERIOR JUN 12 1905

TRIBAL ENROLLMENT OF PARENTS

Name of Father	Year	County	Name of Mother	Year	County
1 John Baskus	dead	Non Citz	Christina Baskus	dead	Non Citz

About the year 1885 No.1 was married to John Tully Haley, a recognized and enrolled citizen by blood of the Choctaw Nation, who is identified (as John Tulliheli), upon the 1885 Choctaw Census Roll, Boktuklo[sic] Co., No. 107, and who died about 1887.

~~No.1 originally listed for enrollment on Choctaw card #D- 138 April 29/99 transferred to this card May 15, 1905 See decision of March 27, 1905~~

Date of Application for Enrollment.	Transfer date
April 29/99	May 15, 1905

RESIDENCE: COUNTY. **Choctaw Nation** **Choctaw Roll** *(Not Including Freedmen)* CARD NO.
POST OFFICE: Hugo, I.T. FIELD NO. 5920

Dawes' Roll No.	NAME	Relationship to Person First Named	AGE	SEX	BLOOD	TRIBAL ENROLLMENT Year	County	No.
15888	1 Chatau, George		15	M	1/4	1896	Kiamitia	2700
	2							
	3							
	4							
	5							
	6							
	7							
	8							
	9							
	10							
	11							
	12							
	13							
	14							
	15							
	16							
	17							

ENROLLMENT
~~OF NOS.~~ 1 ~~HEREON~~
APPROVED BY THE SECRETARY
OF INTERIOR JUN 12 1905

TRIBAL ENROLLMENT OF PARENTS

	Name of Father	Year	County	Name of Mother	Year	County
1	George Harrell		Non Citz	Sissy Mc Coy	dead	
2						
3						
4						
5						

6 ~~No.1 on 1896 roll as George Chantaw~~[sic]
7 No.1 is the son of Sissy Mc Coy, deceased, a recognized citizen by blood of the Choctaw Nation
8 No.1 originally listed for enrollment on Choctaw card #D- 142 5/8/99;
~~transferred to this card May 15, 1905 See decision of Feb. 3, 1905~~

Date of Application for Enrollment.	Transfer date
5/8/99	May 15, 1905

RESIDENCE: Towson COUNTY. **Choctaw Nation** Choctaw Roll *(Not Including Freedmen)*
POST OFFICE: Fowlerville, I.T.

Dawes' Roll No.		NAME	Relationship to Person First Named	AGE	SEX	BLOOD	TRIBAL ENROLLMENT Year	County	No.
IW 1436	1	Williams, Etta		23	F	I.W.			
	2								
	3								
	4								
	5								
	6								
	7								
	8								
	9								
	10								
	11								
	12								
	13								
	14								
	15								
	16								
	17								

ENROLLMENT OF NOS. 1 HEREON APPROVED BY THE SECRETARY OF INTERIOR JUN 12 1905

TRIBAL ENROLLMENT OF PARENTS

	Name of Father	Year	County	Name of Mother	Year	County
1	Jim Bell	dead	Non Citz	Mary Bell		Non
2						
3						
4						
5						

6 On Feb. 23, 1899 No.1 and Charles Williams, a recognized citizen by blood of the
7 Choctaw Nation, were married. His roll No. is 3717
8 No.1 was subsequently divorced from said Charles Williams.

10 No.1 originally listed for enrollment on Choctaw card #D- 155 5/11/909;
11 transferred to this card May 15, 1905. See decision of April 28, 1905

Date of Application for Enrollment.	transfer date
5/11/99	May 15, 1905

RESIDENCE: COUNTY. **Choctaw Nation** Choctaw Roll *(Not Including Freedmen)* CARD NO.
POST OFFICE: Spencerville, I.T. FIELD NO. 59

Dawes' Roll No.	NAME	Relationship to Person First Named	AGE	SEX	BLOOD	TRIBAL ENROLLMENT Year	County	No.
IW 1437	1 Williams, Annie		25	F	I.W.			
	2							
	3							
	4							
	5							
	6							
	7							
	8							
	9							
	10							
	11							
	12							
	13							
	14							
	15							
	16							
	17							

ENROLLMENT
OF NOS. 1 HEREON
APPROVED BY THE SECRETARY
OF INTERIOR JUN 12 1905

TRIBAL ENROLLMENT OF PARENTS

Name of Father	Year	County	Name of Mother	Year	County
1 Jim Daniels	dead	Non Citz	Mary Mounts		Non
2					
3					
4					
5					

6 No.1 was formerly the wife of Edward Roebuck, a recognized and enrolled citizen by
7 blood of the Choctaw Nation, Roll No. 4350. Said parties lived together about seven
8 months, when they separated and were divorced.
No.1 is now the wife of Walter Williams, a white man.
9 No.1 originally listed for enrollment on Choctaw card #D- 158, 5/12/99
10 transferred to this card May 15, 1905. See decision of March 28, 1905
11 For children of No.1 see N.B. (Apr 26-06) #1243

Date of Application for Enrollment.	transfer date
5/12/99	May 15, 1905

E:

ICE: Antlers, I.T.

COUNTY. **Choctaw Nation**

Choct
(Not Includi

	NAME	Relationship to Person First Named	AGE	SEX	BLOOD	TRIBAL ENROLLMENT Year	County	No.
1	Freeman, George		24	M	1/4	1896	Jacks Fork	4540
2	" John	Bro	17	"	1/4	1896	" "	4538

ENROLLMENT
~~OF NOS.~~ 1 and 2 ~~HEREON~~
APPROVED BY THE SECRETARY
OF INTERIOR JUN 12 1905

TRIBAL ENROLLMENT OF PARENTS

	Name of Father	Year	County	Name of Mother	Year	County
1	Frank Freeman		Non Citz	Nancy Freeman	dead	1896 Jacks Fork
2	" "		" "	" "	"	
5	~~No.1 1893 Kiamitia~~	Page 125 #23				
6	No.2 1893 "	Page 125 #24				

Date of Application for Enrollment.

Nos 1 and 2 originally listed for enrollment on Choctaw card #D- 177 5/22/99
~~transferred to this card May 15, 1905 See decision of Feb. 7, 1905~~

May 15, 1905
transfer
date
May 15, 1905

Choctaw By Blood Enrollment Cards 1898-1914

RESIDENCE: COUNTY. **Choctaw Nation** **Choctaw Roll** *(Not Including Freedmen)* CARD NO.
POST OFFICE: Fort Smith, Ark. FIELD NO.

Dawes' Roll No.	NAME	Relationship to Person First Named	AGE	SEX	BLOOD	TRIBAL ENROLLMENT Year	County	No.
IW 1438	1 Foucar, Ida L		48	F	I.W	1896	Skullyville	14745

ENROLLMENT
OF NOS. I HEREON
APPROVED BY THE SECRETARY
OF INTERIOR JUN 12 1905

TRIBAL ENROLLMENT OF PARENTS

Name of Father	Year	County	Name of Mother	Year	County
1 Jos. A. Tibbitts	dead	Non Citz	Louisa A. Tibbitts		Non

No.1 formerly the wife of Campbell LeFlore, a recognized and enrolled citizen by blood of the Choctaw Nation, who is identified on 1885 Choc. Census Roll, Skullyville Co. No. 758; also 1893 Choc. Leased Dist. Pay Roll, Skullyville Co page 35 #329 as Campbell Le Flore Sr.
No.1 on 1896 roll, page 392 #14745 as Ida L LeFlore
also " " " " " #14742 " Ida LeFlore
No.1 on 1885 Choc. Census Roll, Skullyville Co, #759
No.1 originally listed for enrollment on Choctaw card #D- 187 5/31/99
transferred to this card May 15, 1905 See decision of April 1, 1905

Date of Application for Enrollment. 5/31/99

transfer date May 15, 1905

RESIDENCE: Blue COUNTY. **Choctaw Nation** Choctaw Roll (Not Including Freedmen) CARD NO.
POST OFFICE: Durant, I.T. 1/3/06 FIELD NO. 5925

Dawes' Roll No.	NAME	Relationship to Person First Named	AGE	SEX	BLOOD	TRIBAL ENROLLMENT Year	County	No.
IW1439	1 Payton, Nancy C.		52	F	I.W.			

ENROLLMENT
OF NOS. 1 HEREON
APPROVED BY THE SECRETARY
OF INTERIOR JUN 12 1905

TRIBAL ENROLLMENT OF PARENTS

Name of Father	Year	County	Name of Mother	Year	County
1 Finis Johnson		Non Citz	Eliz Johnson		Non Citz

On June 5, 1899 No.1 married Daniel Payton, a recognized and enrolled citizen by blood of the Choctaw Nation Final roll #10225
They lived together for about two months when they separated and were divorced.
No.1 originally listed for enrollment on Choctaw card #D- 338, Aug 18/99 transferred to this card May 15, 1905 See decision of Feb. 7, 1905

P.O. Paoli I.T.

Date of Application for Enrollment. Aug 18/99

transfer date May 15, 1905

RESIDENCE: COUNTY. **Choctaw Nation** Choctaw Roll (Not Including Freedmen) CARD NO.
POST OFFICE: Boswell, I.T. FIELD NO. 5926

Dawes' Roll No.	NAME	Relationship to Person First Named	AGE	SEX	BLOOD	TRIBAL ENROLLMENT Year	County	No.
IW 1440	1 Lewis, John M		50	M	I.W.			
	2							
	3							
	4							
	5							
	6							
	7							
	8							
	9							
	10							
	11							
	12							
	13							
	14							
	15							
	16							
	17							

ENROLLMENT
OF NOS. 1 HEREON
APPROVED BY THE SECRETARY
OF INTERIOR JUN 12 1905

TRIBAL ENROLLMENT OF PARENTS

	Name of Father	Year	County	Name of Mother	Year	County
1	John Lewis	dead	Non Citz	Pruda Lewis	dead	Non Citz
2						
3						
4						
5						

No.1 formerly the husband of Sophia Peters (formerly Sophia Nail who died in 1893), the name of whose son Joe Nail, appears as number 4266 (three-fourths Choctaw Indian by blood), on final roll of Choctaws by blood

~~No.1 originally listed for enrollment on Choctaw card #D- 342, Aug. 21/99 transferred to this card May 15, 1905 See decision of April 22, 1905~~

Date of Application for Enrollment: Aug 21/99

transfer date: May 15, 1905

RESIDENCE: Chickasaw Nation ~~COUNTY.~~
POST OFFICE: M[c] Gee, I.T.

Choctaw Nation

Choctaw Roll *(Not Including Freedmen)*

CARD NO.
FIELD NO. 5927

	NAME	Relationship to Person First Named	AGE	SEX	BLOOD	TRIBAL ENROLLMENT Year	County	No.
	1 Blevins, George W		26	M	I.W.			
15891	2 Rose, Pearl	S. Dau	7	F	1/8			
15892	3 Blevins, James	Son	3	M	1/8			

ENROLLMENT OF NOS. 2 and 3 HEREON APPROVED BY THE SECRETARY OF INTERIOR JUN 12 1905

ENROLLMENT OF NOS. 1 HEREON APPROVED BY THE SECRETARY OF INTERIOR JUN 12 1905

Name of Father	Year	County	Name of Mother	Year	County
1 James Blevins		Non Citz			
2 Cull Rose		" "	Ida Blevins	dead	
3 No.1			" "		

On April 5, 1899 No.1 was married to Ida Blevins, formerly Ida Rose (nee Ida Boswell), a recognized and enrolled citizen by blood of the Choc Nation, who is identified (as Ida Rose) on the 1893 Choc Leased Dist Payment Roll, Kiamitia Co, page 126,
~~Nos. 1,2,3 originally listed for enrollment on Choctaw card #D- 353, 1 and 2 ^enrolled^ Aug 24/99 and No.3 Oct. 6/99; transferred to this card May 15, 1905 See decision of March~~

Date of Application for Enrollment.
Aug 24/99

transfer date
May 15, 1905

RESIDENCE: Atoka COUNTY. **Choctaw Nation** Choctaw Roll *(Not Including Freedmen)* CARD NO.
POST OFFICE: Kiowa, I.T. FIELD NO. 5928

Dawes' Roll No.	NAME	Relationship to Person First Named	AGE	SEX	BLOOD	TRIBAL ENROLLMENT Year	County	No.
IW 1441	1 Campbell, John		78	M	I.W.			
	2							
	3							
	4							
	5							
	6							
	7							
	8							
	9							
	10							
	11							
	12							
	13							
	14							
	15							
	16							
	17							

ENROLLMENT
OF NOS. 1 HEREON
APPROVED BY THE SECRETARY
OF INTERIOR JUN 12 1905

TRIBAL ENROLLMENT OF PARENTS

	Name of Father	Year	County	Name of Mother	Year	County
1	Pat Campbell	dead	Non Citz	Nancy Campbell	dead	Non Citz
2						
3						
4						
5						

~~No.1 was formerly the husband of Mary Campbell (formerly Folsom) a recognized citizen~~ by blood of the Choctaw Nation, the name of whose daughter, Sarah E. Ridgeway, by said marriage appears as #11630, upon the lists prepared by this Commission.
~~No.1 originally listed for enrollment on Choctaw card #D- 423 Sept 4/99 transferred to this card May 15, 1905 See decision of April 28, 1905~~

Date of Application for Enrollment.

Sept 4/99

transfer date

May 15, 1905

RESIDENCE: Blue COUNTY. **Choctaw Nation** **Choctaw Roll** *(Not Including Freedmen)* CARD NO.
POST OFFICE: Caddo, I.T. FIELD NO. 5929

Dawes' Roll No.		NAME	Relationship to Person First Named	AGE	SEX	BLOOD	TRIBAL ENROLLMENT Year	County	No.
IW 1442	1	Boydstun, Mary Jane	First Named	27	F	I.W.	1896	Blue	14576
	2								
	3								
	4								
	5								
	6								
	7								
	8								
	9								
	10								
	11								
	12								
	13								
	14								
	15								
	16								
	17								

ENROLLMENT
~~OF NOS.~~ 1 ~~HEREON~~
APPROVED BY THE SECRETARY
OF INTERIOR JUN 12 1905

TRIBAL ENROLLMENT OF PARENTS

	[illegible]ther	Year	County	Name of Mother	Year	County
1				Selina Stewart	dead	Non Cit
2						
3						
4						
5						

~~No.1 was formerly the wife of Daniel H. Gardner, a recognized and enrolled citizen by blood~~
of the Choctaw Nation whose name appears as #10743 upon the lists prepared by this
Commission.
~~No.1 is now the wife of George A. Boydstun, on Choctaw card #3698, I.W. 1125.~~
~~No.1 originally listed for enrollment on Choctaw card #D-345 Aug 22/99;~~
transferred to this card May 15, 1905 See decision of March 28, 1905
For child of No1 see NB (Apr 26 '06) #1089

Date of Application for Enrollment. Aug 28/99

transfer date May 15, 1905

RESIDENCE: Atoka COUNTY. **Choctaw Nation** Choctaw Roll (Not Including Freedmen) CARD NO.
POST OFFICE: Atoka, I.T. FIELD NO. 5930

Dawes' Roll No.		NAME	Relationship to Person First Named	AGE	SEX	BLOOD	TRIBAL ENROLLMENT Year	County	No.
IW 1443	1	Stewart, John		76	M	I.W.			
	2								
	3								
	4								
	5								
	6	ENROLLMENT OF NOS. 1 HEREON APPROVED BY THE SECRETARY OF INTERIOR JUN 12 1905							
	7								
	8								
	9								
	10								
	11								
	12								
	13								
	14								
	15								
	16								
	17								

TRIBAL ENROLLMENT OF PARENTS

	Name of Father	Year	County	Name of Mother	Year	County
1	W. B. Stewart	dead	Non Citz	Henrietta Stewart	dead	Non Citz
2						
3						
4						
5						

~~No.1 formerly husband of Nancy Jane Stewart, a recognized Choctaw by blood.~~ Said Nancy Jane Stewart and No.1 admitted by U.S. Indian Agent, Oct. 12, 1889. Said decision of U.S. Indian Agent approved by Acting Sec. of the Interior on Nov. 19, 1889.
~~No.1 originally listed for enrollment on Choctaw card #D-420 Sept 2/99~~
~~transferred to this card May 15, 1905 See decision of March 29, 1905~~

Date of Application for Enrollment. Sept 2/99

transfer date May 15, 1905

[...]E: Gaines COUNTY. **Choctaw Nation** Choctaw Roll (Not Including Freedmen) CARD NO.
[...]CE: Bower, I.T. FIELD NO. 5[...]

	NAME	Relationship to Person First Named	AGE	SEX	BLOOD	TRIBAL ENROLLMENT Year	County	No.
1	Jennings, James C		22	M	1/2	1896	Gaines	6623
2	" Ida Leona	Wife	18	F	I.W.			
3	" Donnie May	Dau	2mo	F	1/4			
4								
5								
6								
7								
8	ENROLLMENT							
9	OF NOS. 1 and 3 HEREON							
10	APPROVED BY THE SECRETARY OF INTERIOR JUN 12 1905							
11								
12	ENROLLMENT							
13	OF NOS. 2 HEREON APPROVED BY THE SECRETARY							
14	OF INTERIOR JUN 12 1905							
15								
16	For child of Nos 1&2 see NB (Apr 26 '06) Card #636							
17								

TRIBAL ENROLLMENT OF PARENTS

	Name of Father	Year	County	Name of Mother	Year	County
1	R.P. Jennings		Gaines	Eliza Jennings	dead	
2	S.J. Metcalf		non citizen	Self Metcalf		Non[...]
3	No.1			No.2		
4						
5						

6 No.1 on 1885 Choc. Census Roll, Gaines Co. #628, as James C. Jennings
7 No.1 " 1893 " Pay " " " page 28, #257 as James Jennings
8 No.1 also on 1894 Cherokee strip payment roll, Sequoyah Dist. #759 as Jennie Jennings
No.1 is a son of Richard P. Jennings, a recognized and enrolled citizen by blood of the
9 Choctaw Nation. Final roll #13144, Choctaw card #4763
10 No.3 born July 19, 1902: enrolled Sept. 20, 1902
11 Nos 1,2 and 3 originally listed for enrollment on Choc. cards #D-493 and D-791, Nos 1 and 3 on card #D-493, Sept 14/99 and Sept 20/02. No 2 on card #D-791, Sept 16, 1902; trans-
12 ferred to this card May 15, 1905. See decision of Feb. 17, 1905
13 No application filed until was ever made to the Commission for enrollment of
14 Nos 1,2 and 3 as Cherokees.

	Date of Application for Enrollment.	transfer date
17	Sept 1/99	May 15, 1905

RESIDENCE: COUNTY. **Choctaw Nation** Choctaw Roll (Not Including Freedmen) CARD NO.
POST OFFICE: Pauls Valley, I.T. FIELD NO. 5932

Dawes' Roll No.	NAME	Relationship to Person First Named	AGE	SEX	BLOOD	TRIBAL ENROLLMENT Year	County	No.
15895	1 Boswell, Frank		28	M	1/4	1893	Kiamitia	Page 125 No. 17
IW 1589	2 " Mary	Wife	26	F	I.W.			
	3							
	4							
	5							
	6							
	7							
	8							
	9							
	10							
	11							
	12							
	13							
	14							
	15							
	16							
	17							

ENROLLMENT OF NOS. 1 HEREON APPROVED BY THE SECRETARY OF INTERIOR JUN 12 1905

ENROLLMENT OF NOS. 2 HEREON APPROVED BY THE SECRETARY OF INTERIOR NOV 26 1906

TRIBAL ENROLLMENT OF PARENTS

Name of Father	Year	County	Name of Mother	Year	County
1 Charley Boswell	dead	non citizen	Ellen Boswell	dead	Kiamitia
2 William Holland		" "	Sallie Holland		Non-citiz

No.1 is the son of Ellen Boswell, a recognized citizen by blood of the Choc. Nation
No.1 on 1893 Pay Roll, Kiamitia Co, page 125 No. 17 as G.W. Boswell
No.1 originally listed for enrollment on Choctaw card #D- 713 April 29, 1902; transferred to this card May 15, 1905 See decision of Feb. 3, 1905

For child of No1 see NB (Apr 26-06) Card #452

No.2 transferred from Choctaw Card # D- 713; July 29, 1906; See decision of July 13, 1906

#1

Date of Application for Enrollment. April 29/02

Date of Transfer to this Card. May 15, 1905

Choctaw By Blood Enrollment Cards 1898-1914

RESIDENCE: COUNTY. **Choctaw Nation** **Choctaw Roll** *(Not Including Freedmen)* CARD NO.
POST OFFICE: Cairo, I.T. FIELD NO. 5933

Dawes' Roll No.	NAME	Relationship to Person First Named	AGE	SEX	BLOOD	TRIBAL ENROLLMENT Year	County	No.
15896	1 Johnson, Thomas		14	M	Full	1896	Tobucksy	6677
	2							
	3							
	4							
	5							
	6							
	7							
	8							
	9							
	10							
	11							
	12							
	13							
	14							
	15							
	16							
	17							

ENROLLMENT OF NOS. 1 HEREON APPROVED BY THE SECRETARY OF INTERIOR JUN 12 1905

TRIBAL ENROLLMENT OF PARENTS

Name of Father	Year	County	Name of Mother	Year	County
1 Noel Johnson	dead	Choctaw	Molsey Seely	dead	Atoka
2					
3					
4					
5					

6 No.1 also on 1893 Pay Roll, Atoka Co., page 55, No. 579 as Thomas Johnson
7 No.1 originally listed for enrollment on Choctaw card #D- 925, Dec. 24, 1902
8 transferred to this card May 15, 1905

Date of Application for Enrollment.	Date of transfer to this card.
Dec 24/02	May 15, 1905

RESIDENCE: COUNTY. **Choctaw Nation** **Choctaw Roll** *(Not Including Freedmen)* CARD NO.
POST OFFICE: Redoak, I.T. FIELD NO. 5934

Dawes' Roll No.	NAME	Relationship to Person First Named	AGE	SEX	BLOOD	TRIBAL ENROLLMENT Year	County	No.
15897	1 Wesley, Thomas	First Named	11	M	Full	1896	Sugar Loaf	12928

ENROLLMENT
OF NOS. 1 HEREON
APPROVED BY THE SECRETARY
OF INTERIOR JUN 12 1905

TRIBAL ENROLLMENT OF PARENTS

Name of Father	Year	County	Name of Mother	Year	County
1 Slaughter Wesley	Dead	Choctaw	Lizzie Shauna Wesley	dead	Choctaw

6 ~~No.1 originally listed for enrollment on Choctaw card #D-923 Dec 24, 1902~~
7 transferred to this card [sic] 15, 1905

~~Date of Application for Enrollment.~~ Dec 24/02

~~Date of transfer to this card~~ May 15, 1905

RESIDENCE: COUNTY. **Choctaw Nation** **Choctaw Roll** *(Not Including Freedmen)* CARD NO.
POST OFFICE: Caddo, I.T. FIELD NO. 5935

Dawes' Roll No.	NAME	Relationship to Person First Named	AGE	SEX	BLOOD	TRIBAL ENROLLMENT Year	County	No.
15898	1 Goforth, Cordelia		19	F	1/2	1896	Jackson	368
	2							
	3							
	4							
	5							
	6							
	7							
	8							
	9							
	10							
	11							
	12							
	13							
	14							
	15							
	16							
	17							

ENROLLMENT
OF NOS. 1 HEREON
APPROVED BY THE SECRETARY
OF INTERIOR Jun 12 1905

TRIBAL ENROLLMENT OF PARENTS

	Name of Father	Year	County	Name of Mother	Year	County
1	Nelson Anukwiatubbi	dead	Choctaw	Nancy Deaton		non citizen
2						
3						
4						
5						

No.1 on 1896 Choc. Census Roll, page 10, No. 368 as Cordelia Anukwiatubbi
Husband of No.1 is on Chickasaw card #1639; final roll #4390
No.1 originally listed for enrollment on Choctaw card #R-214
~~No.1 transferred to this card May 15, 1905, see decision of April 22, 1905~~

Date of Application for Enrollment.
April 9/02

Date of transfer to this card.
May 15, 1905

RESIDENCE: Tishomingo COUNTY. **Choctaw Nation** Choctaw Roll (Not Including Freedmen) CARD NO.
POST OFFICE: Tishomingo, I.T. FIELD NO. 5936

Dawes' Roll No.	NAME	Relationship to Person First Named	AGE	SEX	BLOOD	TRIBAL ENROLLMENT Year	County	No.
IW 1444	1 Bolin, John		56	M	I.W.			

ENROLLMENT
OF NOS. 1 HEREON
APPROVED BY THE SECRETARY
OF INTERIOR JUN 12 1905

TRIBAL ENROLLMENT OF PARENTS

Name of Father	Year	County	Name of Mother	Year	County
1 Hugh Bolin	dead	Non Citz	Polly Bolin	dead	Non Citz

On March 25, 1874 No.1 married Laura Jackson, a recognized and enrolled citizen by blood of the Choctaw Nation, whose name (as Laura Kelly) appears as #14815 upon the lists prepared by this Commission. They lived together for about one year when they separated and were divorced

No.1 originally listed for enrollment on Choctaw card #D-323, Aug. 15/99 transferred to this card May 15, 1905 See decision of March 29, 1905

Date of Application for Enrollment. Aug 12/99

Date of transfer to this card May 15, 1905

RESIDENCE: Tobucksy COUNTY. **Choctaw Nation** **Choctaw Roll** *(Not Including Freedmen)* CARD NO.
POST OFFICE: Stuart, I.T. FIELD NO. 5937

Dawes' Roll No.		NAME	Relationship to Person First Named	AGE	SEX	BLOOD	TRIBAL ENROLLMENT Year	County	No.
IW 1445	1	Wilson, Mary		33	F	I.W.			
	2								
	3								
	4								
	5								
	6								
	7								
	8								
	9								
	10								
	11								
	12								
	13								
	14								
	15								
	16								
	17								

ENROLLMENT OF NOS. 1 HEREON APPROVED BY THE SECRETARY OF INTERIOR JUN 12 1905

TRIBAL ENROLLMENT OF PARENTS

	Name of Father	Year	County	Name of Mother	Year	County
1	Nath. Collins		non cit.	Susan Collins	dead	non cit.
2						
3						
4						
5						

6 No.1 formerly the wife of Frank Victor, a recognized citizen by blood of the Choctaw Nation,
7 who died about 1886.

8 ~~No.1 originally listed for enrollment on Choctaw card #D- 431 9/5/99~~
9 ~~transferred to this card May 15, 1905 See decision of Feb. 7,1905~~

Date of Application for Enrollment.	Date of transfer to this card
9/5/99	May 15, 1905

17 P.O. Cabaniss I.T. 1/26/06

RESIDENCE: COUNTY. **Choctaw Nation** **Choctaw Roll** *(Not Including Freedmen)* CARD NO.
POST OFFICE: So. Mc Alester, I.T. FIELD NO. 5938

Dawes' Roll No.	NAME	Relationship to Person First Named	AGE	SEX	BLOOD	TRIBAL ENROLLMENT Year	County	No.
IW 1446	1 Gordon, Haywood P	First Named	49	M	I.W.	1896	Gaines	14564
	2							
	3							
	4							
	5							
	6							
	7							
	8							
	9							
	10							
	11							
	12							
	13							
	14							
	15							
	16							
	17							

ENROLLMENT
~~OF NOS. 1 HEREON~~
APPROVED BY THE SECRETARY
OF INTERIOR JUN 12 1905

TRIBAL ENROLLMENT OF PARENTS

Name of Father	Year	County	Name of Mother	Year	County
1 M.B. Gordon	dead	Non Cit.	Alvina Gordon	dead	Non Cit.
2					
3					
4					
5					

6 No.1 formerly husband of Verneda Cowen a recognized and enrolled citizen by blood of the
7 Choctaw and Creek Nations, who is identified on 1896 Choctaw Census Roll, Gaines Co.
8 #4685. Verneda Cowen enrolled as a citizen by blood of the Creek Nation, final roll #1322
No.1 on 1896 roll Gaines Co, #14564 as H.P. Gordon
9 No.1 originally listed for enrollment on Choctaw card #D- 458 9/7/99;
10 transferred to this card May 15, 1905 See decision of Feb. 3, 1905

Date of Application for Enrollment.	Date of transfer to this card
9/7/99	May 15, 1905

RESIDENCE: Tobucksy COUNTY. **Choctaw Nation** **Choctaw Roll** *(Not Including Freedmen)* CARD NO.
POST OFFICE: Alderson, I.T. FIELD NO. 5939

Dawes' Roll No.	NAME	Relationship to Person First Named	AGE	SEX	BLOOD	TRIBAL ENROLLMENT Year	County	No.
	[Norman, Emma		24	F	I.W.	1896	Tobucksy	14466
	2							
	3							
	4							
	5							
	6							
	7							
	8							
	9							
	10							
	11							
	12							
	13							
	14							
	15							
	16							
	17							

ENROLLMENT
OF NOS. 1 HEREON
APPROVED BY THE SECRETARY
OF INTERIOR JUN 12 1905

TRIBAL ENROLLMENT OF PARENTS

	Name of Father	Year	County	Name of Mother	Year	County
1	T. G. Wilks		non citizen	Belle Wilks		non-citizen
2						
3						
4						
5						

6 ~~No.1 formerly wife of William H. Davis a recognized and enrolled citizen by blood of the~~
7 Choctaw Nation, final roll #12823, Choc. card #4638
No.1 now the wife of B.L. Norman, a white man.
8 ~~No.1 originally listed for enrollment on Choctaw card #D- 472 Sept 9-1899~~
9 ~~transferred to this card May 15, 1905 See decision of Feb. 7, 1905~~

Date of Application for Enrollment.	Date of transfer to this card
Sept 9/99	May 15, 1905

RESIDENCE: Choctaw Nation ~~COUNTY.~~ **Choctaw Nation** **Choctaw Roll** *(Not Including Freedmen)* CARD NO.
POST OFFICE: Nixon, Ind. Ter. FIELD NO. 59

Dawes' Roll No.	NAME	Relationship to Person First Named	AGE	SEX	BLOOD	TRIBAL ENROLLMENT Year	County	No.
IW 1448	1 Plummer, Minnie		29	F	I.W.			

ENROLLMENT
OF NOS. 1 HEREON
APPROVED BY THE SECRETARY
OF INTERIOR JUN 12 1905

TRIBAL ENROLLMENT OF PARENTS

	Name of Father	Year	County	Name of Mother	Year	County
1	Parkes Bacon		non citizen	Sarah Bacon		non ci

No.1 is the wife of Walter G. Plummer, a recognized and enrolled citizen by blood of the Choctaw Nation Choc. card #4113, final roll #11533

No.1 originally listed for enrollment on Choctaw card #D- 601 Dec 11, 1900; ~~transferred to this card May 15, 1905 See decision of Feb. 17, 1905~~

For child of No.1 see N.B. (Apr 26, 1906) card No. 244
" " " " " " (Mar 3 '05) " " 287

Date of Application for Enrollment.	Date of transfer to this card
Dec. 11/1900	May 15, 1905

RESIDENCE: COUNTY. **Choctaw Nation** **Choctaw Roll** *(Not Including Freedmen)* CARD NO.
POST OFFICE: Gillham, Arkansas FIELD NO. 5941

Dawes' Roll No.		NAME	Relationship to Person First Named	AGE	SEX	BLOOD	TRIBAL ENROLLMENT Year	County	No.
IW 1449	1	Heflin, William H		53	M	I.W.			
	2								
	3								
	4								
	5								
	6								
	7								
	8								
	9								
	10								
	11								
	12								
	13								
	14								
	15								
	16								
	17								

ENROLLMENT
OF NOS. 1 HEREON
APPROVED BY THE SECRETARY
OF INTERIOR JUN 12 1905

TRIBAL ENROLLMENT OF PARENTS

	Name of Father	Year	County	Name of Mother	Year	County
1	Wm R. Heflin	dead	white-man	Roxanna Heflin	dead	non-citizen
2						
3						
4						
5						

6 On Aug. 30, 1891 No.1 was married to Kizzie Hampton, a recognized and enrolled citizen by
7 blood of the Choctaw Nation. On final roll #10957 as Kizzie Wilmoth, Choctaw card #3870
No.1 is father of Lena L. Heflin on Choctaw card #3892
8 ~~No.1 originally listed for enrollment on Choctaw card #D-686 -~~
9 ~~transferred to this card May 15, 1905 See decision of Feb. 7, 1905~~

Date of Application for Enrollment.	Date of transfer to this card
Aug 24/99	May 15, 1905

RESIDENCE: COUNTY. **Choctaw Nation** Choctaw Roll (Not Including Freedmen) CARD NO.
POST OFFICE: Bennington, I.T. FIELD NO. 5942

Dawes' Roll No.	NAME	Relationship to Person First Named	AGE	SEX	BLOOD	TRIBAL ENROLLMENT Year	County	No.
IW 1450	1 Bingham, James B		40	M	I.W.			

ENROLLMENT OF NOS. 1 HEREON APPROVED BY THE SECRETARY OF INTERIOR Jun 12 1905

TRIBAL ENROLLMENT OF PARENTS

	Name of Father	Year	County	Name of Mother	Year	County
1	Elias Bingham	dead	non citizen	Mary Bingham	dead	non-citizen

On Nov. 17, 1885 No.1 was married to Lizzie Bingham (nee Tims) a recognized and enrolled citizen by blood of the Choctaw Nation, who is identified (as Lizzie Tims) upon the 1893 Choc Leased Dist. Payment Roll, Towson Co. #356 and also on 1896 Choc. Census Roll, Towson Co. #12122, and who died about the year 1896.

No.1 originally listed for enrollment on Choctaw card #D-854 Dec. 4 1902 transferred to this card May 15, 1905 See decision of March 28, 1905

Date of Application for Enrollment.	Date of transfer to this card
Dec 4/02	May 15, 1905

RESIDENCE: COUNTY. **Choctaw Nation** **Choctaw Roll** *(Not Including Freedmen)* CARD NO.

POST OFFICE: Indianola, I.T. FIELD NO. 5943

Dawes' Roll No.	NAME	Relationship to Person First Named	AGE	SEX	BLOOD	TRIBAL ENROLLMENT Year	County	No.
IW 1451	1 Beams, Levina Victoria							
	2							
	3							
	4							
	5							
	6							
	7							
	8							
	9							
	10							
	11							
	12							
	13							
	14							
	15							
	16							
	17							

ENROLLMENT
OF NOS. 1 HEREON
APPROVED BY THE SECRETARY
OF INTERIOR JUN 12 1905

TRIBAL ENROLLMENT OF PARENTS

Name of Father	Year	County	Name of Mother	Year	County
1 Rufus Kendrick	dead	non citz	Jane Kendrick		non citz
2					
3					
4					
5					

On Jan. 19, 1901 No.1 was married to William T. Beams, a recognized and enrolled citizen by blood of the Choctaw Nation, Choc card #5710, final roll #15512.
No.1 originally listed for enrollment on Choctaw card #D-968 - Dec. 23, 1902; transferred to this card May 15, 1905. See decision of Feb. 7, 1905

Date of Application for Enrollment.	Date of transfer to this card
Dec 23/02	May 15, 1905

[Re]sidence:	County. **Choctaw Nation**	**Choctaw Roll** *(Not Including Freedmen)*	Card No.
[Pos]t Office: Ardmore, I.T.			Field No.

[Da]wes' [Ro]ll No.	NAME	Relationship to Person First Named	AGE	SEX	BLOOD	TRIBAL ENROLLMENT Year	County	No.
[14]452	1 Nichols, Maggie B		26	F	I.W.			
	2							
	3							
	4							
	5							
	6							
	7							
	8							
	9							
	10							
	11							
	12							
	13							
	14							
	15							
	16							
	17							

ENROLLMENT
~~OF NOS.~~ 1 ~~HEREON~~
APPROVED BY THE SECRETARY
OF INTERIOR JUN 12 1905

TRIBAL ENROLLMENT OF PARENTS

Name of Father	Year	County	Name of Mother	Year	County
1 L. G. Copeland		non citizen	Betty Copeland		non citizen
2					
3					

4 On Sept 8, 1896 No.1 made application to this Commission for the admission to citizenship in
5 the Chickasaw Nation as Mrs. M. Brenda Nichols (1896 Chick. Citizenship Docket Case #255).
No.1 claiming her right through her husband S.W. Nichols, a recognized and enrolled citizen by
6 ~~blood of the Chick Nation whose name appears as Stanwaite Nichols, card #605 final roll #4422.~~
7 On Nov. 23, 1896 this Commission denied said application, no appeal was taken. Said
8 Stanwaite Nichols, husband of No.1 is also a recognized and enrolled citizen by blood of the
Choctaw Nation; identified on 1896 Choc. Census Roll page 249, #9847 as Waitie Nicholas.
9 ~~On Jan. 12, 1903 Stanwaite Nichols husband of No.1 came before this Commission and elected~~
10 for himself and his two children to be finally enrolled as citizens by blood of the Chick Nation
11 No.1 on 1896 Choc Census Roll, page 396, #14905 as Maggie Nicholas; enrolled thereon as a
citizen by intermarriage of said nation.
12 ~~No.1 originally listed for enrollment on Chick card #605. transferred~~
13 to this card May 15, 1905. See decision of March 29, 1905
14
15
16
17

Date of Application for Enrollment.	Date of transfer to this card
Oct. 5/98	May 15, 1905

RESIDENCE: COUNTY. **Choctaw Nation** **Choctaw Roll** *(Not Including Freedmen)* CARD

POST OFFICE: Durant, I.T. FIELD

Dawes' Roll No.	NAME	Relationship to Person First Named	AGE	SEX	BLOOD	TRIBAL ENROLLMENT Year	County	No.
IW 1453	1 M^c^Daniel, Cammie		20	F	I.W.			

ENROLLMENT OF NOS. 1 HEREON APPROVED BY THE SECRETARY OF INTERIOR JUN 12 1905

TRIBAL ENROLLMENT OF PARENTS

Name of Father	Year	County	Name of Mother	Year	County
1 J. A. Todd		non-citz	Nannie Todd		non-citz

~~No.1 is the wife of Marvin M^c^Daniel, a recognized and enrolled citizen by blood of the~~ Choctaw Nation; Choctaw card #5394, final roll #13660

No.1 originally listed for enrollment on Choctaw card #D-379 - Sept, 23, 1902; ~~transferred to this card May 15, 1905. See decision of Jan. 8 1905~~

No.1 was married to Marvin M^c^Daniel September 14, 1902

Record as to enrollment of No.1 forwarded Department March 14, 1906

Record returned. See opinion of Assistant Attorney General of March 15, 1906 in case of ~~Omer R. Nicholson~~

For child of No.1 see NB (Mar 3, 1905) card #399

" " " " " " (April 26, 1906) " #175

Date of Application for Enrollment.	Date of transfer to this card
Sept 23/02	May 15, 1905

RESIDENCE: Chickasaw Nation COUNTY [redacted] Choctaw Nation | Choctaw Roll (Not Including Freedmen) | CARD NO.
POST OFFICE: Bailey. I[redacted] | FIELD NO. 5946

Dawes' Roll No.	NAME	Relationship to Person First Named	AGE	SEX	BLOOD	TRIBAL ENROLLMENT Year	County	No.
IW 1454	1 Miller, Virginia P		25	F	I.W.			
	2							
	3							
	4							
	5							
	6							
	7							
	8							
	9							
	10							
	11							
	12							
	13							
	14							
	15							
	16							
	17							

ENROLLMENT OF NOS. 1 HEREON APPROVED BY THE SECRETARY OF INTERIOR JUN 12 1905

TRIBAL ENROLLMENT OF PARENTS

Name of Father	Year	County	Name of Mother	Year	County
1 James K. P. Rucker	dead	non-citizen	Virginia E. Rucker		non-citizen

5 John M Miller, husband of No 1, is part Choctaw and part Chickasaw. He is on 1893 Choc.
6 Leased Dist. Payment Roll, Atoka Co., #813 as John Miller.
John M. Miller, husband of No.1 is on Chick. card #1278, final roll #3683.
7 " " " " " " has been recognized and enrolled as a citizen by blood of the
8 Choc. Nation.
9 No.1 transferred from Chickasaw Card #D-453 to this card May 15, 1905;
See decision of March 29, 1905.
10 No.1 not entitled to enrollment as Chick by intermarriage because she was not married
11 under Chickasaw law
12 For child of No.1 see Chickasaw NB (March 13, 1905) #195

Date of Application for Enrollment. July 1/02

Date of transfer to this card May 15, 1905

RESIDENCE: COUNTY. **Choctaw Nation** Choctaw Roll (Not Including Freedmen) CARD NO.
POST OFFICE: McAlester, I.T. - c/o Aven Kelton FIELD NO. 5947

Dawes' Roll No.	NAME	Relationship to Person First Named	AGE	SEX	BLOOD	TRIBAL ENROLLMENT Year	County	No.
IW 1455	1 McLain, Susan A		31	F	I.W.			
	2							
	3							
	4							
	5							
	6							
	7							
	8							
	9							
	10							
	11							
	12							
	13							
	14							
	15							
	16 c/o Aven Kelton							
	17							

ENROLLMENT
~~OF NOS.~~ 1 ~~HEREON~~
APPROVED BY THE SECRETARY
OF INTERIOR JUN 12 1905

TRIBAL ENROLLMENT OF PARENTS

	Name of Father	Year	County	Name of Mother	Year	County
1	Hugh Winner		non citz.	Emma Blake		Choctaw
2						
3						
4						
5						

6 No.1 formerly wife of William A. McLain a recognized and enrolled citizen by blood of the Choctaw Nation Choc. card #3132 final roll #9082.
7 ~~No.1 originally listed for enrollment on Choctaw card #3132, Aug 2/99~~
8 ~~transferred to this card May 15, 1905 See decision of April 1, 1905~~

Date of Application for Enrollment.	Date of transfer to this card
Aug 2/99	May 15, 1905

RESIDENCE: Chickasaw Nation COUNTY. **Choctaw Nation** **Choctaw Roll** *(Not Including Freedmen)* CARD NO.
POST OFFICE: Antioch, Ind. Ter. FIELD NO. 5948

Dawes' Roll No.		NAME	Relationship to Person First Named	AGE	SEX	BLOOD	TRIBAL ENROLLMENT Year	County	No.
DP 4/10/06	1	Beard, Tennessee	Named	43	F	I.W.			
	2								
	3								

REFUSED JAN 28 1907

COPY OF DECISION FORWARDED APPLICANT JAN 28 1907

COPY OF DECISION FORWARDED ATTORNEY FOR APPLICANT. JAN 28 1907

COPY OF DECISION FORWARDED ATTORNEYS FOR CHOCTAW AND CHICKASAW NATIONS. JAN 28 1907

RECORD FORWARDED DEPARTMENT. JAN 28 1907

TRIBAL ENROLLMENT OF PARENTS

	Name of Father	Year	County	Name of Mother	Year	County
1	David Betts	Dead	noncitizen	Mary Damron		

No.1 placed on this card, May 24, 1905, under decision of Commission of that date holding application was made within time prescribed by act of Congress approved July 1, 1902 (32 Stat 641)

Date of Application for Enrollment.

ACTION APPROVED BY SECRETARY OF INTERIOR. FEB 28 1907

NOTICE OF DEPARTMENTAL ACTION FORWARDED ATTORNEYS FOR CHOCTAW AND CHICKASAW NATIONS. APR 6 1907

NOTICE OF DEPARTMENTAL ACTION FORWARDED ATTORNEY FOR APPLICANT. APR 6 1907

NOTICE OF DEPARTMENTAL ACTION MAILED APPLICANT. APR 6 1907

MAY 24 1905

RESIDENCE: Choctaw Nation COUNTY. **Choctaw Nation** **Choctaw Roll** *(Not Including Freedmen)* CARD NO.
POST OFFICE: Durant, Ind. Ter. FIELD NO. 5949

Dawes' Roll No.		NAME	Relationship to Person First Named	AGE	SEX	BLOOD	TRIBAL ENROLLMENT Year	County	No.
IW 1505	1	Maddoc, Elliah C	Named	44	F	I.W.			
	2								
	3								
	4								
	5								
	6								
	7								
	8								
	9								
	10								
	11								
	12								
	13								
	14								
	15								
	16								
	17								

ENROLLMENT
OF NOS. 1 HEREON
APPROVED BY THE SECRETARY
OF INTERIOR NOV 27 1905

GRANTED SEP 30 1905

TRIBAL ENROLLMENT OF PARENTS

	Name of Father	Year	County	Name of Mother	Year	County
1	William Vaughan	Dead	noncitizen	Mary Elizabeth Vaughan	Dead	noncitizen

No.1 placed on this card, May 24th 1905 under decision of Commission of that date holding application was made for enrollment of No.1 within time prescribed by act of Congress approved July 1, 1902 (32 Stat 641)

Date of Application for Enrollment.

~~No.1 formerly wife of John Carshial (John Carshall) a recognized Choctaw who died about 1890.~~

For children of No1 see NB (Apr 26 '06) #1147

Date of transfer to this card
May 24, 1905

RESIDENCE: Chickasaw Nation COUNTY. Choc
POST OFFICE: Roena, Ind. Ter.

Dawes' Roll No.	NAME	Relationship to Person First Named	AGE	SEX	BLOOD	TRIBAL ENROLLMENT Year	County	No.
I.W. 1485	1 Askew, Mollie	First Named	32	F	I.W.			

GRANTED
JUN 27 1905

ENROLLMENT
OF NOS. One HEREON
APPROVED BY THE SECRETARY
OF INTERIOR AUG 22 1905

TRIBAL ENROLLMENT OF PARENTS

Name of Father	Year	County	Name of Mother	Year	County
1 Doctor Caruthers	dead	non-citizen	Katie Caruthers	dead	non

Name of No.1 placed on this card May 24, 1905, and application heard on its merit under Departmental instructions of April 24, 1905 (I.T.D. 1679, 3306, 3638, 2886-1905).
No.1 is the wife of Bee Askew Choctaw roll card #343, final roll of citizens by blood of the Choctaw Nation No. 14273.

transfer
date
MAY 24 1905

5951 [sic]
5951

RESIDENCE: Choctaw Nation COUNTY. **Choctaw** ... Roll (... Freedmen) CARD NO.
POST OFFICE: Stringtown, I.T. FIELD NO.

Dawes' Roll No.		NAME	Relationship to Person First Named	AGE	SEX	BLOOD	TRIBAL ENROLLMENT Year	County	No.
IW 1506	1	Newkirk, Sarah M		31	F	IW			
	2								
	3								
	4								
	5								
	6								
	7								
	8								
	9								
	10								
	11								
	12								
	13								
	14								
	15								
	16								
	17								

ENROLLMENT
OF NOS. 1 HEREON
APPROVED BY THE SECRETARY
OF INTERIOR NOV 27 1905

GRANTED SEP 30 1905

TRIBAL ENROLLMENT OF PARENTS

	Name of Father	Year	County	Name of Mother	Year	County
1	Heram Jones		noncitizen	Minervia Stowers		non...
2						
3						
4						
5						

~~Name of No.1 placed on this card June 22d, 1905 in accordance with a decision of the~~
Commission of that date holding application was made within time prescribed by act of
Congress approved July 1, 1902
(32 Stat 641)

Date of Application for Enrollment

No.1 formerly wife of Dixon Kemp (Dickson Camp) 1885 Red River
now deceased.

Aug 1/99

[redacted]E: Choctaw Nation COUNTY. **Choctaw Nation** **Choctaw Roll** *(Not Including Freedmen)* CARD NO. [redacted]
[redacted]CE: Stigler, Ind. Ter. FIELD NO. 5[redacted]

[redacted]	NAME	Relationship to Person First Named	AGE	SEX	BLOOD	TRIBAL ENROLLMENT Year	County	No.
IW 1486	1 Beagles, Allen	Named	53	M	I.W.			
	2							
	3							
	4							
	5							
	6							
	7							
	8							
	9							
	10							
	11							
	12							
	13							
	14							
	15							
	16							
	17							

ENROLLMENT
OF NOS. One HEREON
APPROVED BY THE SECRETARY
OF INTERIOR AUG 22 1905

TRIBAL ENROLLMENT OF PARENTS

	Name of Father	Year	County	Name of Mother	Year	Cou[redacted]
1	Edmund Beagles	dead	non-citizen	Polly Beagles	dead	non-citiz[redacted]
2						
3						

4 No1 restored to roll by Departmental authority of January 19, 1909 (File 5-51)
~~Enrollment of No.1 cancelled by Department March 4, 1904~~
5 No.1 placed on this card June 22d, 1905 in accordance with decision of the Commission of
6 ~~that date holding application was made within the time prescribed by act of Congress~~
7 approved July 1, 1902 (32 Stat 641)
8 No.1 denied by Dawes Commission under act of Congress approved June 10, 1896
(1896 Choctaw case #11). No appeal.
9 ~~No.1 is the husband of Annie Hurt, approved roll of Choctaws by blood 9068~~
10 See decision of June 22, 1905 enrolling No.1 No.1 divorced from Annie Hurt in 1896
11 For children of No1 see NB (Apr 26-1906) #1087
12 No.1 denied by Commission in 1896 Choctaw case #11. No appeal.
13
14
15
16 Date o[redacted] to thi[redacted]
17 PO Mannsville IT 10/22/06 JUN 2[redacted]

RESIDENCE: COUNTY. **Choctaw Nation** Choctaw Roll (Not Including Freedmen) CARD NO.
POST OFFICE: Ardmore, Ind. Ter. FIELD NO. 5953

Dawes' Roll No.	NAME	Relationship to Person First Named	AGE	SEX	BLOOD	TRIBAL ENROLLMENT Year	County	No.
IW 1487	1 Eitel, Annie	First Named	31	F	I.W.			
	2							
	3							
	4							
	5							
	6							
	7							
	8							
	9							
	10							
	11							
	12							
	13							
	14							
	15							
	16							
	17							

ENROLLMENT
OF NOS. One HEREON
APPROVED BY THE SECRETARY
OF INTERIOR AUG 29 1905

TRIBAL ENROLLMENT OF PARENTS

Name of Father	Year	County	Name of Mother	Year	County
1					
2					
3					
4					

No.1 formerly the wife of William C. Davis, who was admitted to citizenship in the Choctaw Nation by an act of the Choctaw Council approved Oct. 13, 1894, and whose name appears upon the 1896 Choctaw Census Roll, Blue Co, #3544

~~No.1 is now the wife of Charlie Eitel, a noncitizen white man.~~

~~No.1 originally listed for enrollment on Choctaw card #R-141; transferred to this card~~ July 17, 1905. See decision of June 6, 1905

~~Date of transfer~~ to this card.
July 16-1905

RESIDENCE: Sans Bois COUNTY. **Choctaw Nation** Choctaw Roll (Not Including Freedmen) CARD NO.
POST OFFICE: Cowlington, I.T. FIELD NO.

Dawes' Roll No.		NAME	Relationship to Person First Named	AGE	SEX	BLOOD	TRIBAL ENROLLMENT Year	County	No.
IW 1507	1	Cowlington, Caroline		49	F	I.W.	1896	Skullyville	14380
15963	2	" John A	Son	21	M	1/16			
15964	3	" A. D.	"	16	"	1/16			
15965	4	" Oramittie	Dau	13	F	1/16			
	5								
	6								
	7								
	8								
	9	For child of No2 see NB (Apr 26-06) Card #366							
	10								
	11	ENROLLMENT							
	12	OF NOS. 2,3 and 4 HEREON APPROVED BY THE SECRETARY							
	13	OF INTERIOR NOV 27 1905							
	14	ENROLLMENT							
	15	OF NOS. 1 HEREON							
	16	APPROVED BY THE SECRETARY OF INTERIOR NOV 27 1905							
	17								

TRIBAL ENROLLMENT OF PARENTS

	Name of Father	Year	County	Name of Mother	Year	County
1	John Fox	dead	non citizen	Sarah Fox	dead	non citi
2						
3						
4						
5						

Nos 1 to 4 incl. admitted by Commission as citizens by blood in 1896 Case #741
No appeal.
No.1 admitted as an intermarried citizen in 1896 by Commission Case #766
No appeal.
No.1 formerly wife of Wm A. Harris, a recognized Choctaw now deceased. Now wife of Anderson F. Cowling who was denied by C.C.C.C. Feb. 29, 1904 Case #25
Nos. 1 to 4 incl. originally listed for enrollment on Choctaw card #D- 235 transferred to this card.

6/13/99 Date of Application for Enrollment.

June 22, 1905 Nos 1 to 4 enrolled by Comm
June 26, 1905 protest of attorney for Nation filed
June 30, 1905 record and protest forwarded [illegible]
Sept. 12-1905- Decision of Commission of June 22, 1905 enrolling Nos. 1,2,3 and 4 affirmed by the Department (I.T.D. 10910-1905)

RESIDENCE: COUNTY. **Choctaw Nation** **Choctaw Roll** *(Not Including Freedmen)* CARD NO.

POST OFFICE: Pauls Valley, I.T. FIELD NO. 59

Dawes' Roll No.	NAME	Relationship to Person First Named	AGE	SEX	BLOOD	TRIBAL ENROLLMENT Year	County	No.
IW 1488	1 Waide, Whit M		24	M	I.W.			

ENROLLMENT OF NOS. One HEREON APPROVED BY THE SECRETARY OF INTERIOR AUG 22 1905

TRIBAL ENROLLMENT OF PARENTS

Name of Father	Year	County	Name of Mother	Year	County
1 Wm E. Waide	dead	non citizen	Innie T. Waide	dead	non citi

No.1 is the husband of Helen F. Waide (nee Carr), a recognized and enrolled citizen by blood of the Choctaw Nation. Choctaw card #149; roll #295

No.1 originally listed for enrollment on Choctaw card #D- 594 Dec. 6, 1900: transferred to this card July 17, 1905 See decision of June 30, 1905

For child of No.1 see N.B. (Apr 26, 1906) Card No. 151

Date of Application for Enrollment. Dec 6/1900

Date of transfer to this card. July 16, 1905

Choctaw By Blood Enrollment Cards 1898-1914

RESIDENCE: COUNTY. **Choctaw Nation** **Choctaw Roll** *(Not Including Freedmen)* CARD NO.

POST OFFICE: Ryan, I.T. FIELD NO. 59

Dawes' Roll No.	NAME	Relationship to Person First Named	AGE	SEX	BLOOD	TRIBAL ENROLLMENT Year	County	No.
IW 1489	1 ~~Gann, William Newton~~	~~Named~~	~~46~~	~~M~~	~~I.W.~~			
	2							
	3							
	4							
	5							
	6							
	7							
	8							
	9							
	10							
	11							
	12							
	13							
	14 ENROLLMENT							
	15 OF NOS. One HEREON							
	16 APPROVED BY THE SECRETARY OF INTERIOR AUG 22 1905							
	17							

TRIBAL ENROLLMENT OF PARENTS

	Name of Father	Year	County	Name of Mother	Year	County
1	~~Sam Gann~~	~~Dead~~	~~Non Citz~~	~~Nancy Gann~~	~~Dead~~	~~Non~~
2						
3						
4						

5 No.1 admitted by Commission in 1896 Choctaw case #1010; admit[ted by] U.S.
6 Court No appeal to C.C.C.C.

7 ~~No.1 formerly husband of Sarah E. Stidham, a recognized and enrolled citizen by blood of~~
8 the Choctaw Nation. On Choctaw card #445; roll #856 a Sarah E. Cook; but whose
9 enrollment was cancelled by the Department on July 8, 1904, she having died Nov. 28, 1900
No.1 originally listed for enrollment on Choctaw card #5194 9/24/98; transferred to this
10 ~~card July 17, 1905 See decision of June 6, 1905~~
11 ~~Enrollment of No.1 cancelled by order of Department March 4, 1907;~~
12 No.1 restored to roll by Departmental authority of January 19, 1909 (File 5-51)

Date of Application for Enrollment. 9/24/98

~~Date of transfer~~ to this card. July 16, 1905

Choctaw By Blood Enrollment Cards 1898-1914

RESIDENCE: Choctaw Nation ~~COUNTY~~. **Choctaw Nation** Choctaw Roll (*Not Including Freedmen*) 5957
POST OFFICE: Legal, Ind. Ter.

Dawes' Roll No.	NAME	Relationship to Person First Named	AGE	SEX	BLOOD	TRIBAL ENROLLMENT Year	County	No.
15931	1 Wade, Sampson	First Named	62	M	Full	1896	Atoka	13993
15932	2 " Byington	Son	5	"	"			
	3							
	4							
	5							
	6							
	7							
	8							
	9							
	10 ENROLLMENT OF NOS. 1 and 2 HEREON							
	11 APPROVED BY THE SECRETARY OF INTERIOR AUG 23 1905							
	12							
	13 Nos 1 and 2 originally listed for enrollment on							
	14 Choctaw card #D- 996; transferred to this card							
	15 July 17, 1905							
	16							
	17							

TRIBAL ENROLLMENT OF PARENTS

Name of Father	Year	County	Name of Mother	Year	County
1 Cornelius Wade	dead	Choctaw		dead	Choctaw
2 No.1			Silsey Wade	"	"
3					
4					
5					
6					
7					
8 No.1 on 1885 Choctaw census roll Tobucksy County					
9 No.1 " 1893 " leased district payment roll; Tobucksey[sic] Co page 99; No. 831					
~~No.1 " 1896 " census roll Atoka County; page 367; No. 13993~~					
10 ~~No.2 born Aug. 28, 1897~~					
11					
12					
13					
14					
15					
16					
17					

RESIDENCE: COUNTY. **Choctaw Nation** **Choctaw Roll** *(Not Including Freedmen)* CARD NO.
POST OFFICE: Wister, Ind. Ter. FIELD NO. 5958

Dawes' Roll No.	NAME	Relationship to Person First Named	AGE	SEX	BLOOD	TRIBAL ENROLLMENT Year	County	No.
IW 1540	1 McAlvain, Bell		20	F	I.W.			
	2							
	3							
	4							
	5							
	6							
	7							
	8							
	9							
	10							
	11							
	12							
	13							
	14							
	15							
	16							
	17							

GRANTED
NOV 11 1905

ENROLLMENT
OF NOS. 1 HEREON
APPROVED BY THE SECRETARY
OF INTERIOR MAR 14 1906

TRIBAL ENROLLMENT OF PARENTS

Name of Father	Year	County	Name of Mother	Year	County
1 Frank Howell		noncitizen	Mollie Howell		noncitizen
2					
3					
4					

5 No.1 placed hereon under order of Commissioner to the Five Civilized Tribes of July 25, 1905,
6 holding that application was made for her enrollment within the time provided by the act of
7 Congress approved July 1, 1902 (32 Stat 641)

Date of Application
for Enrollment.

9 No.1 is wife of Louis Riley McAlvain No5 on Choctaw card 2225 Choctaw roll 6448

Date of transfer
to this card.
JUL 25 1905

RESIDENCE: Choctaw Nation COUNTY. **Choctaw Nation** **Choctaw Roll** (Not Including Freedmen) CARD NO.
POST OFFICE: Stuart, Ind. Ter. FIELD NO. 5959

Dawes' Roll No.	NAME	Relationship to Person First Named	AGE	SEX	BLOOD	TRIBAL ENROLLMENT Year	County	No.
15948	1 LeFlore, Isaac		35	M	Full	1893	Tobucksy	501
IW 1508	2 " Mason	Wife	33	F	I.W.			
15949	3 " Jincy	Dau	3	F	1/2			
15950	4 " Wicy	Dau	1	F	1/2			

ENROLLMENT OF NOS. 2 HEREON APPROVED BY THE SECRETARY OF INTERIOR Nov. 27, 1905

ENROLLMENT OF NOS. 1,3 and 4 HEREON APPROVED BY THE SECRETARY OF INTERIOR Nov. 24, 1905

TRIBAL ENROLLMENT OF PARENTS

Name of Father	Year	County	Name of Mother	Year	County
1 Billy LeFlore	Dead	Choctaw	Malissie	Dead	Choctaw
2 James Spitta	Dead		Locinda		
3 No.1			No.2		
4 No.1			No.2		

Notify :Preslie B. Cole Atty South M[c]Alester of approval.

No.2 Probable duplicate of Creek Roll No 7141

~~April 17, 1905 the Commission to the Five Civilized Tribes rendered decision holding that it was without authority to receive application for enrollment of Nos. 1 to 4 inclusive.~~

August 5, 1905 Department directed enrollment of Nos. 1, 3 and 4 as citizens by blood and No.2 as citizen by intermarriage of Choctaw Nation (I.T.D 8840-1905) D.C. #38283-1905)

~~No.1 on 1893 Leased District Roll as Isaac La Flore~~

For child of Nos. 1&2 see NB (Apr 26-06) card #845

Date of transfer to this card.

Date of Application for Enrollment. Aug 16, 1905

RESIDENCE: Atoka COUNTY. **Choctaw Nation** Choctaw Roll (*Not Including Freedmen*) CARD NO.
POST OFFICE: Citra, Ind. Ter FIELD NO. 5960

Dawes' Roll No.	NAME	Relationship to Person First Named	AGE	SEX	BLOOD	TRIBAL ENROLLMENT Year	County	No.
16002	1 Jackson, Mary		50	F	Full	1896	Tobucksy	6640
	2							
	3							
	4							
	5							
	6							
	7							
	8							
	9							
	10							
	11							
	12							
	13							
	14							
	15							
	16							
	17							

ENROLLMENT
OF NOS. 1 HEREON
APPROVED BY THE SECRETARY
OF INTERIOR Jun 16 1906

Granted
Mar 14 1906

TRIBAL ENROLLMENT OF PARENTS

Name of Father	Year	County	Name of Mother	Year	County
1 ~~~~~~~~~~~~~~~	Dead	Choctaw	~~~~~~~~~~~~	Dead	Choctaw
2					
3					
4					

5 ~~No.1 also on 1893 roll, Atoka County, page 98, No. 954 as Mollie Solomon~~
6 No.1 is wife of Shoniko Jackson, on Chickasaw freedman card #170
7 Application made for enrollment of No.1 by her husband at Stonewall, I.T. September 6, 1898
8 ~~No.1 originally listed for enrollment on Choctaw card #D-567 also on D #1001;~~
9 transferred to this card September 22, 1905
10 See testimony taken May 19, 1904 and March 1, 1905.

Date of Application for Enrollment.	Date of transfer to this card.
Sept 6/98	Sep 22, 1905

RESIDENCE: COUNTY. **Choctaw Nation** **Choctaw Roll** *(Not Including Freedmen)* CARD NO.
POST OFFICE: Monroe, I.T. FIELD NO. 5961

Dawes' Roll No.	NAME	Relationship to Person First Named	AGE	SEX	BLOOD	TRIBAL ENROLLMENT Year	County	No.
IW 1541	1 Harris, Frances		20	F	I.W.			
	2							
	3							
	4							
	5							
	6 ENROLLMENT							
	7 OF NOS. 1 HEREON ~~APPROVED BY THE SECRETARY~~							
	8 OF INTERIOR MAR 14 1906							
	9							
	10							
	11 ~~GRANTED~~							
	12							
	13 NOV 11 1906							
	14							
	15							
	16 ~~Guy P Cobb Atty.~~							
	17							

TRIBAL ENROLLMENT OF PARENTS

Name of Father	Year	County	Name of Mother	Year	County
1 Jack Wise	dead	non citizen	J. W. Wise		noncitizen
2					
3					
4					
5					
6					

7 Henry Harris, husband of No.1 is on Choctaw card #2272 Roll #6583
~~No.1 placed on this card September 28th, 1905 in accordance with order of the~~
8 ~~Commission to the Five Civilized Tribes of that date holding application was made within time~~
9 prescribed by act of Congress approved July 1, 1902 (32 Stat 641)

Date of Application for Enrollment.

Date of Transfer to this Card. SEP 28, 1905

POST OFFICE: Bower, Ind. Ter. (Not Including Freedmen) FIELD NO. 3962

Dawes'	NAME	Relationship to Person First Named	AGE	SEX	BLOOD	TRIBAL ENROLLMENT Year	County	No.
	Hagewood, Mary J		57	F	I.W.	1896	Gaines	14609

ENROLLMENT
OF NOS.
APPROVED
OF INTERIOR

TRIBAL ENROLLMENT OF PARENTS

Name of Father	Year	County	Name of Mother	Year	County
Jesse Wilson	Dead			Dead	

No.1 was married August 2, 1869 to Leroy Tiner, a Choctaw Indian, Newton Tiner, son by said marriage on Choctaw card #4477 Roll #12432
No.1 now wife of M. L. Hagewood, a non citizen

No.1 transferred from Choctaw Card R112. See decision of Octob

transferred
date
OCT 21 1905

Choctaw By Blood Enrollment Cards 1898-1914

RESIDENCE:
POST OFFICE: Durant

Choctaw Nation Choctaw (Not Including Fr

CARD NO.
FIELD NO. 59

Dawes' Roll No.	NAME	Relationship to Person First Named	AGE	SEX	BLOOD	TRIBAL ENROLLMENT Year	County	No.
IW 1510	1 Rogers, Lavega		47	M	I.W.	1885	Atoka	
	2							
	3							
	4							
	5							
	6							
	7							
	8							
	9							
	10							
	11							
	12							
	13							
	14							
	15							
	16							
	17							

ENROLLMENT
OF NOS. 1 HEREON
APPROVED BY THE SECRETARY
OF INTERIOR NOV 27 1905

TRIBAL ENROLLMENT OF PARENTS

Name of Father	Year	County	Name of Mother	Year	County
1 George Rogers	Dead	Cherokee	Palina Rogers		noncitizen
2					
3					
4					
5					

6 No.1 was married on October 2, 1897 to Isabelle Rogers
7 who is identified on the Atoka County 1885 census roll and
1893 leased district payment roll and who died about 1898
8 ~~Now married to Mary Grantham, a white woman~~.
9
10 No.1 transferred from Choctaw Card # D- 534. See decision of October 4, 1905

Date of Application for Enrollment.	Date of transfer to this card
Dec 5/99	OCT 20 1905

COUNTY. ...en, Arkansas **Choctaw Nation** Choctaw Roll (Not Including Freedmen) CARD NO. FIELD NO.

	...E	Relationship to Person First Named	AGE	SEX	BLOOD	TRIBAL ENROLLMENT Year	County	
1511	1 Durant, Jennie		46	F	I.W.			
	2							
	3							
	4							
	5							
	6							
	7							
	8							
	9							
	10							
	11							
	12							
	13							
	14							
	15							
	16							
	17							

ENROLLMENT
OF NOS. 1 HEREON
APPROVED BY THE SECRETARY
OF INTERIOR NOV 27 1905

TRIBAL ENROLLMENT OF PARENTS

Name of Father	Year	County	Name of Mother	Year	
1 William Smith	dead	non-citizen	Nancy Smith	dead	
2					
3					
4					
5					

6 No.1 was formerly wife of Taylor Durant Choctaw roll by blood #11463

7 No.1 transferred from Choctaw Card # D- 418. See decision of September 5, 1905

Date of Application for Enrollment. Sept 2/99

Date of transfer to this card SEP 21 1905

RESIDENCE: Chickasaw Nation COUNTY. **Choctaw Nation** Choctaw Roll NO.
POST OFFICE: Pauls Valley I.T. (Not Including Freedmen) No. 5965

Dawes' Roll No.	NAME	Relationship to Person First Named	AGE	SEX	BLOOD	TRIBAL ENROLLMENT Year	County	No.
I.W. 1512	1 Moore, Idummea		35	F	I.W.	1896	Tobucksy	14817

ENROLLMENT
~~OF NOS.~~ 1 ~~HEREON~~
APPROVED BY THE SECRETARY
OF INTERIOR NOV 27 1905

TRIBAL ENROLLMENT OF PARENTS

Name of Father	Year	County	Name of Mother	Year	County
1 John Seybold	dead	noncitizen	Amanda		noncitizen

~~No1 on 1896 roll as Idunlia Moore~~
No.1 was formerly wife of Allen Moore, identification on th
1893 and 1896 Choctaw Rolls
No.1 transferred from Choctaw Card # D- 447, See decision 1905

Date of Application for Enrollment. Sept 2/99

Date of transfer to this card OCT 2

RESIDENCE: COUNTY. **Choctaw Nation** **Choctaw Roll** *(Not Including Freedmen)* CARD NO.
POST OFFICE: Brooken, Ind. Ter. FIELD NO. 5966

Dawes' Roll No.		NAME	Relationship to Person First Named	AGE	SEX	BLOOD	TRIBAL ENROLLMENT Year	County	No.
15966	1	Freeman, William	First Named	28	M	1/8	1896	Jacks Fork	4539
IW1513	2	" Joanna	Wife	28	F	I.W.			
15967	3	" James Richard	son	2	M	1/16			
	4								
	5								
	6								
	7								
	8								
	9								
	10								
	11								
	12								
	13								
	14								
	15								
	16								
	17								

ENROLLMENT OF NOS. 1 and 3 HEREON APPROVED BY THE SECRETARY OF INTERIOR Nov 27 1905

ENROLLMENT OF NOS. 2 HEREON APPROVED BY THE SECRETARY OF INTERIOR Nov 27 1905

TRIBAL ENROLLMENT OF PARENTS

	Name of Father	Year	County	Name of Mother	Year	County
1						
2						
3						
4						
5						

6 No.1 on 1893 Pay Roll Kiamitia County Page 125 No. 22

8 No.3 born March 31, 1900. Proof of birth filed December 24, 1902.

9 Nos. 1 to 3 transferred from Choctaw Card # D-240. See decision of October 6, 1905.

11 For child of Nos 1&2 see NB (Apr 26-06) card #499.

Date of Application for Enrollment.

Date of transfer to this card Oct 22 1905

17 P.O. Chant, I.T. 6/14/99

RESIDENCE: Choctaw Nation COUNTY. **Choctaw Nation** **Choctaw Roll** (Not Including Freedmen) CARD NO.
POST OFFICE: Howe, Ind. Ter. FIELD NO. 59[illegible]

Dawes' Roll No.	NAME	Relationship to Person First Named	AGE	SEX	BLOOD	TRIBAL ENROLLMENT Year	County	No.
IW 1514	1 Hickman, Samuel		59	M	IW	1896	Sugar Loaf	14605

ENROLLMENT OF NOS. 1 HEREON APPROVED BY THE SECRETARY OF INTERIOR NOV 27 1906

TRIBAL ENROLLMENT OF PARENTS

Name of Father	Year	County	Name of Mother	Year	County
1 John Hickman	dead	noncitizen	Betsey Hickman	dead	noncitizen

~~No.1 on 1896 Choctaw roll as Sam Hickman. No1 also on 1885 Choctaw roll,~~
Sugar Loaf County No. 323

~~No.1 is father of Mary Britton Choctaw card #2247, Martha Johnson Choctaw care #2388 and Austin Hickman Choctaw card #2264 Roll No 6568~~

No.1 transferred from Choctaw Card # D- 953 See decision of October 2, 1905

Date of Application for Enrollment. Dec 17/02

~~Original copy of record herein forwarded Department for use in adjudication of Choctaw case~~ of Thomas G. Ashford in compliance with Departmental request of March 22, [illegible]

For child of No1 see NB (Apr 26 '06) No 1121

OCT 18 1905
~~transfer date~~
~~to this card~~

RESIDENCE:
POST OFFICE: Crowder Ind [redacted] ation

Choctaw Roll
(Not Including Freedmen)

Dawes' Roll No.	NAME	Relationship to Person First Named	AGE	SEX	BLOOD	TRIBAL ENROLLMENT Year	County	No.
IW 1515	1 Freeman, Zona		26	F	I.W.			
	2 Gardner, Rosetta	Dau	7	F	1/4			

ENROLLMENT OF NOS. 1 HEREON APPROVED BY THE SECRETARY OF INTERIOR NOV 27 1905

TRIBAL ENROLLMENT OF PARENTS

Name of Father	Year	County	Name of Mother	Year	County
1 Wm Webb		noncitizen	Liddy Webb		noncitizen
2 Wilson W Gardner		Blue	No.1		

5 No.1 was formerly wife of Wilson W. Gardner, 1896 Choctaw Census Roll, Blue
6 County No. 4893

7 ~~Nos. 1 and 2 transferred from Choctaw Card # D-473 See decision of October 5, 1905~~

9 No2 Dismissed October [illegible] Died prior to September 25, 1902

Date of Application for Enrollment.
Sept 9/99

~~Date of transfer to this card~~
OCT 18 1905

RESIDENCE: Choctaw Nation COUNTY. **Choctaw Nation** **Choctaw Roll** (Not Including Freedmen) CARD NO.
OFFICE: Krebs, Indian Territory FIELD NO. 5969

...ves' No.		NAME	Relationship to Person First Named	AGE	SEX	BLOOD	TRIBAL ENROLLMENT Year	County	No.
	1	Gelling, Edward J	Named	59	M	I.W.			
/23	2								

REFUSED
DEC 29 1905

COPY OF DECISION FORWARDED ATTORNEYS FOR CHOCTAW AND CHICKASAW NATIONS.
DEC 29 1905

COPY OF DECISION FORWARDED ATTORNEY FOR APPLICANT.
DEC 29 1905

COPY OF DECISION FORWARDED APPLICANT DEC 29 1905

RECORD FORWARDED DEPARTMENT.
DEC 29 1905

TRIBAL ENROLLMENT OF PARENTS

	Name of Father	Year	County	Name of Mother	Year	County
1	Edward Gelling	Dead	non citizen	Ann Gelling		noncitizen

ACTION APPROVED BY SECRETARY OF INTERIOR.
MAR 6 1906

NOTICE OF DEPARTMENTAL ACTION FORWARDED ATTORNEYS FOR CHOCTAW AND CHICKASAW NATIONS. MAR 14 1906

No.1 placed hereon under order of the Commissioner to the Five Civilized Tribes of November 9, 1905 holding that application was made for his enrollment under act of Congress of July 1, 1902 (32 Stat. 641)

June 18, 1906 Motion for rehearing forwarded Department
Nov. 21 1906 Motion denied by Dept.
Dec. 5, 1906 Parties interested notified.

MAR 14 1906

NOTICE OF DEPARTMENTAL ACTION MAILED APPLICANT.
MAR 14 1906

Date of Application for Enrollment.
NOV 9 1905

RESIDENCE: COUNTY. **Choctaw Nation** Choctaw Roll (Not Including Freedmen) CARD NO.
POST OFFICE: Scipio, Ind. Ter. FIELD NO. 5[illegible]

Dawes' Roll No.		NAME	Relationship to Person First Named	AGE	SEX	BLOOD	TRIBAL ENROLLMENT Year	County	No.
IW 1542	1	Burnes, Buckner	Named	61	M	I.W.			
	2								
	3								
	4								
	5								
	6								
	7								
	8								
	9								
	10								
	11								
	12								
	13								
	14								
	15	Dec. 27, 1905 Decision of Commissioner to Five Civilized Tribes of Dec. 26, 1905							
	16	Feb. 23, 1906 this action approved by Department							
	17								

ENROLLMENT
OF NOS. 1 HEREON
APPROVED BY THE SECRETARY
OF INTERIOR MAR 14 1906

TRIBAL ENROLLMENT OF PARENTS

	Name of Father	Year	County	Name of Mother	Year	C[illegible]
1	Willis Burnes	Dead	noncitizen	Keziah Burnes	Dead	Nonci[illegible]
2						
3						
4						
5						
6	~~No.1 was admitted in 1896 Choctaw case #886~~					
7						
8	No.1 transferred from Choctaw Card # D- 283. See decision of December 26, 1905					
9	~~No.1 was formerly married to Isabella LeFlore, a citizen by blood of the Choctaw Nation who~~					
10	died Feb. 6, 1879. His child by said marriage, Henry F Burns[sic] is enrolled at No. 8872 upon					
11	the approved roll of citizens of the Choctaw Nation.					
12						
13						
14						
15						
16				Date of Application for Enrollment.		transfer date to this card
17				Aug 1/99		DEC 30 1905

RESIDENCE: Chickasaw Nation COUNTY. **Choctaw Nation** Choctaw Roll (*Not Including Freedmen*) CARD NO.
POST OFFICE: Lindsay, Ind. Ter. FIELD NO. 597

Dawes' Roll No.	NAME	Relationship to Person First Named	AGE	SEX	BLOOD	TRIBAL ENROLLMENT Year	County	No.
	1 ~~Reynolds, John W~~	~~Named~~	~~31~~	~~M~~	~~I.W.~~			
	2							
	3 REFUSED							
	4							
	5 DECISION RENDERED	APR 28	1906					
	6 COPY OF DECISION FORWARDED							
	7 ATTORNEY FOR APPLICANT.	APR 28	1906					
	8							
	9 COPY OF DECISION FORWARDED ATTORNEYS FOR CHOCTAW AND							
	10 CHICKASAW NATIONS.	APR 28	1906					
	11							
	12 COPY OF DECISION FORWARDED							
	13 APPLICANT	APR 28	1906					
	14							
	15 RECORD FORWARDED DEPARTMENT.							
	16	APR 28		1906				
	17							

TRIBAL ENROLLMENT OF PARENTS

	Name of Father	Year	County	Name of Mother	Year	County
1	~~John Reynolds~~	~~Dead~~	~~noncitizen~~	~~Martha Reynolds~~	~~Dead~~	~~nonciti~~
2						
3				ACTION APPROVED		
4				SECRETARY OF INTERIOR APR 18 1907		
5				NOTICE OF DEPARTMENTAL ACTION		
6				FORWARDED ATTORNEYS FOR CHOCTAW AND CHICKASAW NATIONS. APR 18 1907		
7						

8 ~~No.1 placed hereon under order of the Commissioner to the Five Civilized Tribes~~
9 of Nov. 11, 1905 holding that application was made for his enrollment within the time provided
10 by the act of Congress of July 1, 1902 (32 Stat.641) NOTICE OF DEPARTMENTAL ACTION FORWARDED ATTORNEY FOR APPLICANT.

Date of Application for Enrollment.

11 ~~May 29, 1906 Motion for review and reconsideration forwarded Department.~~ APR 18 1907
12 NOTICE OF DEPARTMENTAL ACTION MAILED APPLICANT.
13 July 27, 1906 Motion for rehearing forwarded Department
Mar 16-07 " " " denied by "
14
15 For children of No1 see NB (Apr 26-06) #1249.
16 NOV 1
17 P.O. Ego, I.T. 3/15/06

Choctaw By Blood Enrollment Cards 1898-1914

RESIDENCE: Creek Nation COUNTY [redacted] Choctaw Roll CARD NO.
POST OFFICE: Wetumpka, I.T. Box # [redacted] (Not Including Freedmen) FIELD NO. 5972

Dawes' Roll No.	NAME	Relationship to Person First Named	AGE	SEX	BLOOD	TRIBAL ENROLLMENT Year	County	No.
IW 1549	1 Carter, John W.	First Named	43	M	I.W.	1896	Atoka	14425
	2							
	3							
	4							
	5							
	6							
	7							
	8							
	9							
	10							
	11							
	12							
	13							
	14							
	15							
	16							
	17							

ENROLLMENT OF NOS. 1 HEREON APPROVED BY THE SECRETARY OF INTERIOR MAR 14 1906

TRIBAL ENROLLMENT OF PARENTS

Name of Father	Year	County	Name of Mother	Year	County
1 Vivian Carter	Dead	Non Citz	Millie Carter		Non-Citz
2					
3					
4					

No.1 restored to roll by Departmental authority [illegible]
~~Enrollment of No.1 cancelled by Department [illegible]~~
No.1 on 1896 toll as Jno. W. Carter
~~No.1 was rejected by the Dawes Commission in 1896, Choc. case #982: no appeal.~~
No.1 was formerly husband of Annie I. Lewis, citizen by blood of Choctaw Nation, whose name appears upon the 1893 Leased District Roll, Atoka County, as No. 192: said Annie I. Lewis died in 1894.

No.1 transferred from Choctaw Card # D- 7-D308: see decision of December 28, 1905.

~~Date of~~ Application for Enrollment. Aug 8/98

Date of transfer to this card January 13, 1906

RESIDENCE: COUNTY. **Choctaw Nation**   **Choctaw Roll** *(Not Including Freedmen)*   CARD NO.

POST OFFICE: Wesley, I.T.   FIELD NO. 5[redacted]

Dawes' Roll No.	NAME	Relationship to Person First Named	AGE	SEX	BLOOD	TRIBAL ENROLLMENT Year	County	No.
IW 1544	1 Smith, Albert		28	M	I.W.			
	2							
	3							
	4							
	5							
	6							
	7							
	8							
	9							
	10							
	11							
	12							
	13							
	14							
	15							
	16							
	17							

ENROLLMENT
OF NOS. 1 HEREON
APPROVED BY THE SECRETARY
OF INTERIOR MAR 14 1906

TRIBAL ENROLLMENT OF PARENTS

	Name of Father	Year	County	Name of Mother	Year	County
1	L. E. Smith		Non-Citz	Alice Smith		Non-Citz
2						
3						
4						
5						

~~No.1 formerly husband of Ella Moore, citizen by blood of Choc. Nation, whose name appears, on 1893 Leased District Roll, Chickasaw District, as No. 418: also on 1896 Census Roll, Chickasaw District as No. 8913; said Ella Moore died January 27, 1901.~~

No.1 transferred from 7-D-483; See decision of December 28, 1905

For child of No.1 see NB (Apr 26-06) #1247

Date of Application for Enrollment. Sept 12/99

Date of transfer to this card January 13, 1906

E:
ICE:

COUNTY. **Choctaw Nation** Choctaw Roll (Not Including Freedmen) CARD NO. FIELD NO. 5974

NAME	Relationship to Person First Named	AGE	SEX	BLOOD	TRIBAL ENROLLMENT Year	County	No.
1 Reynolds, Dora		23	F	I.W.	1896	Gaines	14519
2							
3							
4							
5							
6							
7							
8 No 1 deceased							
9 Notify J.N. Fletcher							
Hartshorne, I.T.							
10 R.W. Higgins attorney							
11 (So. M^c^Alester, I.T.)							
12 R.B. Coleman							
13 So. M^c^Alester, I.T.							
2/23/06							
14							
15							
16							
17							

ENROLLMENT OF NOS. 1 HEREON APPROVED BY THE SECRETARY OF INTERIOR MAR 14 1906

TRIBAL ENROLLMENT OF PARENTS

	Name of Father	Year	County	Name of Mother	Year	County
1						
2						
3						
4						
5						

6 No 1 was formerly wife of Franklin Freeny (deceased) citizen by blood of Choc. Nation,
7 whose name appears on 1893 Leased District Roll, Gaines Co, as No. 169;
also on 1896 Census Roll, Gaines County as No. 3986 said Franklin Freeny died in 1900.
8 In November 1900, No.1 married Will Reynolds, an alleged Cherokee by blood.
9 No1 transferred from Choctaw Card # D- 7-R-97. See decision of November 13, 1905

Date of Application for Enrollment. Sept 1/99

Date of transfer to this card January 13, 1906

RESIDENCE: COUNTY. **Choctaw Nation** Choctaw Roll (Not Including Freedmen) CARD NO.
POST OFFICE: South McAlester, I.T. FIELD NO. 597

Dawes' Roll No.	NAME	Relationship to Person First Named	AGE	SEX	BLOOD	TRIBAL ENROLLMENT Year	County	No.
IW 1546	1 De Poister, Mary E		46	F	I.W.	1885	Sugar Loaf	514
	2							
	3							
	4							
	5							
	6							
	7							
	8							
	9							
	10							
	11							
	12							
	13							
	14							
	15							
	16							
	17							

ENROLLMENT OF NOS. 1 HEREON APPROVED BY THE SECRETARY OF INTERIOR MAR 14 1906

TRIBAL ENROLLMENT OF PARENTS

Name of Father	Year	County	Name of Mother	Year	County
1 Thos. Ruddle	Dead	Non Citz	Catherine Ruddle	Dead	Non-Citz

No1 was formerly wife of J. H. Parnell, citizen by blood of Choctaw Nation, whose name as "Haywood P. Parnell" appears upon approved roll as No. 6112, on Choctaw card #2120. No.1 and J. H. Parnell separated in 1886 and were subsequently divorced; and in 1900 she married one DePoister - a non-citizen.

No.1 transferred from 7-D-269; see decision of November 6, 1905.

Date of Application for Enrollment.	Date of transfer to this card
Aug 1/99	November 22, 1905

RESIDENCE: Chickasaw Nation COUNTY. **Choctaw Nation** Choctaw Roll (Not Including Freedmen) CARD NO.
POST OFFICE: Ada, Ind. Ter. FIELD NO. 5976

Dawes' Roll No.	NAME	Relationship to Person First Named	AGE	SEX	BLOOD	TRIBAL ENROLLMENT Year	County	No.
IW 1620	1 Rogers, Emma		32	F	I.W.			

GRANTED
DEC 31 1906

COPY OF DECISION FORWARDED APPLICANT DEC 31 1906

COPY OF DECISION FORWARDED ATTORNEY FOR APPLICANT. DEC 31 1906

COPY OF DECISION FORWARDED ATTORNEYS FOR CHOCTAW AND CHICKASAW NATIONS. DEC 31 1906

ENROLLMENT OF NOS. 1 HEREON APPROVED BY THE SECRETARY OF INTERIOR FEB 12 1907

TRIBAL ENROLLMENT OF PARENTS

Name of Father	Year	County	Name of Mother	Year	County

No.1 placed hereon by order of Commissioner to Five Civilized Tribes of January 11, 1906, holding that application was made for her enrollment within the time provided by the act of Congress approved July 1, 1902 (32 Stat. 641)

For children of No.1 see NB (Apr 26-06) #1262

No.1 was formerly married to Jimmerson Jones, now deceased, a recognized and enrolled citizen of the Choctaw Nation whose name appears on the 1885 Census roll, Gaines County.

Date of Application for Enrollment.

July 7, 1905

Listed on this card JAN 11 1906

RESIDEN ickasaw Nation COUNTY. **Choctaw Nation** Choc CARD NO.
POST OF Lebanon, I.T. (Not Inclu FIELD NO. 597

Dawes Roll No	NAME	Relationship to Person First Named	AGE	SEX	BLOOD	TRIBAL ENROLLMENT Year	County	No.
IW 156	kew, Josephine		49	F	I.W.			

ENROLLMENT
OF NOS. 1 HEREON
APPROVED BY THE SECRETARY
OF INTERIOR AUG 2 1906

TRIBAL ENROLLMENT OF PARENTS

Nar er	Year	County	Name of Mother	Year	
Joshua	Dead	noncitizen	Mary Fowler	Dead	nonc

No.1 is mother of Daniel P. Askew Ch rd #343 Roll #14272

No.1 was wife of Aaron Askew, who ttted by U.S. Indian Agent Feb. 8, 1895
~~Her children by him appear on Chocta 343 Roll Nos 14272 to 14277 inclusive~~
No 1 placed on this card under an orde Commissioner to the Five Civilized Tribes of January 11, 1906, holding that applica made for her enrollment within the time provided by the act of Congress approved July 1, 1902 (32 Stat. 641)

Date of Application for Enrollment.

PO 3/6/06 Madill I.T. c/o Lula O'Key
~~PO [Illegible] I.T. 2/13/06~~

NTED APR 16 1906

Date of transfer to this card JAN 11 1906

Choctaw By Blood Enrollment Cards 1898-1914

RESIDENCE: Blue
POST OFFICE: Durant I.T.
COUNTY. **Choctaw Nation**
Choctaw Roll *(Not Including Freedmen)*
CARD NO.
FIELD NO. 5978

Dawes' Roll No.	NAME	Relationship to Person First Named	AGE	SEX	BLOOD	TRIBAL ENROLLMENT Year	County	No.
IW 1590	1 Turner, Hattie	First Named	21	F	IW			
	2							
	3							
	4							
	5							
	6							
	7							
	8							
	9							
	10							
	11							
	12							
	13							
	14							
	15							
	16							
	17							

ENROLLMENT
~~OF NOS.~~ 1 ~~HEREON~~
APPROVED BY THE SECRETARY
OF INTERIOR NOV 26 1906

TRIBAL ENROLLMENT OF PARENTS

	Name of Father	Year	County	Name of Mother	Year	County
1	G.P. Stout		noncitizen	Anna Stout		noncitizen
2						
3						
4						
5						

6 No.1 was formerly wife of Thomas Starks Choctaw roll card #3639 Roll 10288

7

8 No.1 placed on this card under order of Commissioner to Five Civilized Tribes of January 11, ~~1906 holding that application was made for her enrollment within the time provided by the act of~~

9 Congress approved July 1, 1902 (32 Stat. 641)

Date of Application for Enrollment.

GRANTED
APR 25 1906

Date of transfer to this card
JAN 11 1906

RESIDENCE: Chick[redacted] Nation COUNTY. **Choctaw Nation** **Choctaw Roll** (Not Including Freedmen) CARD NO.
POST OFFICE: M[redacted] I.T. FIELD NO. 597[redacted]

Dawes' Roll No.	NAME	Relationship to Person First Named	AGE	SEX	BLOOD	TRIBAL ENROLLMENT Year	County	No.
IW1567	1 Askew, Mollie		18	F	I.W.			
	2							
	3							
	4							
	5							
	6							
	7							
	8							
	9							
	10							
	11							
	12							
	13							
	14							
	15							
	16							
	17							

ENROLLMENT OF NOS. 1 HEREON APPROVED BY THE SECRETARY OF INTERIOR AUG 2 - 1906

TRIBAL ENROLLMENT OF PARENTS

Name of Father	Year	County	Name of Mother	Year	County
1 Newt Walker		noncitizen	Mary Walker		noncitizen

No.1 placed hereon under order of the Commissioner to the Five Civilized Tribes of January 11, 1906, holding that application was made for her enrollment within the time ~~provided by the act of Congress approved July 1, 1902 (32 Stat. 641)~~

Date of Application ~~for Enrollment.~~

No.1 is wife of Lee Askew, Choctaw card #202 Roll #14241

~~For child of No.1 see NB (Mar 3'05) #360~~

GRANTED APR 25 1906

Date of transfer to this card JAN 11 1906

RESIDENCE: COUNTY. **Choctaw Nation** **Choctaw Roll** *(Not Including Freedmen)* CARD NO.

POST OFFICE: Brock, I.T. FIELD NO. 59

Dawes' Roll No.	NAME	Relationship to Person First Named	AGE	SEX	BLOOD	TRIBAL ENROLLMENT Year	County	No.
	1 Henry. Lizzie	Named	42	F	I.W.			

REFUSED

DECISION RENDERED APR 28 1906

COPY OF DECISION FORWARDED ATTORNEYS FOR CHOCTAW AND CHICKASAW NATIONS. APR 28 1906

COPY OF DECISION FORWARDED ATTORNEY FOR APPLICANT APR 28 1906

COPY OF DECISION FORWARDED APPLICANT APR 28 1906

RECORD FORWARDED DEPARTMENT APR 28 1906

TRIBAL ENROLLMENT OF PARENTS

Name of Father	Year	County	Name of Mother	Year	County
1 Thomas Holden		noncitizen	Holden		noncitizen

No.1 was formerly wife of Isaac Folsom, a Choctaw Indian.

~~No.1 placed hereon under order of Commissioner to the Five Civilized Tribes of January 20, 1906, holding that application was made for her enrollment within the time~~ provided by the act of Congress approved July 1, 1902 (32 Stat. 641)

ACTION APPROVED BY SECRETARY OF INTERIOR. MAR 4 1907

NOTICE OF DEPARTMENTAL ACTION FORWARDED ATTORNEYS FOR CHOCTAW AND CHICKASAW NATIONS. APR 17 1907

NOTICE OF DEPARTMENTAL ACTION FORWARDED ATTORNEY FOR APPLICANT. APR 17 1907

NOTICE OF DEPARTMENTAL ACTION MAILED APPLICANT. APR 17 1907

Date of Application for Enrollment.

~~transfer date~~ JAN 20 1906

RESIDENCE: COUNTY. **Choctaw Nation** **Choctaw Roll** *(Not Including Freedmen)* CARD NO.
POST OFFICE: Keota, Ind. Ter. FIELD NO. 5981

Dawes' Roll No.	NAME	Relationship to Person First Named	AGE	SEX	BLOOD	TRIBAL ENROLLMENT Year	County	No.
IW 1588	1 Workman, Dora	First Named	28	F	IW			

ENROLLMENT
OF NOS. 1 HEREON
APPROVED BY THE SECRETARY
OF INTERIOR AUG 2 - 1906

TRIBAL ENROLLMENT OF PARENTS

Name of Father	Year	County	Name of Mother	Year	County
1 J. H. Hickey	Dead	noncitizen	S.E. Banks		noncitizen

No.1 placed hereon under order of Commissioner to the Five Civilized Tribes of January 20, 1906, holding that application was made for her enrollment within the time provided by the act of Congress approved July 1, 1902 (32 Stat. 641).

Date of Application for Enrollment.

No.1 was formerly wife of Charles M. James Choctaw roll card #2511 Roll 7291

GRANTED
APR 25 1906

transferred date
JAN 20 1906

RESIDENCE: COUNTY. **Choctaw Nation** **Choctaw Roll** *(Not Including Freedmen)* CARD NO.
POST OFFICE: Madill, I.T. FIELD NO. 59[illegible]

Dawes' Roll No.	NAME	Relationship to Person First Named	AGE	SEX	BLOOD	TRIBAL ENROLLMENT Year	County	No.
IW 1550	1 Omo, Julia	First Named	43	F	I.W.			

ENROLLMENT OF NOS. 1 HEREON APPROVED BY THE SECRETARY OF INTERIOR MAY 28 1906

TRIBAL ENROLLMENT OF PARENTS

Name of Father	Year	County	Name of Mother	Year	County
1 Robert Biggar	dead	non-citizen	Jane Biggar	dead	non-[illegible]

No.1 restored to roll by Departmental authority of January [illegible]

No.1 denied in 1896 case #1407. No appeal.

Enrollment of No.1 cancelled by order of Department [illegible]

No.1 formerly wife George W Buckholts, a recognized and enrolled citizen by blood of Choctaw Nation; whose name appears as #15181 upon a list prepared by Commission and approved by Department May 9, 1904; they were married in 1873 or 1874 and fourteen years later, divorced.

No.1 transferred to this card from Choctaw card #5225, January 12, 1906; See decision of December 27, 1905.

Now Julia Elmore

Date of Application for Enrollment.

P.O Sulphur

PO Box M Fayetteville Ark

9-26-98

c/o Madam Chira

RESIDENCE: Choctaw Nation COUNTY. **Choctaw Nation** Choctaw Roll (Not Including Freedmen) CARD NO.
POST OFFICE: Soper, Ind. Ter. FIELD NO. 59[illegible]

Dawes' Roll No.	NAME	Relationship to Person First Named	AGE	SEX	BLOOD	TRIBAL ENROLLMENT Year	County	No.
IW 1672	1 Lee, C.W.D.	First Named	46	M	I.W.			

REFUSED
DECISION RENDERED APR 28 1906

COPY OF DECISION FORWARDED
ATTORNEYS FOR CHOCTAW AND CHICKASAW NATIONS. APR 28 1906

COPY OF DECISION FORWARDED
ATTORNEY FOR APPLICANT. APR 28 1906

COPY OF DECISION FORWARDED
APPLICANT APR 28 1906

RECORD FORWARDED DEPARTMENT APR 28 1906

ENROLLMENT
OF NOS. One HEREON
APPROVED BY THE SECRETARY
OF INTERIOR MAR 4 1907

TRIBAL ENROLLMENT OF PARENTS

Name of Father	Year	County	Name of Mother	Year	County
1 Charley Lee	Dead	noncitizen	Malissa Lee	Dead	non-c[illegible]

ACTION APPROVED BY
SECRETARY OF INTERIOR DEC -6 1906

NOTICE OF DEPARTMENTAL ACTION
FORWARDED ATTORNEYS FOR CHOCTAW
AND CHICKASAW NATIONS. DEC -6 1906

~~No.1 placed hereon under an order of the Commissioner to the Five Civilized Tribes of February~~ 20, 1906, holding that application was made for his enrollment within the time provided by the act of Congress approved July 1, 1902.

No.1 was admitted by Dawes Commission in 1896 Choctaw case #1209

~~No.1 was formerly husband of Ellen Taylor a recognized and enrolled citizen by blood of the~~ Choctaw Nation, now deceased.

Feb. 27, 1907 Recommendation to Department that No.1 be enrolled [illegible]

March 4, 1907 Department rescinds action of Nov. 22, 1906 and approves enrollment of No.1

NOTICE OF DEPARTMENTAL ACTION
FORWARDED ATTORNEY FOR APPLICANT.
DEC -6 1906

transfer date
to this card FEB 20 1906

RESIDENCE: Choctaw Nation COUNTY. **Choctaw Nation** **Choctaw Roll** *(Not Including Freedmen)* CARD NO.
POST OFFICE: Muse, Ind. Ter. FIELD NO. 598

Dawes' Roll No.	NAME	Relationship to Person First Named	AGE	SEX	BLOOD	TRIBAL ENROLLMENT Year	County	No.
IW 1569	1 Chaffin, Dorellar		27	F	I.W.			
	2							
	3							
	4							
	5							
	6							
	7							
	8							
	9							
	10							
	11							
	12							
	13							
	14							
	15							
	16							
	17							

ENROLLMENT
~~OF NOS.~~ 1 ~~HEREON~~
APPROVED BY THE SECRETARY
OF INTERIOR AUG 2 - 1906

TRIBAL ENROLLMENT OF PARENTS

Name of Father	Year	County	Name of Mother	Year	County
1 J.W. Newsome	Dead	noncitizen	Malinda Newsom	Dead	noncitizen

No.1 was formerly wife of James Johnston, deceased, whose name appears on 1885 Choctaw Census Roll Wade County No. 417.

No.1 placed hereon under order of Commissioner to the Five Civilized Tribes of February 20, 1906, holding that application was made for her enrollment within the time provided by the act of Congress approved July 1, 1902

Date of Application for Enrollment.

GRANTED
APR 24 1906

Date of transfer to this card
FEB 20 1906

RESIDENCE: COUNTY. **Choctaw Nation** **Choctaw Roll** *(Not Including Freedmen)* CA

POST OFFICE: Rubottom, I.T. FI

Dawes' Roll No.	NAME	Relationship to Person First Named	AGE	SEX	BLOOD	TRIBAL ENROLLMENT Year	County	No.
	1 Sorrels, Thomas J	Named	28	M	I.W.			

REFUSED

DECISION RENDERED APR 28 1906

COPY OF DECISION FORWARDED ATTORNEYS FOR CHOCTAW AND CHICKASAW NATIONS. APR 28 1906

COPY OF DECISION FORWARDED ATTORNEY FOR APPLICANT. APR 28 1906

COPY OF DECISION FORWARDED APPLICANT APR 28 1906

RECORD FORWARDED DEPARTMENT. APR 28 1906

TRIBAL ENROLLMENT OF PARENTS

Name of Father	Year	County	Name of Mother	Year	County
1 Joseph Sorrels	Dead	noncitizen	Nancy Sorrels	Dead	nonc

No.1 placed hereon February 20, 1906, under order of Commissioner to the Five Civilized Tribes of February 20, 1906, holding that application was made for his enrollment within the time provided by the act of Congress approved July 1, 1902

Date of Application for Enrollment.

transferred date FEB 20 1906

[redacted]E: Chickasaw Nation COUNTY. **Choctaw Nation** **Choctaw Roll** *(Not Including Freedmen)* CARD NO. [redacted]
[redacted]ICE: Dolberg, I.T. FIELD NO. 59[redacted]

	NAME	Relationship to Person First Named	AGE	SEX	BLOOD	TRIBAL ENROLLMENT Year	County	No.
IW 1570	1 Hardin, Bettie		25	F	IW			
	2							
	3							
	4							
	5							
	6							
	7							
	8							
	9							
	10							
	11							
	12							
	13 ENROLLMENT							
	14 OF NOS. 1 HEREON ~~APPROVED BY THE SECRETARY~~							
	15 OF INTERIOR AUG 2 - 1906							
	16							
	17							

TRIBAL ENROLLMENT OF PARENTS

Name of Father	Year	County	Name of Mother	Year	County
1 Leo Maxwell		noncitizen	Minerva Maxwell		[redacted]
2					
3					
4					
5					

6 No.1 placed hereon under order of Commissioner to the Five Civilized Tribes of Feb. 26, 1906
7 holding that application was made for her enrollment within the time provided by the act of
8 Congress approved July 1, 1902 **Date of Application for Enrollment.**

9 No 1 was formerly wife of Jackson Baker, Choctaw card No. 1849 approved roll of citizens by
10 blood of Choctaw Nation #5273

~~transferred~~
date
FEB 26 1906

GRANTED
APR 24 1906

17 PO Pontotoc 12/19/95

Choctaw By Blood Enrollment Cards 1898-1914

RESIDENCE: COUNTY. **Choctaw Nation** Choctaw Roll *(Not Including Freedmen)* CARD NO.
POST OFFICE: Coleman, I.T. FIELD NO. 5987

Dawes' Roll No.	NAME	Relationship to Person First Named	AGE	SEX	BLOOD	TRIBAL ENROLLMENT Year	County	No.
IW 1571	1 Bruton, Thomas		40	M	I.W.			
	2							
	3							
	4							
	5							
	6							
	7							
	8							
	9							
	10							
	11							
	12							
	13							
	14							
	15							
	16							
	17							

ENROLLMENT OF NOS. 1 HEREON APPROVED BY THE SECRETARY OF INTERIOR AUG 2- 1906

TRIBAL ENROLLMENT OF PARENTS

Name of Father	Year	County	Name of Mother	Year	County
1					
2					
3					
4					

No.1 was formerly married to Mary James deceased whose name appears on 1885 Choctaw Census Roll Tobucksy County, No. 922

No. 1 placed hereon under order of Commissioner to the Five Civilized Tribes of February 26, 1906, holding application was made for his enrollment within the time provided by the act of Congress approved July 1, 1902

Date of Application for Enrollment.

Ages given as of this date FEB 26 1906

GRANTED JUN 13 1906

RESIDENCE: Choctaw Nation COUNTY. **Choctaw Nation** **Choctaw Roll** *(Not Including Freedmen)* CARD NO.
POST OFFICE: Soper, I.T. FIELD NO. 5988

Dawes' Roll No.	NAME	Relationship to Person First Named	AGE	SEX	BLOOD	TRIBAL ENROLLMENT Year	County	No.
4/18/06	Williams, J A	Named	23	M	I.W.			

DECISION RENDERED JUN 22 1906

REFUSED JUN 22 1906

COPY OF DECISION FORWARDED ATTORNEYS FOR CHOCTAW AND CHICKASAW NATIONS. JUN 22 1906

COPY OF DECISION FORWARDED ATTORNEY FOR APPLICANT. JUN 22 1906

COPY OF DECISION FORWARDED APPLICANT JUN 22 1906

RECORD FORWARDED DEPARTMENT. JUN 22 1906

TRIBAL ENROLLMENT OF PARENTS

Name of Father	Year	County	Name of Mother	Year	County
Bill Williams	Dead	noncitizen	Nannie Williams	dead	noncitizen

ACTION APPROVED BY SECRETARY OF INTERIOR. DEC 13 1906

NOTICE OF DEPARTMENTAL ACTION FORWARDED ATTORNEYS FOR CHOCTAW AND CHICKASAW NATIONS. DEC 28 1906

No 1 placed hereon under order of Commissioner to the Five Civilized Tribes of March 14, 1906 holding that application was made for his enrollment within the time provided by the act of Congress approved July 1, 1902 (32 Stat, 641).

Date of Application for Enrollment.

No 1 was formerly married to Fannie Crowder 1896 Choctaw Roll Kiamitia County No. 2728 now deceased. No.3 on Choctaw card #1445 and is father of Lena Williams Choctaw Roll No. 4035.

NOTICE OF DEPARTMENTAL ACTION FORWARDED ATTORNEY FOR APPLICANT. DEC 28 1906

NOTICE OF DEPARTMENTAL ACTION MAILED APPLICANT. DEC 28 1906

Ages given as of this date MAR 14 1906

RESIDENCE: Chickasaw Nation COUNTY. **Choctaw Nation** **Choctaw Roll** (Not Including Freedmen) CARD NO.
POST OFFICE: Lindsay, I.T. FIELD NO. 5989

Dawes' Roll No.	NAME	Relationship to Person First Named	AGE	SEX	BLOOD	TRIBAL ENROLLMENT Year	County	No.
IW 1572	1 Burkes, Sarah P		20	F	I.W.			
	2							
	3							
	4							
	5							
	6							
	7							
	8							
	9							
	10							
	11							
	12							
	13							
	14							
	15							
	16							
	17							

ENROLLMENT
OF NOS. 1 HEREON
APPROVED BY THE SECRETARY
OF INTERIOR AUG 2 - 1906

TRIBAL ENROLLMENT OF PARENTS

Name of Father	Year	County	Name of Mother	Year	County
1 W. H. M^c^Daniels		noncitizen	M. L. M^c^Daniels		noncitizen
2					
3					
4					
5					

6 No.1 was married December 29, 1901, to John G Burkes Jr Choctaw card #77 Roll 1417

No.1 placed hereon March 23, 1906, under order of Commissioner to the Five Civilized Tribes of that date holding application was made for her enrollment within time prescribed by act of Congress approved July 1, 1902 (32 Stat 641)

Date of Application for Enrollment.

GRANTED
APR 24 1906

Ages given as of this date
MAR 23 1906

RESIDENCE: Choctaw Nation COUNTY. **Choctaw Nation** **Choctaw Roll** *(Not Including Freedmen)* CARD NO.
POST OFFICE: Allen, I.T. FIELD NO. 5990

Dawes' Roll No.	NAME	Relationship to Person First Named	AGE	SEX	BLOOD	TRIBAL ENROLLMENT Year	County	No.
IW 1573	1 Krebbs, Susie Bell	First Named	19	F	IW			
	2							
	3							
	4							
	5							
	6							
	7							
	8							
	9							
	10							
	11							
	12							
	13							
	14							
	15							
	16							
	17							

ENROLLMENT
~~OF NOS.~~ 1 ~~HEREON~~
APPROVED BY THE SECRETARY
OF INTERIOR AUG 2 - 1906

TRIBAL ENROLLMENT OF PARENTS

Name of Father	Year	County	Name of Mother	Year	County
1 John Allen		noncitizen	Amanda Paralee Allen		noncitizen
2					
3					

4 No.1 was married September 16, 1900 to Benjamin Krebbs, Choctaw card #4008, Roll 14388

5

6 No.1 placer hereon under order of Commissioner to the Five Civilized Tribes of March 24, ~~1906, holding application was made for her enrollment within time provided by act of Congress~~

7 of July 1, 1902 (32 Stat 641)

Date of Application ~~for Enrollment.~~

8

9 For child of No.1 see NB (Apr 26-06) Card #416

GRANTED
APR 24 1906

~~Ages given as of this date~~
MAR 23 1906

RESIDENCE: Chickasaw Nation COUNTY. **Choctaw Nation** **Choctaw Roll** *(Not Including Freedmen)* CARD NO.
POST OFFICE: Arthur, I.T. FIELD NO.

Dawes' Roll No.	NAME	Relationship to Person First Named	AGE	SEX	BLOOD	TRIBAL ENROLLMENT Year	County	No.
IW 1574	1 Sanner, Lou		21	F	I.W.			
	2							
	3							
	4							
	5							
	6							
	7							
	8							
	9							
	10							
	11							
	12							
	13							
	14							
	15							
	16							
	17							

ENROLLMENT
OF NOS. 1 HEREON
~~APPROVED BY THE SECRETARY~~
OF INTERIOR AUG 2 - 1906

TRIBAL ENROLLMENT OF PARENTS

	Name of Father	Year	County	Name of Mother	Year	County
1	Tom Chapman		noncitizen	Sallie Chapman		nc
2						
3						
4						
5						

6 No.1 was married December 2, 1900 to Willie Sanner, Choctaw card 409 Roll 14288

7 ~~No.1 placed hereon under order of Commissioner to Five Civilized Tribes of March 24, 1906,~~
8 ~~holding application was made for her enrollment within time provided by act of Congress~~
9 approved July 1, 1902 (32 Stat 641) **Date of Application for Enrollment.**

GRANTED
APR 24 1906

~~Ages given as~~ of this date
MAR 24 1906

RESIDENCE: COUNTY. **Choctaw N[redacted] Roll** CARD NO.
POST OFFICE: (Freedmen) FIELD NO. 5[redacted]

Dawes' Roll No.	NAME	Relationship to Person First Named	AGE	SEX	BLOOD	TRIBAL ENROLLMENT Year	County	No.
	1 Crawford, Emma		23	F	I.W.			
	2							
	3							
	4							
	5							
	6							
	7							
	8							
	9							
	10							
	11							
	12							
	13							
	14							
	15							
	16							
	17							

TRIBAL ENROLLMENT OF PARENTS

Name of Father	Year	County	Name of Mother	Year	County

ACTION APPROVED BY SECRETARY OF INTERIOR. MAR 4 190[redacted]

NOTICE OF DEPARTMENTAL ACTION APR 5 1907 FORWARDED ATTORNEYS FOR CHOCTAW AND CHICKASAW NATIONS.

NOTICE OF DEPARTMENTAL ACTION APR 5 1907 FORWARDED ATTORNEY FOR APPLICANT.

No.1 is deceased and was represented by Gus Crawford her husbands brother

NOTICE OF DEPARTMENTAL ACTION MAILED APPLICANT. APR 5 1907

~~No.1 was married July 31, 1900, to Henry Crawford, Choctaw care #3619 who was admitted by~~ Dawes Commission in 1896 Choctaw case No. 17 now deceased. Her child by him Flora May Crawford, on approved Choctaw roll No. 14375.

~~No.1 placed hereon under order of Commissioner to Five Civilized Tribes of March 24, 1906,~~ holding application was made for her enrollment within time provided by act of Congress approved July 1, 1902 (32 Stat 641)

REFUSED FEB 15 1907

RECORD FORWARDED DEPARTMENT. FEB 15 1907

Ages given as of this date MAR 24 1906

RESIDENCE: COUNTY. **Choctaw Nation** Choctaw Roll (Not Including Freedmen) CARD NO.
POST OFFICE: Power I.T. FIELD NO. 5993

Dawes' Roll No.	NAME	Relationship to Person First Named	AGE	SEX	BLOOD	TRIBAL ENROLLMENT Year	County	No.
16003	1 Long, James S	First Named	45	M	1/8	1896	Sans Bois	7704
16004	2 " Joseph	Bro	31	M	1/8	~~1896~~	~~" "~~	~~7701~~
16005	3 " Forbis	Bro	27	M	1/8	~~1896~~	~~" "~~	~~7702~~

ENROLLMENT OF NOS. 1, 2 and 3 HEREON APPROVED BY THE SECRETARY OF INTERIOR JUN 16 1906

Nos. 1,2 and 3 restored to roll by Departmental authority of January 19, 1909 (File 5-51)
Enrollment of Nos 1,2 and 3 cancelled by order of Department of March

TRIBAL ENROLLMENT OF PARENTS

Name of Father	Year	County	Name of Mother	Year	County
~~1 Jake Long~~	~~Dead~~	~~Choctaw~~	~~Jane H Long~~		~~noncitizen~~
~~2 " "~~	~~"~~	~~"~~	~~" "~~		~~"~~
~~3 " "~~	~~"~~	~~"~~	~~" "~~		~~"~~

No.1 is husband of Letitia C. Featherstone on Choctaw card #4520

~~Nos. 1 to 3 transferred from Choctaw 2338~~
~~For children of No.3 see NB (April 26-06) Card No. 872~~
Jan. 19, 1905 Decision rendered refusing Nos 1 to 3 inclusive.
February 23, 1906 Decision of Commission to Five Civilized Tribes
~~of January 19, 1905 reversed by Department and enrollment~~
~~of Nos 1 to 3 directed (I.T.D. 22343192-1905) DC 10936-1905~~

Date of Application for Enrollment. 6/14/99

~~Ages given as of this date~~ APR 2- 1906

P.O. M^c^Alester I.T.
3/7/07

RESIDENCE: Chickasaw Nation COUNTY. **Choctaw Nation** Choctaw Roll (*Not Including Freedmen*) CARD NO.
POST OFFICE: Marlow, Ind. Ter. FIELD NO. 5994

Dawes' Roll No.	NAME	Relationship to Person First Named	AGE	SEX	BLOOD	TRIBAL ENROLLMENT Year	County	No.
16006	1 Holloway, Mattie	First Named	30	F	1/16	1896	Chick District	6179
16007	2 " Jessie	Son	9	M	1/32	"	" "	6181
16008	3 " Willie	"	7	"	"			
16009	4 " Hallie Hazel	Dau	5	F	"			
16010	5 Bolensiefen, Ivey	"	12	"	"			
	6							
	7							
	8							
	9							
	10							
	11							
	12							
	13							
	14							
	15							
	16							
	17							

ENROLLMENT
~~OF NOS. 1,2,3,4 and 5 HEREON~~
APPROVED BY THE SECRETARY
OF INTERIOR Jun 16 1906

TRIBAL ENROLLMENT OF PARENTS

Name of Father	Year	County	Name of Mother	Year	County
1 T.J. O'Quinn	dead	non-citizen	Mary O'Quinn		Choctaw
2 J. M. Holloway		" "	No.1		"
3 " " "		" "	No.1		"
4 " " "		" "	No.1		"
5					

6 Nos 1 to 5 inclusive restored to roll by Departmental authority of February 20, 1909 (File 5-51)
~~Enrollment of Nos 1 to 5 cancelled by order of Department February 23, 1907~~
7 ~~Nos. 1,2,3,4 and 5 transferred from M.C.R. #458 Apr 11, 1906~~
8 ~~Nos. 1,2,3,4 and 5 enrolled by direction of Department (Apr 4, 1906, I.T.D. 4222-1906) in~~
9 conformity with opinion of Asst. Atty. General of Mar. 10, 1906 in case of William
10 C. Thompson, et al.

11 ~~Child of No.1 on NB (Apr. 26-06) card #290~~

12

13

14

15 ~~Date of Application~~ for Enrollment. — Ages given as of this date Apr 11th 1906

16

17 June 21/1900

RESIDENCE: Chickasaw Nation COUNTY. **Choctaw Nation** **Choctaw Roll** *(Not Including Freedmen)* CARD NO.
POST OFFICE: Marlow, Ind. Ter. FIELD NO. 5995

Dawes' Roll No.		NAME	Relationship to Person First Named	AGE	SEX	BLOOD	TRIBAL ENROLLMENT Year	County	No.
16011	1	Thompson, Rufus O		48	M	1/16	1896	Chick District	12542
IW 1575	2	" Martha Louisiana	Wife	35	F	I.W.	"	" "	12543
	3								
	4								
	5								
	6								
	7								
	8								
	9								
	10								
	11								
	12								
	13								
	14								
	15								
	16								
	17								

ENROLLMENT
OF NOS. 1 HEREON
APPROVED BY THE SECRETARY
OF INTERIOR JUN 16 1906

ENROLLMENT
OF NOS. 2 HEREON
APPROVED BY THE SECRETARY
OF INTERIOR AUG 2- 1906

TRIBAL ENROLLMENT OF PARENTS

	Name of Father	Year	County	Name of Mother	Year	County
1	John Thompson	Dead	Claims Choctaw	Mary J Thompson		Non Citizen
2	Ed. C. Calhoun		Non Citizen	Frances Calhoun		" "
3						
4						
5						

Nos 1 and 2 transferred to this card from M.C.R. #581, Apr 11, 1906, their enrollment having been directed by the Department, Apr. 4, 1906 (I.T.D. 4222-1906) in conformity with opinion of the Asst. Atty General of Mar. 10, 1906, in case of William C. Thompson, et al.

Date of Application for Enrollment.
Aug 13/1900

Ages hereon given as of this date Apr. 11, 1906

RESIDENCE: Chickasaw Nation COUNTY.
POST OFFICE: Marlow, Ind. Ter.

Choctaw Nation

Choctaw Roll
(Not Including Freedmen)

CARD NO.
FIELD NO. 5996

Dawes' Roll No.	NAME	Relationship to Person First Named	AGE	SEX	BLOOD	TRIBAL ENROLLMENT Year	County	No.
16012	1 O'Quin[sic], Mary E		50	F	1/8	1896	Chick. Dist.	10028
16013	2 " James Walter	Son	19	M	1/16	"	" "	10030
16014	3 " Dora E	Dau	17	F	"	"	" "	10031
16015	4 " Thomas M	Son	15	M	"	"	" "	10029
16016	5 " Ora May	Dau	12	F	"	"	" "	10032

ENROLLMENT OF NOS. 1,2,3,4 and 5 HEREON APPROVED BY THE SECRETARY OF INTERIOR Jun 16 1906

For child of No.2 see NB (Apr 26-06) card #355
" children " No.3 " " " " #356

TRIBAL ENROLLMENT OF PARENTS

	Name of Father	Year	County	Name of Mother	Year	County
1	John T. Thompson	Dead	Claims Choctaw	Mary I Kerr		Non Citizen
2	Thomas J O'Quinn		non-citizen	No.1		Claims Choctaw
3	" " "		" "	"		" "
4	" " "		" "	"		" "
5	" " "		" "	"		" "

Nos. 1 to 5 inclusive restored to roll by Departmental authority of February 20, 1909 (File 5-51)
~~Enrollment of Nos 1 to 5 inclusive cancelled by order of Department of February 23, 1907~~

No.1 on 1896 Roll as Elza O'quinn
~~No.2 " " " " Jas. W. Oquinn[sic]~~
No.3 " " " " Dosia E. "
No.5 " " " " Osia M "

Nos. 1,2,3,4 and 5 transferred to this card from M.C.R. #7124 Apr. 11, 1906, their ~~enrollment having been ordered by the Department Apr. 4, 1906 (I.T.D. 4222-1906)~~ in conformity with opinion of the Asst. Atty General of Mar. 10, 1906, in case of William C. Thompson, et al.

DATE OF APPLICATION FOR ENROLLMENT
MAR 19 1906

Date of transfer to this card Apr. 11, 1906

RESIDENCE: Chickasaw Nation COUNTY. **Choctaw Nation** **Choctaw Roll** *(Not Including Freedmen)* CARD NO.
POST OFFICE: Marlow, Ind. Ter. FIELD NO. 5997

Dawes' Roll No.		NAME	Relationship to Person First Named	AGE	SEX	BLOOD	TRIBAL ENROLLMENT Year	County	No.
16017	1	Jones, Winburn	First Named	45	M	15/32	1896	Chick District	7372
IW 1576	2	" Fannie	Wife	42	F	I.W.	"	" "	14712
16018	3	" Peter N	Son	21	M	15/64	"	" "	7373
16019	4	" Eslie[sic]	Dau	19	F	"	"	" "	7374
16020	5	" Thomas	Son	17	M	"	"	" "	7375
16021	6	" Maude C	Dau	14	F	"	"	" "	7376
16022	7	" Jesse H	Son	12	M	"	"	" "	7377
16023	8	" Sallie	Dau	11	F	"	"	" "	7378
16024	9	" Paul	Son	4	M	"			
	10								
	11								
	12	Child of No.4 on NB (Apr 26-06) Card #287							
	13								
	14								
	15								
	16								
	17								

ENROLLMENT OF NOS. 2 HEREON APPROVED BY THE SECRETARY OF INTERIOR Aug 2 1906

ENROLLMENT OF NOS. 1,3,4,5,6,7,8 and 9 HEREON APPROVED BY THE SECRETARY OF INTERIOR Jun 16 1906

TRIBAL ENROLLMENT OF PARENTS

	Name of Father	Year	County	Name of Mother	Year	County
1	Woody Jones	Dead	Choctaw	Mary Jones		Choctaw
2			non citizen			non citizen
3	No 1		claims Choctaw	No.2		
4	"		" "	"		
5	"		" "	"		
6	"		" "	"		
7	"		" "	"		
8	"		" "	"		
9	"		" "	"		

10 Nos. 1to9 inclusive restored to roll by Departmental authority of February 20, 1909 (File 5-51)
11 ~~Enrollment of Nos 1to9 inclusive cancelled by order of Department of February 23, 1907~~
12 Nos. 1to9 inclusive transferred to this card from M.C.R. #310, Apr. 11, 1906, their ~~enrollment having been ordered by the Department Apr. 4, 1906 (I.T.D. 4222-1906,~~
13 4813-1905) in conformity with opinion of the Asst Atty General of Mar 10, 1906
14 in case of William C. Thompson et al. and of Feb. 19, 1906, in case of James S. Long.

16 **Date of Application for Enrollment.** June 18/1900 — transfer date to this card Apr. 11, 1906
17 No.4 P.O. Arthur, I.T. 5/7/06

Choctaw By Blood Enrollment Cards 1898-1914

RESIDENCE: Chickasaw Nation COUNTY. **Choctaw Nation** **Choctaw Roll** *(Not Including Freedmen)* CARD NO.

POST OFFICE: Arthur, Ind. Ter. FIELD NO. **5998**

Dawes' Roll No.		NAME	Relationship to Person First Named	AGE	SEX	BLOOD	TRIBAL ENROLLMENT Year	County	No.
16025	1	McLendon, Burrell F		41	M	1/16	1896	Chickasaw	9484
IW 1577	2	" Corneal[sic]	Wife	42	F	I.W.	"	"	14890
16026	3	" John B	Son	13	M	1/32	"	"	9485
16027	4	" Thomas	"	11	M	1/32	"	"	9486
16028	5	" Ida M	Dau	9	F	1/32	"	"	9487
16029	6	" Ralph	Son	8	M	1/32	"	"	9488
16030	7	" Harry	"	6	M	1/32			
16031	8	" Fannie	Dau	4	F	1/32			

ENROLLMENT OF NOS. 2 HEREON APPROVED BY THE SECRETARY OF INTERIOR Aug 2- 1906

Nos 1to8 inclusive restored to roll by Departmental authority of February 20, 1909 (File 5-51)

Two (2) children of Nos 1&2 on NB (Apr 26-06) Card #289

Nos. 1to 6 denied in 1896 Choctaw Case #1271. No appeal.

Date of Application for Enrollment. Aug. 23, 1900

ENROLLMENT OF NOS. 1,3,4,5,6,7and8 HEREON APPROVED BY THE SECRETARY OF INTERIOR Jun 16 1906

TRIBAL ENROLLMENT OF PARENTS

	Name of Father	Year	County	Name of Mother	Year	County
1	John E. McLendon	Dead	Non Citizen	Asha J McLendon	Dead	Claims Choctaw
2	Dont[sic] Know			Dont Know		
3	No.1			No.2		
4	No.1			No.2		
5	No.1			No.2		
6	No.1			No.2		
7	No.1			No.2		
8	No.1			No.2		

Apr 6, 1906 (I.T.D. 6372-1904) Department affirms Commission's decision of Maar. 15, 1904 in so far as it denies the applicants identification as Miss Choctaws, but reverses said decision, however, in respect to the application of Nos. 1,3,4,5,6, 7 and 8, for enrollment as citizens by blood, and the application of No.2 as a citizen by intermarriage, of the Choctaw Nation, and directs their enrollment as such, in conformity with opinion of Asst. Atty. General of Feb. 19, 1906, in the case of James S. Long, et al.

Nos 1 to 8 inclusive transferred from Choctaw Card M.C.R. 627 Apr 16, 1906.

Enrollment of Nos. 1to 8 inclusive cancelled by order of Department of March 4, 1907

Listed on this card.

Ages given hereon as of Sept. 25 1902 Apr. 16. 1906

E:
CE: Comanche, Ind. Ter. COUNTY. **Choctaw Nation** Choctaw Roll (Not Including Freedmen) CARD NO. FIELD NO. 5999

	NAME	Relationship to Person First Named	AGE	SEX	BLOOD	TRIBAL ENROLLMENT Year	County	No.
1	McLendon, Robert C		44	M	1/16	1896	Jacks Fork	9490
2								
3								
4								
5								
6								
7								
8								
9								
10								
11								
12								
13								
14								
15								
16								
17								

ENROLLMENT
OF NOS. 1 HEREON
APPROVED BY THE SECRETARY
OF INTERIOR JUN 16 1906

TRIBAL ENROLLMENT OF PARENTS

	Name of Father	Year	County	Name of Mother	Year	County
1	John E. McLendon	Dead	Non Citizen	Asha J. McLendon	Dead	Claims Choctaw
2						
3						
4						

5 No1 restored to roll by Departmental authority*of February 20, 1909 (File 5-51)
6 Apr. 5, 1906 (I.T.D. 4870-1903; 2194, 3610, 5932-1904) Department rescinds its decision of
7 July 7, 1904, and reverses the Commission's decision of Nov. 30, 1903, except in so far as said decisions refuse to identify No.1 as a Miss. Choctaw, and directs the enrollment of No.1, as a
8 citizen by blood of the Choctaw Nation, in conformity with opinion of Asst Atty General of
9 Feby 19, 1906, in case of James S. Long, et al
10 Apr. 16, 1906 No.1 transferred from Choctaw Card R206.
Enrollment of No.1 cancelled by Department March 4, 1907
11 For child of No.1 see NB (Apr 26-06) Card #285.

Date of Application for Enrollment. Dec. 1/02

transfer date to this card Apr. 16, 1906

RESIDENCE: Choctaw Nation COUNTY. **Choctaw Nation** **Choctaw Roll** *(Not Including Freedmen)* CARD NO.
POST OFFICE: Colbert, Ind. Ter. FIELD NO. **6000**

Dawes' Roll No.	NAME	Relationship to Person First Named	AGE	SEX	BLOOD	TRIBAL ENROLLMENT Year	County	No.
16033	1 Howard, Thomas J		49	M	1/2	1896	Atoka	6063
IW 1578	2 " Carrie	Wife	36	F	I.W.	"	"	6064
16034	3 " Horace	Son	17	M	1/4	"	"	6067
16035	4 " Lonnie	"	15	M	1/4	"	"	6068
16036	5 " Emery	"	13	M	1/4	"	"	6070
16037	6 " Elmer	"	11	M	1/4	"	"	6069
16038	7 " Bettie Penney	Dau	5	F	1/4			
16039	8 " Dora Lee	"	3	F	1/4			

ENROLLMENT OF NOS. 1,3,4,5,6,7 and 8 HEREON APPROVED BY THE SECRETARY OF INTERIOR June 16 1906

ENROLLMENT OF NOS. 2 HEREON APPROVED BY THE SECRETARY OF INTERIOR Aug 2 1906

TRIBAL ENROLLMENT OF PARENTS

	Name of Father	Year	County	Name of Mother	Year	County
1	Wm Howard	Dead	Non Citizen	Mary Howard	Dead	Choctaw
2			" "			Non Citizen
3	No.1			No.2		
4	No.1			No.2		
5	No.1			No.2		
6	No.1			No.2		
7	No.1			No.2		
8	No.1			No.2		

Nos.1,3,4,5and6 denied by Dawes Commission in 1896, Choctaw Case No 1354. No appeal.
~~Enrollment of Nos.1,2,3,4,5,6,7and8 cancelled by order of Department March 4, 1907.~~
~~Apr. 6, 1906 (I.T.D. 5364-1904) Department reverses the Commission's decision of Mar 15,~~ 1904, except in so far as it denies Nos. 1 to 8 inclusive identification as Miss Choctaws and directs the enrollment of Nos. 1,3,4,5,6,7 and 8 as citizens by blood and No.2 as a citizen by intermarriage of the Choctaw Nation, in conformity with opinion of Asst Atty General of ~~Feb. 19, 1906 in Case of James S. Long et al.~~
Apr. 16, 1906 No 1 to 8 inclusive transferred from M C R 130
Nos. 1,2,3,4,5,6,7 and 8 restored to roll by Departmental authority of January 19, 1904 (File 5-51)

June 8/1900 **Date of Application for Enrollment.**

RESIDENCE: Choctaw Nation COUNTY. **Choctaw Nation** **Choctaw Roll** *(Not Including Freedmen)* CARD NO.
POST OFFICE: Legal, Ind. Ter. FIELD NO. 6001

Dawes' Roll No.		NAME	Relationship to Person First Named	AGE	SEX	BLOOD	TRIBAL ENROLLMENT Year	County	No.
16040	1	Beaver, Gertrude		23	F	1/8	1896	Atoka	1868
16041	2	" Clarence	Son	6	M	1/16	"	"	1869
16042	3	" Nellie	Dau	4	F	1/16			
16043	4	" Myrtle	"	2	F	1/16			
	5								
	6								
	7								
	8								
	9								
	10								
	11								
	12								
	13								
	14								
	15								
	16								
	17								

ENROLLMENT
OF NOS. 1,2,3 and 4 HEREON
APPROVED BY THE SECRETARY
OF INTERIOR Jun 16 1906

TRIBAL ENROLLMENT OF PARENTS

	Name of Father	Year	County	Name of Mother	Year	County
1	Thomas Howard	1896	Atoka #6063	Carrie Howard	1896	Atoka #6064
2	Calvin Beaver		Non Citizen	No.1		
3	" "		" "	"		
4	" "		" "	"		
5						

6 ~~No.1 denied by Dawes Commission in 1896 Choctaw case No 1354 No appeal.~~
7 Apr. 6, 1906 (I.T.D. 5364-1904) Department reverses the Commission's decision of Mar. 15, 1904 except in so far as it denies applicants identification as Miss. Choctaws and directs the
8 ~~enrollment of Nos 1,2,3 & 4 as citizens by blood of the Choctaw Nation, in conformity with~~
9 ~~opinion of Asst. Atty. General of Feb. 19, 1906 in case of James S. Long et al.~~
10 Apr 16, 1906 Nos 1,2,3 & 4 transferred from M.C.R. 5983.

11 ~~For children of No1 see NB (Apr 26 '06) Card #420~~
12 ~~Enrollment of Nos 1 to 4 incl cancelled by order of Department March 4, 1907.~~
13 Nos. 1,2,3 and 4 restored to roll by Departmental authority of January 19, 1909 (File 5-51).

Date of Application for Enrollment.
July 2, 1902

RESIDENCE: COUNTY. **Choctaw Nation** **Choctaw Roll** (Not Including Freedmen) CARD NO.
POST OFFICE: Massey, Ind. Ter. FIELD NO. 6002

Dawes' Roll No.	NAME	Relationship to Person First Named	AGE	SEX	BLOOD	TRIBAL ENROLLMENT Year	County	No.
16044	1 Landram, Janie		29	F	1/4			
16045	2 " Lola May	Dau	6	F	1/8			
16046	3 " Beulah Addison	Dau	2	F	1/8			

ENROLLMENT
~~OF NOS.~~ ~~1,2 and 3~~ ~~HEREON~~
APPROVED BY THE SECRETARY
OF INTERIOR Jun 16 1906

TRIBAL ENROLLMENT OF PARENTS

	Name of Father	Year	County	Name of Mother	Year	County
1	Jim Lee	Dead	Cherokee	Elizabeth Lee	Dead	Choctaw
2	L. W. Landram		non citizen	No.1		
3	" "		"	No.1		

~~June 15, 1904 Departmental decision of January 11, 1902 refusing Nos. 1,2 and 3 rescinded~~
and record returned for further investigation (I.T.D. 182-1902: 4492-1904)
August 4, 1904. Record with report returned to Department
~~April 11, 1906. Enrollment of Nos. 1,2 and 3 as citizens of the Cherokee Nation cancelled by~~
~~Department and their enrollment as Choctaws directed (I.T.D. 3871-1906) D.C.13498-1906~~

Apr. 20, 1906

RESIDENCE: Chickasaw Nation COUNTY. **Choctaw Nation** Choctaw Roll (Not Including Freedmen) CARD NO.
POST OFFICE: Byars, I.T. FIELD NO. 60

Dawes' Roll No.		NAME	Relationship to Person First Named	AGE	SEX	BLOOD	TRIBAL ENROLLMENT Year	County	No.
IW 1591	1	Crawford, Rebecca	First Named	19	F	I.W.			

ENROLLMENT OF NOS. 1 HEREON APPROVED BY THE SECRETARY OF INTERIOR NOV 26 1906

TRIBAL ENROLLMENT OF PARENTS

	Name of Father	Year	County	Name of Mother	Year	County
1	Slusher		noncitizen	Slusher		noncitizen

No.1 wife of Gus Crawford, Choctaw care #3619 approved roll No. 14369

~~No.1 placed hereon under order of Commissioner to Five Civilized Tribes of April 23, 1906, holding application was made for her enrollment within time provided by Act of July 1, 1902~~ (32 Stat 641)

GRANTED JUL 2 1906

Date of Application for Enrollment. APR 23 1906

RESIDENCE: Chickasaw Nation COUNTY. **Choctaw Nation** **Choctaw Roll** *(Not Including Freedmen)* CARD NO.
POST OFFICE: Davis I.T.

Dawes' Roll No.		NAME	Relationship to Person First Named	AGE	SEX	BLOOD	TRIBAL ENROLLMENT Year	County	No.
IW 1579	1	Russell, Calistia		22	F	I.W.			
	2								
	3								
	4								
	5								
	6								
	7								
	8								
	9								
	10								
	11								
	12								
	13								
	14								
	15								
	16								
	17								

ENROLLMENT
OF NOS. 1 HEREON
APPROVED BY THE SECRETARY
OF INTERIOR AUG 2 - 1906

TRIBAL ENROLLMENT OF PARENTS

	Name of Father	Year	County	Name of Mother	Year	County
1	George Green	Dead	noncitizen	Mary Green	Dead	noncitizen
2						
3						
4						

5 No.1 is wife of John Russell Choctaw card #225 approved roll No. 453

6 No.1 placed hereon under order of Commissioner to Five Civilized Tribes of April 23, 1906
7 holding application was made for her enrollment within time provided by act of Congress of
8 July 1, 1902 (32 Stat 641) Date of Application for Enrollment. February 12, [illegible]

GRANTED
JUN 13 1906

age as of
this date
APR 23 1906

RESIDENCE: COUNTY. **Choctaw Nation** Choctaw Roll (Not Including Freedmen) CARD NO.
POST OFFICE: Atoka, Ind. Ter. FIELD NO. 60[illegible]

Dawes' Roll No.	NAME	Relationship to Person First Named	AGE	SEX	BLOOD	TRIBAL ENROLLMENT Year	County	No.
IW 1580	1 Murphy, Pat		45	M	I.W.			
	2							
	3							
	4							
	5							
	6							
	7							
	8							
	9							
	10							
	11							
	12							
	13							
	14							
	15							
	16							
	17							

ENROLLMENT
~~OF NOS.~~ 1 ~~HEREON~~
APPROVED BY THE SECRETARY
OF INTERIOR AUG 2 1906

TRIBAL ENROLLMENT OF PARENTS

Name of Father	Year	County	Name of Mother	Year	County
1 Sam Murphy	dead	non citizen	Rachel Murphy	dead	noncitizen

On March 9, 1892 No.1 was married to Agnes Bohanan, a recognized and enrolled citizen by blood of the Choctaw Nation Card No. 1393 - final roll No. 3842. They lived together for a period of about two or three years when they separated and were divorced.
~~No.1 transferred from Choctaw card No. D-749 May 9, 1906. See decision of April 24/1906.~~

~~Date of Application~~ for Enrollment.
May 8/99

Choctaw By Blood Enrollment Cards 1898-1914

RESIDENCE: COUNTY. **Choctaw Nation** **Choctaw Roll** *(Not Including Freedmen)* CARD NO.

POST OFFICE: Howe, I.T. FIELD NO. 6[redacted]

Dawes' Roll No.	NAME	Relationship to Person First Named	AGE	SEX	BLOOD	TRIBAL ENROLLMENT Year	County	No.
[redacted]	[redacted]mmons, Ellen	First Named	57	F	IW			

ENROLLMENT
OF NOS. 1 HEREON
APPROVED BY THE SECRETARY
OF INTERIOR NOV 26 1906

TRIBAL ENROLLMENT OF PARENTS

Name of Father	Year	County	Name of Mother	Year	County
Wilt Barnes	Dead	noncitizen	Diana Barnes		nonc[redacted]

No.1 placed hereon under order of Commissioner to Five Civilized Tribes of June 23, 1906, holding application was made for her enrollment within the time provided by the act of Congress approved July 1, 1902 (32 Stat 641)

Date of Application for Enrollment.

No.1 was formerly wife of Jimmie Simmons, deceased, whose son Willie Simmons, by ae former wife appears on Choctaw card #2380, approved roll of citizens by blood of Choctaw Nation No. 6905.

Jimmie Simmons eas James Simmons, is identified on 1885 Choctaw Census Roll, Sugar Loaf, and also on 1893 Leased District Payment Roll, Red River Co.

GRANTED JUL 18 1906

age as of this date JUL 3- 1906

Choctaw By Blood Enrollment Cards 1898-1914

RESIDENCE: COUNTY. **Choctaw Nation** **Choctaw Roll** *(Not Including Freedmen)* CARD NO.
POST OFFICE: Atoka FIELD NO. 6007

Dawes' Roll No.	NAME	Relationship to Person First Named	AGE	SEX	BLOOD	TRIBAL ENROLLMENT Year	County	No.
IW 1614	1 McGahey, Martha J		44	F	I.W.	1896	Jacks Fork	14880

ENROLLMENT
OF NOS. 1 HEREON
APPROVED BY THE SECRETARY
OF INTERIOR Feb. 12, 1907

TRIBAL ENROLLMENT OF PARENTS

Name of Father	Year	County	Name of Mother	Year	County
Josiah Stout	Dead	non-citizen	Nancy Stout	Dead	Noncitizen

No.1 restored to roll by Departmental authority of January 19, 1909 (File 5-51)

No.1 was married to J.F. McGahey (deceased) a recognized citizen by blood of the Choctaw Nation, September 13, 1874

Enrollment of No.1 cancelled by order of Department March 4, 1907

No.1 was rejected by Dawes Commission in 1896, in case #1268 page 411 Docket "C" No appeal

On March 7, 1906 the Dept. rescinded its action of May 22, 1904 adverse to claimant and returned record to Commissioner for further investigation and readjudication.

No.1 transferred to this card from Choctaw R. 208 June 21, 1906: See decision of June 5, 1906.

Decision of June 5/06 affirmed by Dept Oct. 30/06

Dec 5/99 Date of Application for Enrollment.

RESIDENCE: COUNTY. **Choctaw Nation** **Choctaw Roll** *(Not Including Freedmen)* [redacted] No. 6008
POST OFFICE:

Dawes' Roll No.	NAME	Relationship to Person First Named	AGE	SEX	BLOOD	TRIBAL ENROLLMENT Year	County	No.
D.P.	1 Price, Mary E			F	I.W.			
	2							
	3							
	4							
	5							
	6							
	7							
	8							
	9							
	10							
	11							
	12							
	13							
	14							
	15							
	16							
	17							

ACTION APPROVED BY SECRETARY OF INTERIOR. MAR 2- 1907

NOTICE OF DEPARTMENTAL ACTION FORWARDED ATTORNEYS FOR CHOCTAW AND CHICKASAW NATIONS APR 4- 1907

NOTICE OF DEPARTMENTAL ACTION FORWARDED ATTORNEY FOR APPLICANT. APR 4- 1907

NOTICE OF DEPARTMENTAL ACTION MAILED APPLICANT. APR 4- 1907

TRIBAL ENROLLMENT OF PARENTS

	Name of Father	Year	County	Name of Mot[redacted]	[redacted]r	County
1						
2						
3						
4						

No.1 placed on this card July 14, 1906 under order of Commissioner to the Five Civilized Tribes of July 10, 1906, holding that application was made for her enrollment within the time limited by the provisions of the Act of Congress approved April 26, 1906.

REFUSED FEB 14 1907

RECORD FORWARDED DEPARTMENT. FEB 14 1907

Jul 14-06

RESIDENCE: COUNTY. **Choctaw Nation** Choctaw Roll (*Not Including Freedmen*) FIELD NO. [redacted]

POST OFFICE: Melton, Ind. Ter.

Dawes' Roll No.	NAME	Relationship to Person First Named	AGE	SEX	BLOOD	TRIBAL ENROLLMENT Year	County	No.
IW1615	1 Dailey, Belle		51	F	I.W.			

ENROLLMENT OF NOS. 1 HEREON APPROVED BY THE SECRETARY OF INTERIOR FEB 12 1907

GRANTED NOV -6 1906

TRIBAL ENROLLMENT OF PARENTS

Name of Father	Year	County	Name of Mother	Year	County
1 Wiley Garrett		Cherokee	Amanda Collins		non citizen

No.1 placed on this card under order of Commissioner to Five Civilized Tribes of July 10, 1906, holding that application was made for her enrollment within the time limited by the provisions of the Act of Congress approved April 26, 1906.

Date of Application for Enrollment.

No.1 was formerly wife of J. H. (or Jack) Foster, a recognized citizen by blood of the Choctaw Nation who died about 1875.

age as of this date July 14, 1906

Choctaw By Blood Enrollment Cards 1898-1914

RESIDENCE: COUNTY. **Choctaw Nation** **Choctaw Roll** *(Not Including Freedmen)* CARD NO.

POST OFFICE: Ego, Ind. Ter.

Dawes' Roll No.		NAME	Relationship to Person First Named	AGE	SEX	BLOOD	TRIBAL ENROLLMENT Year	County	No.
DP 7/31/06	1	~~Wilson, Emaline~~	Named	~~67~~	~~F~~	~~I.W.~~			
	2								
	3								
	4								
	5								
	6								
	7								
	8								
	9								
	10								
	11								
	12								
	13								
	14								
	15								
	16								
	17								

TRIBAL ENROLLMENT OF PARENTS

	Name of Father	Year	County	Name of Mother	Year	County
1	Benjamin Lowery			Charity Lowery	dead	
2						
3						
4						
5						

6 No.1 placed on this card under order of Commissioner to Five Civilized Tribes of July 10,
7 1906, holding that application was made for her enrollment within the time limited by the
8 provisions of the Act of Congress approved July 1, 1902

Date of Application for Enrollment.

15 REFUSED AUG 11 1906

16 Aug. 11, 1906, Record forwarded Department — July 14, 1906

17 Jan. 22-1907 [Illegible...]

E: | COUNTY. | Choctaw Nation | Choctaw Roll (Not Including Freedmen) | CARD NO.
CE: Wister, Ind. Ter. | | | | FIELD NO. 60

NAME	Relationship to Person First Named	AGE	SEX	BLOOD	TRIBAL ENROLLMENT Year	County	No.
1 Choate, Eliza		31	F	1/2			
2							
3 REFUSED	OCT 2 1906						
4							
5 COPY OF DECISION FORWARDED APPLICANT	OCT 2 1906						
6							
7 COPY OF DECISION FORWARDED ATTORNEY FOR APPLICANT	OCT 2 1906						
8							
9 COPY OF DECISION FORWARDED ATTORNEYS FOR CHOCTAW AND	OCT 2 1906						
10 CHICKASAW NATIONS.							
11							
12 RECORD FORWARDED DEPARTMENT.							
13	OCT 2 1906						
14							
15							
16							
17							

TRIBAL ENROLLMENT OF PARENTS

Name of Father	Year	County	Name of Mother	Year	County
1 Sam Page			Sallie Page		
2					
3 ACTION APPROVED BY		FEB 15 1907			
4 SECRETARY OF INTERIOR.					
5 NOTICE OF DEPARTMENTAL ACTION FORWARDED ATTORNEYS FOR CHOCTAW		FEB 28 1907			
6 AND CHICKASAW NATIONS.					
7 NOTICE OF DEPARTMENTAL ACTION FORWARDED ATTORNEY FOR APPLICANT.		FEB 28 1907			
8					
9 NOTICE OF DEPARTMENTAL ACTION MAILED APPLICANT.		FEB 28 1907			
10					
11					
12 No.1 placed on this card under order of Commissioner of July 16, 1906, holding that application					
13 was made for her enrollment within the time limited by the provisions of the Act of Congress					
13 approved April 26, 1906					
14 Date of Application for Enrollment.					
15					
16					
17					July 16, 1906

RESIDENCE: Gaines COUNTY. **Choctaw Nation** Choctaw Roll (Not Including Freedmen) CARD NO.
POST OFFICE: Hartshorne I.T. FIELD NO. 6012

Dawes' Roll No.		NAME	Relationship to Person First Named	AGE	SEX	BLOOD	TRIBAL ENROLLMENT Year	County	No.
16061	1	Battiest, Morris		21	M	Full			
	2								
	3								
	4								
	5								
	6								
	7								
	8								
	9								
	10								
	11								
	12								
	13								
	14								
	15								
	16								
	17								

ENROLLMENT OF NOS. 1 HEREON APPROVED BY THE SECRETARY OF INTERIOR Aug 22 1906

TRIBAL ENROLLMENT OF PARENTS

	Name of Father	Year	County	Name of Mother	Year	County
1		Dead		Icey Hoklotubbe		
2						
3						
4						
5						

6 No.1 transferred from Choctaw D 302 under provisions of act of Congress
7 approved June 21, 1906.

9 No,1 enrolled by special provisions of Act of Congress of June 21, 1906 (34 Stat. 325)

Date of Application for Enrollment.
Aug 8/99

age as of this date
July 25, 1906

RESIDENCE: COUNTY. **Choctaw Nation** **Choctaw Roll** *(Not Including Freedmen)*
POST OFFICE: Roland, I.T.

Dawes' Roll No.	NAME	Relationship to Person First Named	AGE	SEX	BLOOD	TRIBAL ENROLLMENT Year	County	No.
16053	1 McDonald, John		21	M	1/8	1885	Skullyville	515
	2							
	3							
	4							
	5							
	6							
	7							
	8							
	9							
	10							
	11							
	12							
	13							
	14							
	15							
	16							
	17							

ENROLLMENT OF NOS. 1 HEREON APPROVED BY THE SECRETARY OF INTERIOR Aug 22 1906

TRIBAL ENROLLMENT OF PARENTS

Name of Father	Year	County	Name of Mother	Year	County
1 John McDonald		Non-citizen	Sina Thom	Dead	Skullyville
2					
3					
4					
5					

6 No.1 was denied as a Cherokee freedman, July 10, 1903 and on Mch 23, 1906 said
7 decision was affirmed by the Department.
8 For children of No1 see NB (Apr 26-06) #1223

14 No.1 transferred from Choctaw D-249 July 27, 1906: See decision of July 12/06

transfer date JUL 27 1906

Aug 8/99 Date of Application for Enrollment.

RESIDENCE: COUNTY. **Choctaw Nation** **Choctaw Roll** *(Not Including Freedmen)* CARD NO.
POST OFFICE: Chickasha, I.T. FIELD NO. 6014

Dawes' Roll No.		NAME	Relationship to Person First Named	AGE	SEX	BLOOD	TRIBAL ENROLLMENT Year	County	No.
16054	1	Armstrong, Mattie L	First Named	38	F	1/4	~~1896~~	~~Chick Dist~~	~~561~~
16055	2	" Layton B	Son	14	M	1/8	~~1896~~	" "	~~562~~
16056	3	" Bonnie D	Dau	16	F	1/8	~~1896~~	" "	~~563~~
16057	4	" Rebecca K	Dau	4	F	1/8			

Roll 16054 to 16057

Nos. 1,2,3 and 4 restored to roll by Departmental authority of June 15, 1909 (File 5-51).

ENROLLMENT OF NOS. 1, 2, 3 and 4 HEREON APPROVED BY THE SECRETARY OF INTERIOR Aug 22 1906

Feb. 25, 1909 Dept requests report herein
Mar. 12, 1909 Report to Department
~~March 25, 1909 Dept. refers letter of MS Field for report~~
May 4, 1909 Report to Department
See Petition #C-63

TRIBAL ENROLLMENT OF PARENTS

	Name of Father	Year	County	Name of Mother	Year	County
1	~~Wm H. Cundiff~~		~~Non Citizen~~	~~Nancy L. Cundiff~~		~~Choc. Indian~~
2	W.G. Armstrong		" "	No.1		
3	" " "		" "	No.1		
4	" " "		" "	~~No.1~~		

Nos 1 to 3 inclusive denied in 1896 Cases #477 & 478
No4 was born May 20, 1898
~~Enrollment of Nos 1 to 4 incl. cancelled by order of Department March 4, 1907~~
~~No 1 appears on 1896 roll as Mollie B. Armstrong~~
No.2 " " 1896 " " Laten B. Armstrong
No.3 " " 1896 " " Benny D. "
~~Nos 1 to 3 denied by Citizenship Court of Choctaw & Chickasaw Nations Nov. 28- 1904~~

Nos 1 to 4 inclusive transferred from Choctaw card #5108, July 24, 1906: See decision of July 9, 1906

~~Decision of Commission of July 9, 1906 affirmed by Department August 11, 1906~~

Date of Application for Enrollment. 9/2/98 ~~Date of transfer~~ to this card Jul. 24, 1906

RESIDENCE: Chickasaw Nation COUNTY. **Choctaw Nation** **Choctaw Roll** *(Not Including Freedmen)* CARD NO.
POST OFFICE: Tussy, Ind. Ter. FIELD NO. 6015

Dawes' Roll No.		NAME	Relationship to Person First Named	AGE	SEX	BLOOD	TRIBAL ENROLLMENT Year	County	No.
IW1637	1	Brown, William B		66	M	I.W.	1896	Blue	1688
16121	2	" Nancy A	Dau	27	F	1/16	1896	"	1689

Decision of Commissioner to Five Civilized Tribes [illegible...]
opinion of Attorney General of U.S. of February 19, 1907 [illegible...]

ENROLLMENT
OF NOS. 1 & 2 HEREON
APPROVED BY THE SECRETARY
OF INTERIOR MAR 1 - 1907

Duplicate Record Bound See Petition #C 34
Also see Choctaw Cards 6016 to 6029 Ins

TRIBAL ENROLLMENT OF PARENTS

	Name of Father	Year	County	Name of Mother	Year	County
1	Jesse Brown	Dead	Non Citizen	Mary Brown	Dead	Non Citizen
2	No.1			Rebecca Brown	Dead	Choctaw Indian

No.1 on 1896 Census Roll Choctaw Nation as W^m. B. Brown
See decision of Commissioner of Aug. 13-1906 enrolling No.1 as a cit
by intermarriage of the Choctaw Nation and No2 as a citizen by blood
of the Choctaw Nation.
Name of No1 transferred from Choctaw Card 5096 Aug. 13-1906

9/22/98
Date of Application for Enrollment.

transfer date Aug. 13, 1906

RESIDENCE: Chickasaw Nation COUNTY. **Choctaw Nation** **Choctaw Roll** *(Not Including Freedmen)* CARD NO.
POST OFFICE: Tussy, Ind. Ter. FIELD NO. **6016**

Dawes' Roll No.	NAME	Relationship to Person First Named	AGE	SEX	BLOOD	TRIBAL ENROLLMENT Year	County	No.
16122	1 McCarty, Bettie	First Named	23	F	1/16	1896	Blue	1690
16123	2 " Mary Ethel	Dau	1	F	1/32			
	3							
	4							
	5 Decision of Commissioner [illegible...]							
	6							
	7 For children of No.1 see NB (April 26 1906) #916							
	8							
	9							
	10							
	11 ENROLLMENT OF NOS. 1 & 2 HEREON							
	12 APPROVED BY THE SECRETARY							
	13 OF INTERIOR MAR 1 - 1907							
	14							
	15							
	16							
	17							

TRIBAL ENROLLMENT OF PARENTS

Name of Father	Year	County	Name of Mother	Year	County
1 William B Brown	1896	I.W. Choctaw	Rebecca Brown	Dead	Choctaw Indian
2 Oliver McCarty		Non Citizen	No.1		
3					
4					
5					
6 Husband of No.1 is Oliver McCarty a non citizen					
7 No.1 on 1896 Choctaw Census roll as Bettie Brown					
~~No.2 Born Dec. 8-1901~~					
8 See decision of Commissioner of Aug. 13 1906 enrolling Nos. 1 & 2					
9 as citizen by blood of the Choctaw Nation					
10 Name of No.1 transferred from Choctaw Card 5096 Aug. 13-1906.					
11					
12					Date of Application for Enrollment.
13					9/22/98
14					
15 Duplicate record bound [illegible...]					
16 See Choctaw Card 6015					Aug. 13-1996
17 P.O. address Tussy or Robberson I.T.					transfer date

RESIDENCE: Chickasaw Nation COUNTY. **Choctaw Nation** **Choctaw Roll** *(Not Including Freedmen)* CARD NO.
POST OFFICE: Comanche, Ind. Ter. FIELD NO. 6017

Dawes' Roll No.		NAME	Relationship to Person First Named	AGE	SEX	BLOOD	TRIBAL ENROLLMENT Year	County	No.
16124	1	Brown, William N.	First Named	43	M	1/16	1896	Blue	1691
IW 1638	2	" Nancy	Wife	40	F	I.W.	1896	"	1692
16125	3	" Alice	Dau	12	F	1/32	1896	"	1697
16126	4	" George	Son	9	M	1/32	1896	"	1698
16127	5	" Susie	Dau	6	F	1/32	1896	"	1699
16128	6	" Fannie C	Dau	2	F	1/32			
	7								

For child of No1 see NB (Apr 26, 1906) #918
March 1, 1909 Department requests report
~~April 20, 1909 Report to Department~~
June 15, 1909 Department holds case is not analogous to Goldsby case and declines to take action looking to enrollment of applicants June 29, 1909 Parties notified.

ENROLLMENT
OF NOS. 1,2,3,4,5 & 6 HEREON
~~APPROVED BY THE SECRETARY~~
OF INTERIOR Mar. 1-1907

See C. 50
See Choctaw card 6015

TRIBAL ENROLLMENT OF PARENTS

	Name of Father	Year	County	Name of Mother	Year	County
1	William B. Brown	1896	I.W. Choctaw	Rebecca Brown	Dead	Choctaw Indian
2	John Hearne	Dead	Non citizen	Arilla Hearne	Dead	non citizen
3	No.1			No.2		
4	No.1			No.2		
5	No.1			No.2		
6	No.1			No.2		

No.1 on 1896 Choctaw Census Roll as Wm N. Brown
Nos 1-3-4-5&6 enrolled as citizens by blood and No2 as a citizen by intermarriage of Choctaw Nation by decision of Commissioner Aug. 13-1906
~~Nos. 1 to 6 inc. transferred from Choctaw card 5060 Aug 13-1906~~
No.6 Born Feby 11, 1901
Duplicate record bound
Decision of Commissioner to Five Civilized Tribes of August 13, 1906, reversed by Secretary of the Interior in accordance with opinion of Attorney General of U.S. of February 19, 1907, and enrollment of Nos 1 to 6 inclusive, denied by Department.

transfer ~~date~~ Aug 13-1906

5/22/98 Date of Application for Enrollment.

Choctaw By Blood Enrollment Cards 1898-1914

RESIDENCE: Chickasaw Nation COUNTY. **Choctaw Nation** Choctaw Roll (Not Including Freedmen) CARD NO.
POST OFFICE: Comanche, Ind. Ter. FIELD NO. 6018

Dawes' Roll No.	NAME	Relationship to Person First Named	AGE	SEX	BLOOD	TRIBAL ENROLLMENT Year	County	No.
16129	1 Johnston, Sarah		22	F	1/32	1896	Blue	1693
16130	2 " William Erman	Son	2	M	1/64			
	3							

4 Decision of Commissioner to Five Civilized Tribes of August 13, 1906, reversed by Secretary of the Interior in accordance with opinion of Attorney General of U.S. of ~~February 19, 1907, and enrollment of Nos 1&2 denied by Department.~~

8 For children of No.1 see NB (April 26, 1906) #917

ENROLLMENT
OF NOS. 1 & 2 HEREON
~~APPROVED BY THE SECRETARY~~
OF INTERIOR Mar. 1-1907

16 See C. 47

17 See Choctaw card 6015

TRIBAL ENROLLMENT OF PARENTS

Name of Father	Year	County	Name of Mother	Year	County
1 William N. Brown	1896	Choctaw Indian	Nancy J Brown	1896	I. W. Citizen
2 J. A. Johnston		non cit.	No.1		

No.1 on 1896 Choctaw Census Roll as Sarah Brown
No1 is the wife of J.A. Johnston, non citizen.
~~No.2 Born June 30-1900~~
~~Nos 1&2 enrolled as citizens by blood of Choctaw Nation by decision of~~
Commission Aug. 13, 1906
Nos. 1 & 2 transferred from Choctaw Card 5060
~~Duplicate record bound.~~
~~March 1, 1909 Department requests report April 20, 1909. Report to Department~~
June 15, 1909 Department holds case is not analogous to Goldsby case and declines to take action looking to enrollment of applicants
June 29, 1909 Parties notified.

Aug 13-1906 ~~transfer~~ date

5/22/98 Date of Application for Enrollment.

RESIDENCE: Chickasaw Nation COUNTY. **Choctaw Nation** **Choctaw Roll** *(Not Including Freedmen)* CARD NO.
POST OFFICE: Comanche, Ind. Ter. FIELD NO. 6019

Dawes' Roll No.	NAME	Relationship to Person First Named	AGE	SEX	BLOOD	TRIBAL ENROLLMENT Year	County	No.
IW 1639	Brown, Eli W.		31	M	I.W.			
16131	" Becky	Wife	20	F	1/32	1896	Blue	169[?]
16132	" Minnie Gertrude	Dau	2	F	1/64			
16133	" Henry Nitin	Son	1	M	1/64			

For child of Nos 1 and 2 see
NB (April 26, 1906) #920

ENROLLMENT
~~OF NOS.~~ 1,2,3 & 4 ~~HEREON~~
APPROVED BY THE SECRETARY
OF INTERIOR MAR 1 - 1907

Duplicate Record Bound [illegible]
See Choctaw Card 6015

TRIBAL ENROLLMENT OF PARENTS

Name of Father	Year	County	Name of Mother	Year	County
Henry Brown		non Cit	Margaret Brown	Dead	Non Cit
William N Brown	1896	Choctaw	Nancy J Brown	1896	I.W. Choc.
No 1			No.2		
No.1			No.2		

No.2 on 1896 Choctaw Census Roll as Becky Brown
No1 Married to No.2 under Chickasaw Tribal License Aug. 21, 1897
~~No.3 Born Aug 13-1900~~
No.4 " May 21-1902
No.1 enrolled as citizen by intermarriage & Nos 2-3&4 as citizens by blood
of Choctaw Nation by decision of Commissioner Aug. 13-1906
~~Nos 2,3&4 transferred from Choctaw Card 5060 Aug 13-1906~~
No.1 " " " " D.432 Aug 13, 1906

transfer date
Aug. 13-1906

RESIDENCE: Chickasaw Nation COUNTY. **Choctaw Nation** Choctaw Roll (Not Including Freedmen) CARD No.
POST OFFICE: Comanche, Ind. Ter. FIELD No. 6020

Dawes' Roll No.	NAME	Relationship to Person First Named	AGE	SEX	BLOOD	TRIBAL ENROLLMENT Year	County	No.
16134	1 Johnston, Mary		17	F	1/32	1896	Blue	1596
	2							
	3							
	4							
	5							
	6							
	7							
	8							
	9							
	10							
	11 ENROLLMENT OF NOS. 1 HEREON							
	12 APPROVED BY THE SECRETARY							
	13 OF INTERIOR MAR 14 190[?]							
	14							
	15 See CC 47							
	16 Duplicate record bound							
	17 See Choctaw Card 6015							

TRIBAL ENROLLMENT OF PARENTS

Name of Father	Year	County	Name of Mother	Year	County
1 William N Brown	1896	Choctaw	Nancy J Brown	1896	I.W. Choc.
2					
3					
4					
5					
6 No.1 on 1896 Choctaw Census Roll as Mary Brown					
7 No.1 is the wife of Jace J. Johnston non citizen					
8 No.1 enrolled as a citizen by blood of the Choctaw Nation by decision of Commissioner Aug. 13, 1906					
9 No.1 transferred from Choctaw Card 5060					
10					
11 For children of No.1 see N.B (Act of April 26-06) #919					
12					
13					Date of Application for Enrollment.
14					5/22/98
15					transfer
16					date
17					Aug. 13-1906

RESIDENCE: Chickasaw Nation COUNTY. **Choctaw Nation** **Choctaw Roll** (Not Including Freedmen) CARD NO.
POST OFFICE: Comanche, Ind. Ter. FIELD NO. 6021

Dawes' Roll No.	NAME	Relationship to Person First Named	AGE	SEX	BLOOD	TRIBAL ENROLLMENT Year	County	No.
16135	1 Hudson, Mamie	Named	45	F	1/32	1896	Blue	1696
	2							
	3							
	4							
	5							
	6							
	7							
	8							
	9							
	10							
	11 ENROLLMENT OF NOS. 1 HEREON							
	12 APPROVED BY THE SECRETARY							
	13 OF INTERIOR MAR 1 - 1907							
	14							
	15							
	16 Duplicate record bound							
	17 See Choctaw Card 6015							

TRIBAL ENROLLMENT OF PARENTS

Name of Father	Year	County	Name of Mother	Year	County
1 William N. Brown	1896	Choctaw	Nancy J Brown	1896	IW Choc

No.1 on 1896 Choctaw Census Roll as Minnie Brown
No.1 is the wife of ~~~~~ Hudson, non citizen
~~No.1 is also known as Minnie Hudson~~
~~No.1 enrolled as a citizen by blood of the Choctaw Nation by decision~~
of Commissioner Aug 13-190[?]
No.1 transferred from Choctaw Card 5060

~~Date of Application~~ for Enrollment.
5/22/98
transfer date
Aug. 13-1906

RESIDENCE: Chickasaw Nation COUNTY. **Choctaw Nation** **Choctaw Roll** (Not Including Freedmen) CARD NO.
POST OFFICE: Robberson, Ind. Ter. FIELD NO. 6022

Dawes' Roll No.		NAME	Relationship to Person First Named	AGE	SEX	BLOOD	TRIBAL ENROLLMENT Year	County	No.
16136	1	Brown, Caswell M		38	M	1/16	1896	Blue	1701
IW 1640	2	" Amanda	Wife	35	F	I.W.	1896	"	1702
16137	3	" Maudie	Dau	14	F	1/32	1896	"	1703
16138	4	" Willie	Son	10	M	1/32	1896	"	1704
16139	5	" Elbert Knightington	Son	3	M	1/32			
	6								
	7	ENROLLMENT OF NOS. 1,2,3,4 & 5 HEREON APPROVED BY THE SECRETARY OF INTERIOR MAR 1 - 1907							
	8								
	9								
	10								
	11	For child of No.1 see NB (April 26, 1906) #921							
	12								
	13								
	14								
	15								
	16	Duplicate record bound							
	17	See Choctaw Card 6015							

TRIBAL ENROLLMENT OF PARENTS

	Name of Father	Year	County	Name of Mother	Year	County
1	William B. Brown	1896	Choc. I.W.	Rebecca Brown	Dead	Choctaw
2	John Kelly		Non Cit	Cynthia Kelly	Dead	Non Cit
3	No.1			No.2		
4	No.1			No.2		
5	No.1			No.2		
6						
7	No.1 on 1896 Choctaw Census Roll C. M. Brown					
8	No.2 " " " " " Maudy Brown					
9	No.4 " " " " " William Brown					
	Nos 1&2 married Dec 2, 1886					
10	No.5 Born Oct 8, 1899					
11	Nos. 1,3,4 & 5 enrolled as citizens by blood and No.2 as a citizen by					
12	intermarriage of the Choctaw Nation by decision of Commissioner Aug 13-190					
	Nos 1 to 5 inc. transferred from Choctaw Card 5066 Aug 13-1906					
13						
14						
15						
16				Date of Application for Enrollment.		Aug. 13-1906 transfer date
17				9/22/98		

RESIDENCE: Chickasaw Nation COUNTY. **Choctaw Nation** **Choctaw Roll** *(Not Including Freedmen)* CARD NO.
POST OFFICE: Duncan, Ind. Ter. FIELD NO. 6023

Dawes' Roll No.	NAME	Relationship to Person First Named	AGE	SEX	BLOOD	TRIBAL ENROLLMENT Year	County	No.
16140	1 Peck, Polly A		35	F	1/16	1896	Blue	10518
16141	2 " Florence	Dau	13	F	1/32	1896	"	10519
16142	3 " Oscar	Son	11	M	1/32	1896	"	10520
16143	4 " Benjamin	Son	9	M	1/32	1896	"	10521
16144	5 " Andrew	Son	7	M	1/32	1896	"	10522
16145	6 " Otis Dewey	Son	4	M	1/32			
16146	7 " Virgie	Son	1	M	1/32			
	8							
	9							
	10							
	11 ENROLLMENT OF NOS. 1,2,3,4,5,6&7 HEREON							
	12 APPROVED BY THE SECRETARY							
	13 OF INTERIOR MAR 1 - 1907							
	14							
	15							
	16							
	17 See Choctaw Card 6015							

TRIBAL ENROLLMENT OF PARENTS

	Name of Father	Year	County	Name of Mother	Year	County
1	William B. Brown	1896	I.W. Choc	Rebecca Brown	Dead	Choctaw
2	Andrew J Peck		Non Cit.	No.1		
3	"		"	No.1		
4	"		"	No.1		
5	"		"	No.1		
6	"		"	No.1		
7	"		"	No.1		

8 No.1 on 1896 Choctaw Census Roll as Polly Ann Peck
9 No.2 " " " " " " Minnie F. Peck — For child of No1 see NB
10 ~~No.3 " " " " " " Oscar S. Peck~~ — ~~(April 26 1906) #922~~
~~No.4 " " " " " " Benj G. Peck~~
11 Andrew J Peck husband of No.1 and father of Nos 2 to 7 inc. on 1896 Choctaw Census Roll
12 10517 and denied as Intermarried Choctaw by decision of Commissioner of Aug. 13, 1906
Nos 1 to 7 inc. enrolled as citizens by blood of Choctaw Nation by decision of Commissioner Aug 13, 1906
13 ~~Nos 1 to 7 inc. transferred from Choctaw Card 5062 Aug. 13-1906~~
14
15
16 ~~9/22/98~~ Date of Application for Enrollment. Aug. 13-1906 transfer date
17

RESIDENCE: Chickasaw Nation COUNTY. **Choctaw Nation** **Choctaw Roll** (*Not Including Freedmen*) CARD NO.
POST OFFICE: Comanche, Ind. Ter. FIELD NO. 6024

Dawes' Roll No.		NAME	Relationship to Person First Named	AGE	SEX	BLOOD	TRIBAL ENROLLMENT Year	County	No.
16147	1	Brown, George G		30	M	1/16	1896	Blue	1705
IW 1641	2	" Sarah	Wife	25	F	I.W.	1896	"	1706
16148	3	" Willie Emma	Dau	7	F	1/32			
	4	ENROLLMENT							
	5	OF NOS. 1, 2 & 3 HEREON APPROVED BY THE SECRETARY							
	6	OF INTERIOR MAR 1 - 1907							
	7								
	8	March 1, 1909 [Illegible...]							
	9	April 20, 1909 [Illegible...]							
	10	June 15, 1909 [Illegible...] ~~to Goldsby case [illegible...]~~							
	11	enrollment [illegible...]							
	12	Decision of Commissioner [illegible...]							
	13	with opinion of Atty [illegible...]							
	14								
	15								
	16	~~Duplicate Record Bound. See Petition [illegible]~~							
	17	See Choctaw Card 6015							

TRIBAL ENROLLMENT OF PARENTS

	Name of Father	Year	County	Name of Mother	Year	County
1	William B. Brown	1896	I.W. Choc	Rebecca Brown	Dead	Choctaw
2	Perry Johnson		Non Cit	Betty Johnson		Non Cit
3	No.1			No.2		
4						
5						
6						

For children of No.1 see NB (April 26-1906) #923

~~No.1 on 1896 Choctaw Census Roll as Geo. G. Brown~~
~~Nos. 1 & 2 married June 9-1895~~
No.3 Born Mar 22, 1896
Nos 1 and 3 enrolled as citizens by blood and No.2 as a citizen by intermarriage
~~of the Choctaw Nation by decision of Commissioner Aug 13-1906~~
~~Nos. 1 to 3 inc. transferred from Choctaw Card 5095~~

9/22/98 Date of Application for Enrollment.

transfer date ~~Aug. 13-1906~~

RESIDENCE: Chickasaw Nation COUNTY. **Choctaw Nation** Choctaw Roll (Not Including Freedmen) CARD NO.
POST OFFICE: Comanche, Ind. Ter. FIELD NO. 6025

Dawes' Roll No.	NAME	Relationship to Person First Named	AGE	SEX	BLOOD	TRIBAL ENROLLMENT Year	County	No.
16149	1 Nichols, James B		53	M	1/8	1896	Blue	9807
IW 1642	2 " Nancy C	Wife	46	F	I.W.	1896	"	9808
16150	3 " Nancy V	Dau	11	F	1/16	1896	"	9811
	4							
	5 Decision of Commissioner [illegible...]							
	6 opinion of Attorney [illegible...]							
	7							
	8							
	9							
	10							
	11 ENROLLMENT OF NOS. 1, 2 & 3 HEREON							
	12 APPROVED BY THE SECRETARY							
	13 OF INTERIOR MAR 1 - 1907							
	14							
	15							
	16 Duplicate Record Bound See Petition [illegible]							
	17 See Choctaw Card 6015							

TRIBAL ENROLLMENT OF PARENTS

Name of Father	Year	County	Name of Mother	Year	County
1 Wilson Nichols	Dead	Non Cit	Delitha Nichols	Dead	Choctaw
2 Bethel Guest	Dead	Non Cit	Tiny Guest	Dead	Non Cit
3 No.1			No.2		

6 No.1 on 1896 Choctaw Census Roll as J.B. Nicholas
7 No.2 " " " " " " Nancy Nicholas
Nos 1&2 Married Mar 9, 1879
8 No.3 on 1896 Choctaw Census Roll as Velma Nicholas
9 Nos 1&3 enrolled as citizens by blood and No.2 as a citizen by intermarriage
10 of the Choctaw Nation by decision of Commissioner Aug 13-1906
Nos 1,2&3 transferred from Choctaw Card 5100 Aug 13-1906

transfer date

Date of Application for Enrollment. 9/22/98 Aug. 13-1906

RESIDENCE: Chickasaw Nation COUNTY. **Choctaw Nation** Choctaw Roll (Not Including Freedmen) CARD NO.
POST OFFICE: Comanche Ind. Ter. FIELD NO. 60

Dawes' Roll No.	NAME	Relationship to Person First Named	AGE	SEX	BLOOD	TRIBAL ENROLLMENT Year	County	No.
16151	1 Scott, Della May	First Named	19	F	5/16	1896	Blue	981

ENROLLMENT OF NOS. 1 HEREON APPROVED BY THE SECRETARY OF INTERIOR MAR 1 - 1907

For children of No.1 see NB (Apr 26 1906) #924

Decision of Commissioner [illegible...] opinion of Attorney [illegible...]

Duplicate Record Bound See Petition #C 34
See Choctaw Card 6015

TRIBAL ENROLLMENT OF PARENTS

Name of Father	Year	County	Name of Mother	Year	County
1 James B Nichols	1896	Choctaw	Nancy C. Nichols	1896	I.W.

No.1 on 1896 Choctaw Census Roll as Della Nicholas
No.1 is the wife of Burris Scott non-citizen
~~No.1 enrolled as a citizen by blood of the Choctaw Nation by decision of Commissioner Aug 13-1906~~
No.1 transferred from Choctaw Card 5100 Aug 13-1906

transfer date Aug. 13-1906

Date of Application for Enrollment. 9/22/98

RESIDENCE: Chickasaw Nation COUNTY.
POST OFFICE: Comanche, Ind. Ter.

Choctaw Nation

Choctaw Roll *(Not Including Freedmen)*

CARD NO.
FIELD NO. 6027

Dawes' Roll No.		NAME	Relationship to Person First Named	AGE	SEX	BLOOD	TRIBAL ENROLLMENT Year	County	No.
16152	1	Nichols, Orin M	First Named	48	M	1/8	1896	Blue	9812
IW 1643	2	" Amanda M	Wife	42	F	I.W.	1896	"	9813
16153	3	" Maggie M	Dau	16	F	1/16	1896	"	9815
16154	4	" Mettie Myrtle	Dau	12	F	1/16	1896	"	9816
16155	5	" Lonie A	Dau	8	F	1/16	1896	"	9817
	17	See Choctaw Card 6015							

ENROLLMENT
OF NOS. 1,2,3,4&5 HEREON
APPROVED BY THE SECRETARY
OF INTERIOR MAR 1 - 1907

TRIBAL ENROLLMENT OF PARENTS

	Name of Father	Year	County	Name of Mother	Year	County
1	Wilson Nichols	Dead	Non Cit	Delitha Nichols	Dead	Choctaw
2	J. L. Shelton	Dead	Non Cit	Mary Shelton		Non cit
3	No.1			No.2		
4	No.1			No.2		
5	No.1			No.2		

7 No.1 on 1896 Choctaw Census Roll as Ora M. Nicholas
8 No.2 " " " " " " Amanda Nicholas
9 No.3 " " " " " " Maggie "
No.4 " " " " " " Myrtle "
10 No.5 " " " " " " Lona "
11 Nos 1&2 married Oct 20, 1878
12 Nos 1,3,4 & 5 enrolled as citizens by blood and No2 as citizen by intermarriage of the Choctaw Nation by decision of Commissioner Aug 13-1906
13 Nos 1 to 5 inc. transferred from Choctaw Card 5061 Aug 13-1906

Date of Application for Enrollment. 9/22/98

Aug. 13-1906 Date transferred

RESIDENCE: Chickasaw Nation COUNTY. **Choctaw Nation** **Choctaw Roll** (Not Including Freedmen) CARD NO.
POST OFFICE: Comanche, Ind Ter FIELD NO. 6028

Dawes' Roll No.	NAME	Relationship to Person First Named	AGE	SEX	BLOOD	TRIBAL ENROLLMENT Year	County	No.
16156	1 Nichols, James W	First Named	22	M	1/16	1896	Blue	9814
IW 1644	2 " Osa	Wife	20	F	I.W.			
	3							
	4							
	5 For child of No.1 see NB (April 26 1906) #926							
	6							
	7							
	8 ENROLLMENT							
	9 OF NOS. 1 & 2 HEREON APPROVED BY THE SECRETARY							
	10 OF INTERIOR MAR 1 - 1907							
	11							
	12 Decision of Commissioner [illegible...]							
	13 opinion of Attorney [illegible...]							
	14							
	15							
	16 Duplicate Record Bound See Petition #C 34							
	17 See Choctaw Card 6015							

TRIBAL ENROLLMENT OF PARENTS

Name of Father	Year	County	Name of Mother	Year	County
1 Orin M Nichols	1896	Choctaw	Amanda M Nichols	1896	I.W. Choc
2 Billy Richardson		Non Cit	Tennessee Richardson		Non Cit
3					
4					
5					
6 No.1 on 1896 Choctaw Census Roll as James A. Nicholas					
7 Nos 1&2 married April 27-1799					
~~No.1 enrolled as a citizen by blood and No.2 as a citizen by intermarriage~~					
8 ~~of the Choctaw Nation by decision of Commissioner Aug 13-1905~~					
9 No.1 transferred from Choctaw Card 5062 Aug. 13-1906					
10 No.2 " " " " D509 " " "					
11					
12					
13					
14					
15				~~9/22/98~~	Date
16				Date of Application for Enrollment.	transferred
17					Aug. 13-1906

RESIDENCE: Chickasaw Nation COUNTY. **Choctaw Nation** **Choctaw Roll** (Not Including Freedmen) CARD NO.
POST OFFICE: Comanche, Ind Ter FIELD NO. 6029

Dawes' Roll No.		NAME	Relationship to Person First Named	AGE	SEX	BLOOD	TRIBAL ENROLLMENT Year	County	No.
16157	1	Nichols, John W. B.	First Named	28	M	1/16	1896	Blue	9809
IW 1645	2	" Bessie	Wife	22	F	I.W.			
16158	3	" Louie Herman	Son	2	M	1/32			
16159	4	" Golda Ula	Dau	1	F	1/32			
	5								
	6								
	7	ENROLLMENT							
	8	OF NOS. 1,2,3 & 4 HEREON APPROVED BY THE SECRETARY							
	9	OF INTERIOR MAR 1 - 1907							
	10								
	11	For child of No.1 see NB (April 26 1906) #925							
	12								
	13	Decision of Commissioner [illegible]							
	14	opinion of Attorney [illegible]							
	15								
	16	Duplicate Record Bound See Petition [illegible]							
	17	See Choctaw Card 6015							

TRIBAL ENROLLMENT OF PARENTS

	Name of Father	Year	County	Name of Mother	Year	County
1	James B. Nichols	1896	Choctaw	Nancy C. Nichols	1896	I.W. Choc
2	Levi Deaton		Non Cit	R.O. Deaton		Non cit
3	No.1			No.2		
4	No.1			No.2		

~~No.1 on 1896 Choctaw Census Roll as Johnnie Nicholas~~
Nos 1&2 Married June 11, 1895
No.3 Born Aug 19-1900
~~No.4 " Dec 15-1901~~
~~Nos. 1,3&4 enrolled as citizens by blood and No.2 as a citizen by intermarriage~~
of the Choctaw Nation by decision of Commissioner Aug 13-1906
Nos 1,2,3 & 4 transferred from Choctaw Card 5097 Aug. 13-1906

Date of Application for Enrollment. 9/22/98

~~Date~~ transferred Aug. 13-1906

RESIDENCE: COUNTY. **Choctaw Nation** Choctaw Roll (Not Including Freedmen) CARD NO.
POST OFFICE: Sulphur, Ind. Ter. FIELD NO. 60

Dawes' Roll No.	NAME	Relationship to Person First Named	AGE	SEX	BLOOD	TRIBAL ENROLLMENT Year	County	No.
16160	1 Shockley, Ephriam E		33	M	1/16	1893	Chick Dist	498
IW 1646	2 " Ava	Wife	28	F	I.W.			
16161	3 " Mattie	Dau	10	"	1/32	1893	" "	499
16162	4 " Leverett	Son	6	M	1/32			
16163	5 " Elva May	Dau	2	F	1/32			
	6							
	7							
	8							
	9 ENROLLMENT							
	10 OF NOS. 1,2,3,4 and 5 HEREON							
	11 APPROVED BY THE SECRETARY OF INTERIOR MAR 1 1907							
	12							
	13							
	14							
	15							
	16							
	17 Duplicate Record Bound See Petition #C16							

TRIBAL ENROLLMENT OF PARENTS

Name of Father	Year	County	Name of Mother	Year	County
1 John Shockley			Fatima Shockley		
2 John Townsend			Mattie Townsend		
3 No.1			No.2		
4 No.1			No.2		
5 No.1			No.2		
6					
7					
8					

9 Nos 1,3,4 and 5 enrolled as citizens by blood and No.2 as a citizen by
10 intermarriage of the Choctaw Nation by decision of the Commissioner to the Five Civilized Tribes of Mar. 19, 1906.
11 ~~Nos. 1 to 5 incl. transferred from Choctaw card #5109~~
12 For child of Nos 1 and 2 see NB (Apr. 26, 1906) card #773.

16 9/28/98 Date of Application for Enrollment.

Date ~~transferred~~ MAY 20 1906

RESIDENCE: COUNTY. **Choctaw Nation** Choctaw Roll (Not Including Freedmen) CARD NO.
POST OFFICE: Durwood, Ind. Ter. FIELD NO. 6031

Dawes' Roll No.		NAME	Relationship to Person First Named	AGE	SEX	BLOOD	TRIBAL ENROLLMENT Year	County	No.
16164	1	Shockley, Charles L		35	M	1/16	1893	Chick Dist	497
IW 1647	2	" Callie	Wife	24	F	I.W.			
16165	3	" Albert	Son	7	M	1/32			
16166	4	" Hurman	"	5	"	1/32			
16167	5	" Mamie	Dau	3	F	1/32			
	6								
	7								
	8								
	9								
	10								
	11	ENROLLMENT OF NOS. 1,2,3,4 and 5 HEREON							
	12	APPROVED BY THE SECRETARY							
	13	OF INTERIOR MAR 1 1907							
	14								
	15								
	16								
	17	Duplicate Record Bound See Petition #C16							

TRIBAL ENROLLMENT OF PARENTS

	Name of Father	Year	County	Name of Mother	Year	County
1	John E. Shockley			Fatima Shockley		
2	Young Mitchusson			Fanny Mitchusson		
3	No 1			No.2		
4	No.1			No.2		
5	No.1			No.2		

Nos 1,3,4 and 5 enrolled as citizens by blood and No.2 as a citizen by intermarriage of the Choctaw Nation by decision of the Commissioner to the Five Civilized Tribes of March 19, 1906.

~~Nos. 1 to 5 incl. transferred from Choctaw card #5188~~

For child of Nos 1 and 2 see NB (Apr. 26, 19060 card #772.

Date of Application for Enrollment. 9/24/98

Date transferred MAY 20 1906

RESIDENCE: COUNTY. **Choctaw Nation** **Choctaw Roll** *(Not Including Freedmen)* CARD NO.
POST OFFICE: Ardmore, Ind. Ter. FIELD NO. 6032

Dawes' Roll No.	NAME	Relationship to Person First Named	AGE	SEX	BLOOD	TRIBAL ENROLLMENT Year	County	No.
16168	1 West, Lula		29	F	1/16	1893	Chick. Dist.	581
16169	2 " Roy	Son	12	M	1/32	1893	" "	582
16170	3 " Marie	Dau	7	F	1/32			
16171	4 " Corine	"	4	"	1/32			

ENROLLMENT OF NOS. 1 2 3 and 4 HEREON APPROVED BY THE SECRETARY OF INTERIOR MAR 1 1907

Duplicate Record Bound See Petition #C16

TRIBAL ENROLLMENT OF PARENTS

Name of Father	Year	County	Name of Mother	Year	County
1 John Shockley			Fatima Shockley		
2 F. K. West			No.1		
3 " " "			No.1		
4 " " "			No.1		

Nos 1-2-3-4 enrolled as citizens by blood of the Choctaw Nation by decision of the Commissioner to the Five Civilized Tribes of March 19, 1906

Nos 1 to 4 incl transferred from Choctaw card #5191

Date of Application for Enrollment. 9/24/98

MAY

RESIDENCE: COUNTY. **Choctaw Nation** Choctaw Roll (*Not Including Freedmen*) CARD NO.
POST OFFICE: Durwood, I.T. FIELD NO. 6033

Dawes' Roll No.	NAME	Relationship to Person First Named	AGE	SEX	BLOOD	Tribal Enrollment Year	Tribal Enrollment County	Tribal Enrollment No.
16172	1 Shockley, Albert R		22	M	1/32	1893	Chick Dist.	500

ENROLLMENT OF NOS. 1 HEREON APPROVED BY THE SECRETARY OF INTERIOR MAR 1 1907

Duplicate record Bound See Petition #G16

TRIBAL ENROLLMENT OF PARENTS

Name of Father	Year	County	Name of Mother	Year	County
1 William E Shockley			Bettie Shockley		

No.1 enrolled as a citizen by blood of the Choctaw Nation by decision of the Commissioner to the Five Civilized Tribes of March 19, 1906.
No.1 transferred from Choctaw card #5193

Date of Application for Enrollment: 9/24/98

Date transferred: MAY 20 1906

RESIDENCE: COUNTY. **Choctaw Nation** Choctaw Roll (Not Including Freedmen) FIELD NO. [redacted]
POST OFFICE:

Dawes' Roll No.	NAME	Relationship to Person First Named	AGE	SEX	BLOOD	TRIBAL ENROLLMENT Year	County	No.
IW 1648	1 Osborn, Mattie	First Named	46	F	IW			
16173	2 Shockley, John E	Son	16	M	1/16	1893	Chick. Dist	501
	3							
	4							
	5							
	6							
	7							
	8							
	9							
	10							
	11							
	12							
	13							
	14							
	15							
	16							
	17 Duplicate Record Bound See Petition #C[illegible]							

ENROLLMENT OF NOS. 1 and 2 HEREON APPROVED BY THE SECRETARY OF INTERIOR MAR 1 1907

TRIBAL ENROLLMENT OF PARENTS

Name of Father	Year	County	Name of Mother	Year	County
1 Moses Lunsford	Dead	noncitizen	Eliza Lunsford	Dead	noncitizen
2 John Shockley			No.1		

No.1 enrolled as a citizen by intermarriage and No.2 as a citizen by blood of the Choctaw Nation by decision of the Commissioner to the Five Civilized Tribes of March 19, 1906.

~~Nos. 1 and 2 transferred from Choctaw card #5238~~

Date of Application for Enrollment. 10/4/98

~~Date~~ transferred MAY 20 1906

RESIDENCE: COUNTY. **Choctaw Nation** **Choctaw Roll** *(Not Including Freedmen)* CARD NO.
POST OFFICE: Rogers, Texas FIELD NO. 6035

Dawes' Roll No.	NAME	Relationship to Person First Named	AGE	SEX	BLOOD	TRIBAL ENROLLMENT Year	County	No.
SIW 1649	1 Shockley, Pauline		24	F	I.W.			
16174	2 " Albert P	Son	5	M	1/32			
	3							
	4							
	5							
	6							
	7							
	8							
	9							
	10							
	11							
	12							
	13							
	14							
	15							
	16							
	17 Duplicate Record Bound See Petition #C-16							

ENROLLMENT
OF NOS. 1 and 2 HEREON
APPROVED BY THE SECRETARY
OF INTERIOR Mar 1 1907

TRIBAL ENROLLMENT OF PARENTS

Name of Father	Year	County	Name of Mother	Year	County
1 G. W. Du Bose		non-citizen	A. Du Bose		non citizen
2 Albert Sockley[sic]			No.1		

Decision of Commissioner to Five Civilized Tribes of March 19, 1906 reverses by Secretary of the Interior in accordance with opinion of Attorney General of U.S. of February 19, 1907 and enrollment of Nos. 1 and 2 denied by Department.

No.1 enrolled as a citizen by intermarriage and No.2 as a citizen by blood of the Choctaw Nation by decision of the Commissioner to Five Civilized Tribes of March 19, 1906.

Nos 1 and 2 transferred from Choctaw Card #D 51.

March 1, 1909 Department requests report as to persons within this class

April 14, 1909 report to Department.

Date of Application for Enrollment. Sept 24/98

Date transferred May 20 1906

RESIDENCE: COUNTY. **Choctaw Nation** Choctaw Roll (*Not Including Freedmen*) [redacted]6036

POST OFFICE: Ashland, Ind. Ter.

Dawes' Roll No.	NAME	Relationship to Person First Named	AGE	SEX	BLOOD	TRIBAL ENROLLMENT Year	County	No.
IW 1593	1 McLellan, Ada		25	F	I.W.			
	2							
	3							
	4							
	5							
	6							
	7							
	8							
	9							
	10							
	11							
	12							
	13							
	14							
	15							
	16							
	17							

ENROLLMENT OF NOS 1 HEREON APPROVED BY THE SECRETARY OF INTERIOR NOV 26 1906

TRIBAL ENROLLMENT OF PARENTS

Name of Father	Year	County	Name of Mother	Year	County
1 Jim Dobbins		non-citizen	Catherine Dobbins		non-citizen
2					
3					
4					
5					

No.1 placed on this card under order of Commissioner to Five Civilized Tribes of July 9, 1906, holding that application was made for her enrollment within the time limited by the provisions of the Act of Congress approved April 26, 1906.

No.1 is wife of Joseph M. McLellan on Choctaw card #3922. Roll #15324

age as of this date AUG 27 1906

RESIDENCE: Chickasaw Nation COUNTY. **Choctaw Nation** **Choctaw Roll** (Not Including Freedmen) CARD NO.
POST OFFICE: Roff, IT FIELD NO. 60

Dawes' Roll No.	NAME	Relationship to Person First Named	AGE	SEX	BLOOD	TRIBAL ENROLLMENT Year	County	No.
IW 1594	1 Roff, Dottie		22	F	I.W.			
	2							
	3							
	4							
	5							
	6							
	7							
	8							
	9							
	10							
	11							
	12							
	13							
	14							
	15							
	16							
	17 Duplicate Record Bound See Petition #C16							

ENROLLMENT
OF NOS. 1 HEREON
APPROVED BY THE SECRETARY
OF INTERIOR NOV 26 1906

TRIBAL ENROLLMENT OF PARENTS

	Name of Father	Year	County	Name of Mother	Year	County
1						
2						
3						
4						
5						

No.1 placed hereon under departmental instructions of Sept. 19-1906 directing her enrollment as an intermarried citizen of the Choctaw Nation.

No.1 is wife of William D. Roff, Choctaw card #40 Roll #72.

age as of this date
OCT 5 1906

E:
ICE: Hanna, Ark. COUNTY. **Choctaw Nation** **Choctaw Roll** *(Not Including Freedmen)* CARD NO. FIELD NO. 60

	NAME	Relationship to Person First Named	AGE	SEX	BLOOD	TRIBAL ENROLLMENT Year	County	No.
1	Allen, Genelia		45	F	I.W.			
2	" Rovilla	Dau	7	F	1/2			

ENROLLMENT OF NOS. 1 HEREON APPROVED BY THE SECRETARY OF INTERIOR NOV 26 1906

ENROLLMENT OF NOS. 2 HEREON APPROVED BY THE SECRETARY OF INTERIOR NOV 23 1906

TRIBAL ENROLLMENT OF PARENTS

	Name of Father	Year	County	Name of Mother	Year	County
1	George Lewis	dead	non-citizen	Margie Lewis	dead	non-ci
2	John Allen		Nashoba	No.1		

Nos 1&2 transferred from Choctaw card #D-178, September 10, 1906;
See decision of August 24, 1906.

No1 was married to John Allen, Choctaw card #2071, final roll number 5960, August 18, 1894, she lived with him about fifteen months when she separated from him and they were subsequently divorced.

No2 was born July 15, 1895

P.O. Ara, Ind. Ter. 6/4/07

Date of Application for Enrollment. 5/22/99

Date transferred SEP 10 1906

RESIDENCE: COUNTY. **Choctaw Nation** **Choctaw Roll** *(Not Including Freedmen)* CARD No.
POST OFFICE: Terral, Ind. Ter. FIELD No.

Dawes' Roll No.	NAME	Relationship to Person First Named	AGE	SEX	BLOOD	TRIBAL ENROLLMENT Year	County	No.
IW 1596	1 Langley, Samuel Lee	First Named	25	M	I.W.			

ENROLLMENT
OF NOS. 1 HEREON
APPROVED BY THE SECRETARY
OF INTERIOR NOV 26 1906

TRIBAL ENROLLMENT OF PARENTS

Name of Father	Year	County	Name of Mother
1 Geo. B. Langley	dead	non-citizen	Sarah Langley

No.1 is husband of Calcie Lee Langley #4 on Choctaw card #345 whose name appears opposite #14622. They were first married under a U.S. License on November 25, 1900 and on May 6, 1903 were remarried under a Choctaw license.

No.1 transferred from Choctaw card #D.717 July 25, 1906;
See decision of July 9, 1906.

Date of Application for Enrollment. May 7/02

Date

RESIDENCE: COUNTY. Chocta[redacted] 6

POST OFFICE: Garvin, Ind. Ter.

Dawes' Roll No.	NAME	Relationship to Person First Named	AGE	SEX	BLOOD	TRIBAL ENROLLMENT Year	County	No.
16065	1 Forbes, Melvina		14	F	1/2	1896	Red River	4217
	2							
	3							
	4							
	5							
	6							
	7							
	8							
	9							
	10							
	11							
	12							
	13							
	14							
	15							
	16							
	17							

ENROLLMENT
OF NOS. 1 HEREON
APPROVED BY THE SECRETARY
OF INTERIOR NOV 23 1906

TRIBAL ENROLLMENT OF PARENTS

	Name of Father	Year	County	Name of Mother	Year	County
1	Buddy Durant		Choctaw	Martha Mack	dead	non-citizen

No.1 is illegitimate child of a white woman; She was born in Choctaw Nation but did not draw Leased district money in 1893

She was legally adopted by Albert Forbes in Red River County Court Papers of ~~adoption filed Sept 24, 1906.~~

No.1 transferred from Choctaw card #D.938, October 10, 1906;
See decision of September 25, 1906.

Date of Application for Enrollment.
Nov 25/02

Date transferred
OCT 10 1906

RESIDENCE: COUNTY. **Choctaw Nation** **Choctaw Roll** *(Not Including Freedmen)* CARD NO.
POST OFFICE: Stewart, Ind. Ter. FIELD NO. **6041**

Dawes' Roll No.		NAME	Relationship to Person First Named	AGE	SEX	BLOOD	TRIBAL ENROLLMENT Year	County	No.
IW 1597	1	Russell, George		32	M	I.W.			
	2								
	3								
	4								
	5								
	6								
	7								
	8								
	9								
	10								
	11								
	12								
	13								
	14								
	15								
	16								
	17								

ENROLLMENT OF NOS. 1 HEREON APPROVED BY THE SECRETARY OF INTERIOR NOV 26 1906

TRIBAL ENROLLMENT OF PARENTS

	Name of Father	Year	County	Name of Mother	Year	County
1						
2						
3						
4						

~~No.1 was married to Ellen Goens (now deceased) Dec. 25, 1895, lived together five days when they separated and were subsequently divorced.~~
~~Ellen Goens is identified upon 1893 Choctaw Leased District Payment Roll, Jackson County No. 281, and also upon the 1896 Choctaw Census Roll, Jackson County, No. 10884.~~

~~No.1 transferred from Choctaw card #R-258. September 15, 1906; See decision of August 31, 1906.~~

Date of Application for Enrollment. June 2/99

Date of transfer to this card SEP 15 1906

RESIDENCE: COUNTY. **Choctaw Nation** Choctaw Roll (Not Including Freedmen) CARD NO.
POST OFFICE: Albany, Ind. Ter. FIELD NO. 6042

Dawes' Roll No.	NAME	Relationship to Person First Named	AGE	SEX	BLOOD	TRIBAL ENROLLMENT Year	County	No.
IW 1598	1 Ashford, Thomas	Named	54	M	I.W.			
	2							
	3							
	4							
	5							
	6							
	7							
	8							
	9							
	10							
	11							
	12							
	13							
	14							
	15							
	16							
	17							

ENROLLMENT
~~OF NOS.~~ 1 ~~HEREON~~
APPROVED BY THE SECRETARY
OF INTERIOR NOV 26 1906

TRIBAL ENROLLMENT OF PARENTS

Name of Father	Year	County	Name of Mother	Year	County
1 James Ashford	dead	non-citizen	Prudena Ashford	dead	non-citizen
2					
3					
4					
5					

~~No.1 was married to Virginia Airington, a recognized citizen by blood of the Choctaw Nation~~
December 12, 1869, whose son by said marriage appears on final roll of citizens by blood of Choctaw Nation opposite #15066 as James D. Ashford
~~No.1 and wife Virginia Airington, were residents in good faith of Choctaw and resided together continuously in said Nation until her death in 1880, since which time No.1 has~~
continued to live in said Nation up to and including Sept. 25, 1902

~~No.1 transferred from Choctaw card #R-9, August 2, 1906: See decision of July 18, 1906.~~

For children of No.1 see NB (April 26, 1906) #1126

Date of trans[fer] to this ca[rd]
AUG 2 190[6]

Date of Application for Enrollment. April 9/02

RESIDENCE: COUNTY. **Choctaw Nation** **Choctaw Roll** (*Not Including Freedmen*) CARD NO.
POST OFFICE: Duncan I.T. FIELD NO. 6043

Dawes' Roll No.	NAME	Relationship to Person First Named	AGE	SEX	BLOOD	TRIBAL ENROLLMENT Year	County	No.
16112	1 Bumgarner, George A	First Named	20	M	1/32	1896	Choc. Census R	1683
	2						Blue Co	
	3							
	4							
	5							
	6 ENROLLMENT OF NOS. 1 HEREON APPROVED BY THE SECRETARY							
	7 OF INTERIOR Mar 4, 1907							
	8							
	9							
	10							
	11 ENROLLMENT OF NOS. ... HEREON							
	12 APPROVED BY THE SECRETARY OF INTERIOR							
	13							
	14							
	15							
	16							
	17 Granted Oct 15 1906							

TRIBAL ENROLLMENT OF PARENTS

Name of Father	Year	County	Name of Mother	Year	County
1 J. H. Bumgarner		noncitizen	Mary Miller		Choctaw
2					
3					

4 ~~An Aunt of No.1 Nina Lindsey appears on Choctaw card #224, opposite #15361~~

6 No.1 is identified on 1896 Choctaw Census Roll opposite #1683 and opposite his name is the following notation "Enrolled without authority of law"

7 ~~No.1 had application made for him in 1896 Choctaw Citizenship Docket Case #620 as~~

8 George Bumgoner[sic]: Commission rendered its decision denying said application from which

9 n appeal was taken.

10 ~~No.1 placed on this card under order of Commissioner to Five Civilized Tribes of October~~

11 1, 1906 holding that application was made for his enrollment within the time limited by

12 provisions of Congress approved April 26, 1906 (34 Stat. 137)

Date of Application for Enrollment.

17 Oct. 1- 1906

Choctaw By Blood Enrollment Cards 1898-1914

RESIDENCE: COUNTY. Ch
POST OFFICE: Bengal, I.T.

Dawes' Roll No.	NAME	Relationship to Person First Named	AGE	SEX	BLOOD	TRIBAL ENROLLMENT Year	County	No.
IW 1616	1 Loring, Lulie	First Named	48	F	I.W			
	2							
	3							
	4							
	5							
	6							
	7							
	8							
	9							
	10							
	11							
	12							
	13							
	14							
	15							
	16							
	17							

ENROLLMENT
~~OF NOS.~~ 1 ~~HEREON~~
APPROVED BY THE SECRETARY
OF INTERIOR FEB 12 1907

TRIBAL ENROLLMENT OF PARENTS

Name of Father	Year	County	Name of Mother	Year	County
1 Justice Shinn	dead	non-citizen	Lottie Shinn	dead	no
2					
3					
4					
5					

No.1 was formerly wife of William H. Loring whose name appears on Choctaw card #1621 opposite #4594

No.1 transferred Choctaw D-609, November 1, 1906; See decision of October 17, 1906.

Date of Application for Enrollment. Jan 17/01

Date of transfer ~~to this card~~ NOV -1 1906

Choctaw By Blood Enrollment Cards 1898-1914

RESIDENCE: COUNTY. **Choctaw Nation** **Choctaw Roll** *(Not Including Freedmen)* CARD NO.
POST OFFICE: Silo, I.T. FIELD NO. 6045

Dawes' Roll No.	NAME	Relationship to Person First Named	AGE	SEX	BLOOD	TRIBAL ENROLLMENT Year	County	No.
DP 10/18/06	1 Beal, Joseph	Named	4	M	White			

DECISION RENDERED NOV -6 1906
REFUSED
COPY OF DECISION FORWARDED ATTORNEYS FOR CHOCTAW AND CHICKASAW NATIONS NOV -6 1906
COPY OF DECISION FORWARDED ATTORNEY FOR APPLICANT. NOV -6 1906
COPY OF DECISION FORWARDED APPLICANT NOV -6 1906
RECORD FORWARDED DEPARTMENT. NOV -6 1906

TRIBAL ENROLLMENT OF PARENTS

NOV -6 1906

Name of Father	Year	County	Name of Mother	Year	County
1 Andrew Beal	I.W		Bell Beal		Non-citizen

No.1 born July 26, 1898, Birth affidavit filed Dec. 13, 1899
No.1 son of Andrew Beal on 7-3497

ACTION APPROVED BY SECRETARY OF INTERIOR. FEB 27 1907
NOTICE OF DEPARTMENTAL ACTION FORWARDED ATTORNEYS FOR CHOCTAW AND CHICKASAW NATIONS. MAR 13 1907
NOTICE OF DEPARTMENTAL ACTION FORWARDED ATTORNEY FOR APPLICANT MAR 13 1907
NOTICE OF DEPARTMENTAL ACTION MAILED APPLICANT. MAR 13 1907

Oct 18, 1906

RESIDENCE: Choctaw Nation COUNTY. **Choctaw Nation** **Choctaw Roll** *(Not Including Freedmen)* CARD NO.
POST OFFICE: Spiro, I.T. FIELD NO. 6046

Dawes' Roll No.	NAME	Relationship to Person First Named	AGE	SEX	BLOOD	TRIBAL ENROLLMENT Year	County	No.
DP 1/7/1906	1 Avery, Charles M		62	M	I.W.			
	2							
	3							
	4							
	5							
	6 ACTION APPROVED BY							
	7 SECRETARY OF INTERIOR	FEB 28 1907						
	8							
	9 NOTICE OF DEPARTMENTAL ACTION							
	10 FORWARDED ATTORNEYS FOR CHOCTAW AND CHICKASAW NATIONS.		APR 16 1907					
	11 NOTICE OF DEPARTMENTAL ACTION							
	12 FORWARDED ATTORNEY FOR APPLICANT		APR 16 1907					
	13							
	14 NOTICE OF DEPARTMENTAL ACTION MAILED APPLICANT.		APR 16 1907					
	15							
	16							
	17							

TRIBAL ENROLLMENT OF PARENTS

	Name of Father	Year	County	Name of Mother	Year	County
1						
2						
3						
4						
5						
6	No.1 placed hereon under order of the Commissioner to Five Civilized Tribes					
7	of Oct 19-1906 holding that application was made for his enrollment within the time					
8	provided by the act of Congress approved April 26-1906 (34 Stats. 137)					
9						
10						
11						
12						
13						
14						
15	REFUSED		JAN 16 1907			
16						
17	RECORD FORWARDED DEPARTMENT.			JAN 16 1907		

RESIDENCE: Choctaw Nation COUNTY. **Choctaw Nation** Choctaw Roll (Not Including Freedmen) CARD NO.
POST OFFICE: Sutter I.T. FIELD NO. 6047

Dawes' Roll No.	NAME	Relationship to Person First Named	AGE	SEX	BLOOD	TRIBAL ENROLLMENT Year	County	No.
IW 1633	1 Livingston, Mollie		35	F	I.W.			

GRANTED JAN 18 1907

ENROLLMENT OF NOS. 1 HEREON APPROVED BY THE SECRETARY OF INTERIOR FEB 19 1907

TRIBAL ENROLLMENT OF PARENTS

Name of Father	Year	County	Name of Mother	Year	County
1 Jim Sheppard	Dead	Noncitizen	Lithie Sheppard	Dead	Noncitizen

No.1 placed hereon under order of the Commissioner to Five Civilized Tribes of Oct. 19-1906 holding that application was made for her enrollment was made within the time provided by the act of Congress approved April 26-1906 S(34 Stats - 137)

No1 formerly wife of Robert Kincade, enrolled citizen by blood on 7-2697, opposite #7866

RESIDENCE: Blue COUNTY. **Choctaw Nation** Choctaw Roll (Not Including Freedmen) CARD NO.
POST OFFICE: Nail I.T. FIELD NO. 6048

Dawes' Roll No.	NAME	Relationship to Person First Named	AGE	SEX	BLOOD	TRIBAL ENROLLMENT Year	County	No.
iw1617	1 M^c^Lellan, Belle	First Named	21	F	I.W.			
	2							
	3							
	4							
	5							
	6							
	7							
	8							
	9							
	10							
	11							
	12							
	13							
	14							
	15							
	16							
	17							

ENROLLMENT
OF NOS. 1 HEREON
APPROVED BY THE SECRETARY
OF INTERIOR FEB 12 1907

TRIBAL ENROLLMENT OF PARENTS

	Name of Father	Year	County	Name of Mother	Year	County
1						
2						
3						
4						
5						

6 No.1 placed hereon under order of the Commissioner to Five Civilized Tribes of Nov. 6-1906
7 holding that application was made for her enrollment within the time provided by the act of Congress approved April 26-1906
8 ~~No.1 is wife of No.3 on card #3919, Roll 15312 Edmund M^c^Lellan~~
9 For child of No.1 see NB (March 3, 1905) card #571

16 on this card Nov. 6-1906

RESIDENCE: Chickasaw Nation COUNTY. **Choctaw Nation** **Choctaw Roll** *(Not Including Freedmen)* CARD NO.
POST OFFICE: Cornish I.T. FIELD NO. 6049

Dawes' Roll No.	NAME	Relationship to Person First Named	AGE	SEX	BLOOD	TRIBAL ENROLLMENT Year	County	No.
IW 1618	1 Folsom, Lee		20	F	I.W.			
	2							
	3							
	4							
	5							
	6							
	7							
	8							
	9							
	10							
	11							
	12							
	13							
	14							
	15							
	16							
	17							

ENROLLMENT OF NOS. 1 HEREON APPROVED BY THE SECRETARY OF INTERIOR FEB 12 1907

TRIBAL ENROLLMENT OF PARENTS

Name of Father	Year	County	Name of Mother	Year	County
1 John Thatcher		Non Citz	Martha Thatcher	Dead	Non Citz

No.1 placed hereon under order of the Commissioner to Five Civilized Tribes of Nov. 6-1906 holding that application was made for her enrollment within the time provided by the act of Congress approved April 26-1906

No 1 is the wife of William W. Folsom, No 6 on Card No. 4555 Roll 12619
For children of No1 see NB (March 3, 1905) #1258

Date of Application for Enrollment.
12-3-02

~~on this card Nov 16/06~~

RESIDENCE: COUNTY. **Choctaw Nation** Choctaw Roll (Not Including Freedmen) CARD NO.
POST OFFICE: Muskogee IT FIELD NO. 6050

Dawes' Roll No.	NAME	Relationship to Person First Named	AGE	SEX	BLOOD	TRIBAL ENROLLMENT Year	County	No.
	1 Hadnot, Lucretia	Named	45	F				
	2 " Sebrun	Son	12	M				
DP	3 " Artemis	Dau	9	F				
	4 " Freddie	Son	8	M				
	5 " Bessie	Dau	6	F				
	6							
	7							
	8							
	9							
	10							
	11							
	12							
	13							
	14							
	15							
	16							
	17							

REFUSED FEB 15 1907

RECORD FORWARDED DEPARTMENT. FEB 15 1907

TRIBAL ENROLLMENT OF PARENTS

	Name of Father	Year	County	Name of Mother	Year	County
1	John Smith			Mary Smith		
2	Green Hadnot			No.1		
3	" "			"		
4	" "			"		
5	" "			"		

Nos.1-2-3-4 & 5 placed hereon under order of the Commissioner to Five Civilized Tribes of December 31-1906 holding that application was made for their enrollment within the time provided by the act of Congress approved April 26-1906

ACTION APPROVED BY SECRETARY OF INTERIOR. MAR 2- 1907

NOTICE OF DEPARTMENTAL ACTION FORWARDED ATTORNEYS FOR CHOCTAW AND CHICKASAW NATIONS. APR 11 1907

12/31/06

NOTICE OF DEPARTMENTAL ACTION FORWARDED ATTORNEY FOR APPLICANT. APR 11 1907

NOTICE OF DEPARTMENTAL ACTION MAILED APPLICANT APR 11 1907

RESIDENCE: Arkansas COUNTY. **Choctaw Nation** Choctaw Roll (Not Including Freedmen) CARD NO.
POST OFFICE: Fort Smith, Ark FIELD NO. 60[illegible]

Dawes' Roll No.	NAME	Relationship to Person First Named	AGE	SEX	BLOOD	TRIBAL ENROLLMENT Year	County	No.
DP	Simpson. Katie	Named	36	F				

ACTION APPROVED BY SECRETARY OF INTERIOR.

NOTICE OF DEPARTMENTAL ACTION FORWARDED ATTORNEYS FOR CHOCTAW AND CHICKASAW NATIONS. APR 11 1907

NOTICE OF DEPARTMENTAL ACTION FORWARDED ATTORNEY FOR APPLICANT. APR 11 1907

NOTICE OF DEPARTMENTAL ACTION MAILED APPLICANT. APR 11 1907

TRIBAL ENROLLMENT OF PARENTS

Name of Father	Year	County	Name of Mother	Year	County
Jimson Jones					

No.1 placed hereon under order of the Commissioner to Five Civilized Tribes of Jan 2-1907 holding that application was made for her enrollment within the time provided by the act of Congress approved April 26=1906

For children of No1 see NB (Apr 26 '06) Card #1022

REFUSED FEB 16 1907

RECORD FORWARDED DEPARTMENT. FEB 16 1907

Jan 2-07

RESIDENCE: Chickasaw Nation COUNTY. **Choctaw Nation** **Choctaw Roll** *(Not Including Freedmen)* CARD NO.
POST OFFICE: Cliff, I.T. FIELD NO. 6052

Dawes' Roll No.	NAME	Relationship to Person First Named	AGE	SEX	BLOOD	TRIBAL ENROLLMENT Year	County	No.
IW 1619	1 McGahey, Annie		22	F	I.W.			
	2							
	3							
	4							
	5							
	6							
	7							
	8							
	9							
	10							
	11							
	12							
	13							
	14							
	15							
	16							
	17							

ENROLLMENT
OF NOS. 1 HEREON
APPROVED BY THE SECRETARY
OF INTERIOR Feb 12 1907

TRIBAL ENROLLMENT OF PARENTS

Name of Father	Year	County	Name of Mother	Year	County
1 Henry Lawless		Non Citz	Nancy Lawless		Non Citz
2					
3					
4					

~~No.1 placed hereon under order of the Commissioner to Five Civilized Tribes of~~
Dec 17-1906 holding application was made for her enrollment within the time provided by the act of Congress approved April 26-'06

~~No.1 is wife of No.2 on Choctaw Card No. 4403 Roll 12276~~
Arthur D. McGahey
No.1 also on Intermarried Choctaw Roll opposite No. 1661. Notation has been placed opposite that number showing duplicate enrollment.

~~on this card~~
Dec. 17-06
age as of this year

RESIDENCE: Choctaw Nation COUNTY. **Choctaw Nation** **Choctaw Roll** (*Not Including Freedmen*) CARD NO.
POST OFFICE: Coalgate, I.T. FIELD NO. 6053

Dawes' Roll No.		NAME	Relationship to Person First Named	AGE	SEX	BLOOD	TRIBAL ENROLLMENT Year	County	No.
IW 1634	1	Swadley, William T	First Named	57	M	I.W.			
16113	2	" Minerva F	Wife	53	F	1/2	1893	Atoka	947
	3	" John W.W.	Son	32	M	1/4			

ENROLLMENT
OF NOS. 2 HEREON
APPROVED BY THE SECRETARY
OF INTERIOR Mar 4, 1907

Feb. 28, 1907 Recommended to Dept that decision of
Dec. 15, 1906 refusing No.3 he affirmed.
Mch 2-07 Dept affirmed this decision
~~May 28-07 motion for rehearing forwd Dept June 17-07 motion denied by Dept.~~
~~July 13-07 notices sent parties~~

ENROLLMENT
OF NOS. 1 HEREON
APPROVED BY THE SECRETARY
OF INTERIOR Feb. 19, 1907

TRIBAL ENROLLMENT OF PARENTS

	Name of Father	Year	County	Name of Mother	Year	County
1	John Swadley	dead	Non citz	Elizabeth Swadley	dead	Non Citz
2	William Hunter	dead		Margaret Ann Morris	dead	
3	No.1			No.2		

Nos. 1&2 placed hereon under order of the Commissioner to the Five Civilized Tribes of Dec 15-1906 holding that application was made for their enrollment within the time provided by the act of Congress approved April 26-1906

~~No.3 enrolled under Departmental instructions of February 18-1907~~

No.1 restored to roll by Departmental authority of August 9, 1909 (File 5-51)

~~Enrollment of Number 1 cancelled by order of Department of March 2, 1907~~

Dec. 15-1906
on this card

RESIDENCE: Chickasaw Nation COUNTY. **Choctaw Nation** **Choctaw Roll** *(Not Including Freedmen)* CARD NO.
POST OFFICE: Hickory, I.T. FIELD NO. 6054

Dawes' Roll No.	NAME	Relationship to Person First Named	AGE	SEX	BLOOD	TRIBAL ENROLLMENT Year	County	No.
IW 1635	1 Cobb, Agnes		27	F	I.W.			
	2							
	3							
	4							
	5							
	6							
	7							
	8							
	9							
	10							
	11							
	12							
	13							
	14							
	15							
	16							
	17							

ENROLLMENT OF NOS. 1 HEREON APPROVED BY THE SECRETARY OF INTERIOR FEB 19 1907

GRANTED JAN 3 1907

TRIBAL ENROLLMENT OF PARENTS

Name of Father	Year	County	Name of Mother	Year	County
1 John Clary	dead	Non Citz	Lucy Clary		Non Citz
2					
3					
4					
5					

No.1 placed hereon under order of the Commissioner to the Five Civilized Tribes of Jan 3-1907 holding that application was made for his enrollment within the time provided by the act of Congress approved April 26-1906

~~No.1 formerly the wife of Andrew V. Roff No.1 on Choctaw Card No. 39, Roll No. 70~~

on this card 1/3/07

age as of this date

RESIDENCE: COUNTY. **Choctaw Nation** Choctaw Roll (Not Including Freedmen) CARD NO.
POST OFFICE: Keota, I.T. FIELD NO. 6055

Dawes' Roll No.	NAME	Relationship to Person First Named	AGE	SEX	BLOOD	TRIBAL ENROLLMENT Year	County	No.
IW 1621	1 Newman, Julia A		27	F	I.W.			
	2							
	3							
	4							
	5							
	6							
	7							
	8							
	9							
	10							
	11							
	12							
	13							
	14							
	15							
	16							
	17							

ENROLLMENT
OF NOS. 1 HEREON
APPROVED BY THE SECRETARY
OF INTERIOR FEB 12 1907

TRIBAL ENROLLMENT OF PARENTS

Name of Father	Year	County	Name of Mother	Year	County
1 George W. Ballard		Non Citz	E. J. Ballard		Non Citz
2					
3					
4					
5					

No.1 placed hereon under order of the Commissioner to the Five Civilized Tribes of Dec 17-1906 holding that application was made for her enrollment within the time provided by the act of Congress approved April 26-1906

~~No.1 formerly the wife of Cornelius Brandy No1 on Choctaw Card #2424 Roll No 7007~~

on this card
~~12/17/06~~
age as of this ~~date~~

RESIDENCE: Chickasaw Nation ~~COUNTY~~.
POST OFFICE: Marlow, I.T.

Choctaw Nation

Choctaw Roll
(Not Including Freedmen)

CARD NO.
FIELD NO. 6056

Dawes' Roll No.	NAME	Relationship to Person First Named	AGE	SEX	BLOOD	TRIBAL ENROLLMENT Year	County	No.
16066	1 O'Quinn, John T	First Named	30	M	1/16	1896	Chick Dist	10029
IW 1623	2 " Fannie May	Wife	24	F	I.W.			
16067	3 " Ollie Odolphus	Son	6	M	1/32			
	4							
	5							
	6							
	7							
	8							
	9							
	10							
	11							
	12							
	13							
	14							
	15							
	16							
	17							

ENROLLMENT
OF NOS. 1, 2 and 3 HEREON
APPROVED BY THE SECRETARY
OF INTERIOR Mar 4-1907

TRIBAL ENROLLMENT OF PARENTS

Name of Father	Year	County	Name of Mother	Year	County
1 Thomas J O'Quinn			Mary E O'Quinn		
2 Calhoun			Calhoun		
3 No.1			No.2		
4					
5					

Decision of Commissioner to Five Civilized Tribes of January 10, 1907 reversed by Secretary of the Interior in accordance with opinion of Attorney General of U.S. of February 19, 1907 and enrollment of Nos. 1, 2 and 3 denied by Department.
~~No.1 on 1896 Choctaw Census Roll roll as T.E. O'Quinn page 254~~
Nos. 1, 2 and 3 transferred from Choctaw card #R-217 Jan 26, 1907. See decision of Jan. 10, 1907.
For children of Nos. 1 and 2 N.B. 972 (Apr. 26, 1906)
~~March 1, 1909 Department requests report~~
April 22, 1909. Report to Department
June 2, 1909 Department holds case is not analogous to Goldsby case and declines to take action looking to enrollment of these applicants.
~~June 16, 1909. Parties notified.~~

Date of Application for Enrollment: June 21/1900

Date of transfer ~~to this card~~: Jan. 26, 1907

RESIDENCE: Chickasaw Nation ~~COUNTY.~~ **Choctaw Nation** **Choctaw Roll** *(Not Including Freedmen)* CARD NO.
POST OFFICE: Marlow, Ind. Ter. FIELD NO. 6057

Dawes' Roll No.	NAME	Relationship to Person First Named	AGE	SEX	BLOOD	TRIBAL ENROLLMENT Year	County	No.
16068	1 Leddy, Minnie L.		25	F	1/16	1896	Chick. Dist.	8416
	2							
	3							
	4							
	5							
	6							
	7							
	8							
	9							
	10							
	11							
	12							
	13							
	14							
	15							
	16							
	17							

ENROLLMENT
OF NOS. 1 HEREON
APPROVED BY THE SECRETARY
OF INTERIOR MAR 4 - 1907

TRIBAL ENROLLMENT OF PARENTS

Name of Father	Year	County	Name of Mother	Year	County
1 Thomas J O'Quinn			Mary E O'Quinn		
2					
3					
4					
5					

6 No.1 on 1896 roll as Winnie Liddy, page 209
7 No.1 transferred from Choctaw card #R-217 Jan 26, 1907 See decision of Jan 10, 1907

Date of Application for Enrollment. June 21/1900

Date of transfer to this card Jan. 26, 1907

RESIDENCE: Chickasaw Nation ~~COUNTY.~~
POST OFFICE: Marlow, Ind. Ter.

Choctaw Nation

Choctaw Roll (*Not Including Freedmen*)

CARD NO.
FIELD NO. 6058

Dawes' Roll No.	NAME	Relationship to Person First Named	AGE	SEX	BLOOD	TRIBAL ENROLLMENT Year	County	No.
16069	1 Thompson, John T	First Named	38	M	1/16	1896	Chick. Dist	12529
IW 1624	2 " Katie	Wife	30	F	I.W.	1896	" "	15126
16070	3 " Mary Frances	Dau	14	"	1/32	1896	" "	12530
16071	4 " Charles Stanley	Son	13	M	1/32	1896	" "	12532
16072	5 " William Brown	"	10	"	1/32	1896	" "	12531
16073	6 " John Moody	"	8	"	1/32	1896	" "	12533
	7							
	8							
	9							
	10							
	11							
	12							
	13							
	14							
	15							
	16							
	17							

ENROLLMENT
OF NOS. 1,2,3,4,5and6 HEREON
APPROVED BY THE SECRETARY
OF INTERIOR MAR 4- 1907

TRIBAL ENROLLMENT OF PARENTS

Name of Father	Year	County	Name of Mother	Year	County
1 John T. Thompson (Sr)			Mary Jane Thompson		
2 Charlie Calhoun			Frances Calhoun		
3 No.1			No.2		
4 No.1			No.2		
5 No.1			No.2		
6 No.1			No.2		
7					

8 No.1 on 1896 roll as Jno. T. Thompson, page 327
9 No.2 " " " " Kate Thompson, " 401
~~No.3 " " " " Mary F Thompson~~
10 ~~No.4 " " " " Charles Thompson " 327~~
11 No.5 " " " " William Thompson " 327
12 No.6 " " " " Jno M. Thompson " 327
Nos. 1 to 6 incl. transferred from Choctaw card #R-685 Jan 26-07 See decision of Jan.10,1907
13 ~~March 1, 1909 Department requests report~~
14 April 22, 1909 Report to Department
15 June 2, 1909 Department holds case is not analogous to Goldsby case and declines to take
action looking to enrollment of these applicants.
16 ~~June 11, 1909 Parties notified.~~

17 Date of Application for Enrollment. 6/2/1900

Date of transfer to this card Jan. 26-07

RESIDENCE: COUNTY. **Choctaw Nation** **Choctaw Roll** *(Not Including Freedmen)* CARD NO.

POST OFFICE: Lewis, Ind. Ter. FIELD NO. 6059

Dawes' Roll No.	NAME	Relationship to Person First Named	AGE	SEX	BLOOD	TRIBAL ENROLLMENT Year	County	No.
74	Darken, John Henry	First Named	14	M	1/32	1896	Atoka	3626
75	" Charles B, Jr.	Bro	11	"	1/32	1896	"	3627
16076	Welch, Benjamin Oliver	Half Bro	23	"	1/32	1896	"	14020
16077	" Walter	" "	20	"	1/32	1896	"	14021
16078	Lawley, Maultsy J	" Sis	22	F	1/32	1896	"	8348
16079	" Willie May	Dau of No.5	4	"	1/64			

ENROLLMENT OF NOS. 1,2,3,4,5 and 6 HEREON APPROVED BY THE SECRETARY OF INTERIOR MAR 4- 1907

TRIBAL ENROLLMENT OF PARENTS

Name of Father	Year	County	Name of Mother	Year	County
Charles B. Darken			Sarah Jane Darken		
" " "			" " "		
Frank Welch			" " "		
" "			" " "		
" "			" " "		
			No.5		

No.1 on 1896 roll as Jno. Henry Darken
No.2 " 1896 " " Chas. B. "
~~No.3 " 1896 " " Benj. Welch~~
" 5 " 1896 " " Maulsey Lawley page 208
Nos. 1 to 6 incl. transferred from Choctaw card #R-73 Jan. 26, 1907. See decision of Jan. 10,1907.

Date of Application for Enrollment.

Date of transfer to this card Jan 26, 1907

RESIDENCE: Chickasaw Nation COUNTY. **Choctaw Nation** **Choctaw Roll** (Not Including Freedmen) CARD NO.
POST OFFICE: Ardmore I.T. FIELD NO. 6060

Dawes' Roll No.	NAME	Relationship to Person First Named	AGE	SEX	BLOOD	TRIBAL ENROLLMENT Year	County	No.
IW 1622	1 Boydstun, Hattie	Named	26	F	I.W.			
	2							
	3							
	4							
	5							
	6							
	7							
	8							
	9							
	10							
	11							
	12							
	13							
	14							
	15							
	16							
	17							

ENROLLMENT
OF NOS. 1 HEREON
APPROVED BY THE SECRETARY
OF INTERIOR FEB 12 1907

TRIBAL ENROLLMENT OF PARENTS

Name of Father	Year	County	Name of Mother	Year	County
1 W. N. Blackwell	dead	Non Citz	Mollie Black[sic]		

No.1 placed hereon under order of the Commissioner to the Five Civilized Tribes of Nov 16-1906 holding that application was made for her enrollment within the time provided by the act of Congress approved April 26-1906

No.1 is the wife of John F. Boydstun No.1 on Choctaw Card No. 3698
Roll No 10463

~~on this card~~
Nov 16/1906
~~age as of~~
this year

RESIDENCE: COUNTY. **Choctaw Nation** **Choctaw Roll** (*Not Including Freedmen*) CARD NO.

POST OFFICE: Porum, Ind. Ter. FIELD NO. 6061

Dawes' Roll No.	NAME	Relationship to Person First Named	AGE	SEX	BLOOD	TRIBAL ENROLLMENT Year	County	No.
16080	1 Harton, Mattie		38	F	1/16	1896	Atoka	5993
16081	2 " John	Son	20	M	1/32	1896	"	5995
16082	3 " James	"	17	"	1/32	1896	"	5996
16083	4 " Rachel	Dau	15	F	1/32	1896	"	5994
16084	5 " Mary M	"	6	"	1/32	1896	"	5997
16085	6 " Nancy Ella	"	3	"	1/32			

Decision of Commissioner to Five Civilized Tribes of January 10, 1907 reversed by Secretary of the Interior in accordance with opinion of Attorney General of U.S. of February 19, 1907 and enrollment of Nos. 1 to 6 denied by department.

ENROLLMENT OF NOS. 1,2,3,4,5 and 6 HEREON APPROVED BY THE SECRETARY OF INTERIOR Mar 4 1907

TRIBAL ENROLLMENT OF PARENTS

Name of Father	Year	County	Name of Mother	Year	County
1 John D. Thompson			Narcissa Susan Thompson		
2 Franklin M. Harton			No.1		
3 " " "			No.1		
4 " " "			No.1		
5 " " "			No.1		
6 " " "			No.1		

No 4 on 1896 roll as Rachel S. Horton[sic]
No.2 " 1896 " " Johnie "
No.3 " 1896 " " Jimmie "
No.1 " 1896 " " Mattie "
No.5 " 1896 " " Mary M "
Nos.1to6 incl. transferred from Choctaw card #R475 Jan 26, 1907. See decision of Jan 10-1907
For child of No1 see N.B. 976 (Apr 26, 06)
" " " " 2 " N.B. 974 (Apr 26-06)
" " " " 4 " N.B. 975 (Apr 26-06)

Date of Application for Enrollment. 1899

Jan. 26, 1907
Date of transfer to this card

RESIDENCE: Chickasaw Nation ~~COUNTY~~.
POST OFFICE: Rush Springs, Ind. Ter.

Choctaw Nation

Choctaw Roll *(Not Including Freedmen)*

CARD NO.
FIELD NO. **6062**

Dawes' Roll No.	NAME	Relationship to Person First Named	AGE	SEX	BLOOD	TRIBAL ENROLLMENT Year	County	No.
16086	Percival, Jesse	First Named	17	M	1/32	1896	Atoka	10555
16087	" Taylor	Bro	13	"	1/32	1896	"	10556
16088	" Forrest	"	11	"	1/32	1896	"	10557
16089	" Katie	Sister	9	F	1/32	1896	"	10558
16090	" Rebecca	"	6	"	1/32	1896	"	10559
16091	" Narcissa Sadie	"	3	"	1/32			

Decision of Commissioner to Five Civilized Tribes of January 10, 1907 reversed by Secretary of the Interior in accordance with opinion of Attorney General of U.S. of ~~February 19, 1907 and enrollment of Nos. 1 to 6 inclusive denied by department.~~

ENROLLMENT
OF NOS. 1,2,3,4,5 and 6 HEREON
~~APPROVED BY THE SECRETARY~~
OF INTERIOR Mar 4 - 1907

TRIBAL ENROLLMENT OF PARENTS

Name of Father	Year	County	Name of Mother	Year	County
William E. Percival			Narcissa Ella Percival		
" " "			" " "		
" " "			" " "		
" " "			" " "		
" " "			" " "		
" " "			" " "		

~~No.1 on 1896 roll as Jesse Percivill~~[sic]
No.2 " 1896 " " Taylor "
No.3 " 1896 " " Forest "
~~No.4 " 1896 " " Katie "~~
~~No.5 " 1896 " " Rebecca "~~
Nos. 1to6 incl. transferred from Choctaw card #R-225 Jan 26, 1907 See decision of Jan. 10, 1907
~~March 1, 1909 Department requests report.~~
~~April 22, 1909 Report to department~~
June 2, 1909 Department holds case is not analogous to Goldsby case and declines to take action looking to enrollment of these applicants
~~June 16. 1909 Parties notified.~~

~~Date of transfer to this card~~
Jan 26, 1907

RESIDENCE: COUNTY. **Choctaw Nation** Choctaw Roll (Not Including Freedmen) CARD NO.
POST OFFICE: Ninnekah FIELD NO. 6063

Dawes' Roll No.		NAME	Relationship to Person First Named	AGE	SEX	BLOOD	TRIBAL ENROLLMENT Year	County	No.
16092	1	Vaughan, Nannie	First Named	25	F	1/16	1896	Atoka	12631
16093	2	" Hattie	Dau	9	"	1/32	1896	"	12632
16094	3	" Callie	"	7	"	1/32	1896	"	12633
16095	4	" Stella	"	5	"	1/32	1896	"	12634
16096	5	" Roy	Son	4	M	1/32			

~~Decision of Commissioner to Five Civilized Tribes of January 10, 1907 reversed by~~ Secretary of the Interior in accordance with opinion of Attorney General of U.S. of February 19, 1907 and enrollment of Nos. 1to5 inclusive denied by Department.

ENROLLMENT OF NOS. 1,2,3,4 and 5 HEREON APPROVED BY THE SECRETARY OF INTERIOR Mar 4 1907

TRIBAL ENROLLMENT OF PARENTS

	Name of Father	Year	County	Name of Mother	Year	County
1	John Duncan Thompson			Narcissa L. Aaron		
2	Jim Vaughan			No.1		
3	" "			No.1		
4	" "			No.1		
5	" "			No.1		

Surname on 1896 roll as Vaughn
For child of No.1 see N.B. 971 (Apr 26-06)
~~Nos. 1 to 5 incl. transferred from Choctaw Card #R.725 Jan 26, 1907 See decision of Jan. 10, 1907~~
March 1, 1909 Department requests report hereon
April 22, 1909 Report to Department
~~June 2, 1909 Department holds case is not analogous to Goldsby case and declines to take action looking to enrollment of applicants~~
June 16, 1909 Parties notified.

Date of Application for Enrollment. 1899

Jan 26, 1907
Date of transfer to this card

RESIDENCE: Chickasaw Nation COUNTY. **Choctaw Nation** **Choctaw Roll** (Not Including Freedmen) CARD NO.
POST OFFICE: Marlow, Ind. Ter. FIELD NO. 6064

Dawes' Roll No.	NAME	Relationship to Person First Named	AGE	SEX	BLOOD	TRIBAL ENROLLMENT Year	County	No.
16067	1 McCoy, William H	First Named	54	M	1/8	1896	Chick. Dist	9507
IW 1625	2 " Mary G	Wife	47	F	I.W.	1896	" "	14892
16098	3 " Buford T	Son	26	M	1/16	1896	" "	9508
16099	4 Reville, Maud	Dau	21	F	1/16	1896	" "	9509
16100	5 Woolley, Cordie	"	19	"	1/16	1896	" "	9510
16101	6 McCoy, William	Son	11	M	1/16	1896	" "	9511
	7 ~~" Geneva~~	~~Wife of No.3~~	~~25~~	~~F~~	~~I.W.~~			

Decision of Commissioner to Five Civilized Tribes of [illegible...] Feb. 19, 1907 and enrollment [illegible] denied by Department.

ENROLLMENT OF NOS 1,2,3,4,5and6 HEREON APPROVED BY THE SECRETARY OF INTERIOR MAR 4- 1907

DECISION RENDERED Rescinding action of Jan. 26, 1907 FEB 27 1907

TRIBAL ENROLLMENT OF PARENTS

Name of Father	Year	County	Name of Mother	Year	County
1 John McCoy			Matilda McCoy		
2 No.1			No.2		
3 No.1			No.2		
4 No.1			No.2		
5 No.1			No.2		
6 No.1			No.2		
7 ~~Monroe Woolley~~	~~dead~~		~~Caroline Woolley~~		

For children of No.3 see N.B. 977 (Act Apr. 26-06)
" " " No.4 " " 978 " " " "
~~" " " No.5 " " 979 " " " "~~
~~Nos. 1to6 incl. transferred from Choctaw card #R-205 Jan 26-07 See decision of Jan 10-07~~
No.1 on 1896 roll as Wm. H. McCoy
No.5 " 1896 " " Cordia "
~~No.6 " 1896 " " Wm "~~
~~No.7 transferred from Choctaw card R. 205 See decision of Jan. 30, 1907~~

ACTION APPROVED BY SECRETARY OF INTERIOR. MAR 4 1907

NOTICE OF DEPARTMENTAL ACTION MAILED PARTIES HEREIN APR 23 1907

Jan. 26, 1907
~~Date of transfer~~ to this card

Choctaw By Blood Enrollment Cards 1898-1914

RESIDENCE: COUNTY. **Choctaw Nation** **Choctaw Roll** *(Not Including Freedmen)* CARD NO.
POST OFFICE: FIELD NO. 6065

Dawes' Roll No.	NAME	Relationship to Person First Named	AGE	SEX	BLOOD	TRIBAL ENROLLMENT Year	County	No.
IW 1636	1 McBride, Emmette C		38	M	I.W.			
	2							
	3							
	4							
	5							
	6							
	7							
	8							
	9							
	10							
	11							
	12							
	13							
	14							
	15							
	16							
	17		Calloway, Okla					

ENROLLMENT OF NOS. I HEREON APPROVED BY THE SECRETARY OF INTERIOR FEB 19 1907

TRIBAL ENROLLMENT OF PARENTS

Name of Father	Year	County	Name of Mother	Year	County
1 W. D. McBride		noncitizen	M. M. McBride		noncitizen
2					
3					
4					
5					

6 ~~No.1 transferred from Choctaw card D #634 See decision of January 12, 1907~~

7

8 No.1 is husband of Winnie McBride, Choctaw roll card #4298 Roll #12013

~~For child of No.1 see NB (March 3, 195=05) #764~~

June 17/01 Date of Application for Enrollment.

Date of tran[sfer] to this car[d] JAN 28 19[...]

RESIDENCE: Choctaw Nation ~~COUNTY.~~
POST OFFICE: Goodland, Ind. Ter.

Choctaw Nation

Choctaw Roll *(Not Including Freedmen)*

CARD NO.
FIELD NO. 6066

Dawes' Roll No.		NAME	Relationship to Person First Named	AGE	SEX	BLOOD	TRIBAL ENROLLMENT Year	County	No.
9	1	Earnest, George	First Named	15	M	1/64	1896	Towson	9665
0	2	" Willie	Sister	13	F	1/64	1896	"	9666
	3								
	4								
	5								
	6								
	7								
	8								
	9								
	10								
	11								
	12								
	13								
	14								
	15								
	16								
	17								

ENROLLMENT
OF NOS. 1 and 2 HEREON
APPROVED BY THE SECRETARY
OF INTERIOR FEB 21 1907

TRIBAL ENROLLMENT OF PARENTS

	Name of Father	Year	County	Name of Mother	Year	County
1				Onie Norris		Choctaw
2				" "		"
3						
4						
5						

6 Nos.1 and 2 transferred from Choctaw card #D-588. See decision of Jan. 17, 1907.

Date of Application for Enrollment. Oct 29/1900

Date of Transfer to this Card. JAN 17 1907

RESIDENCE: COUNTY. **Choctaw Nation** **Choctaw Roll** *(Not Including Freedmen)* CARD NO.
POST OFFICE: Lebanon, Ind. Ter. FIELD NO. 6067

Dawes' Roll No.	NAME	Relationship to Person First Named	AGE	SEX	BLOOD	TRIBAL ENROLLMENT Year	County	No.
IW1656	1 Goldston, James William	Named	28	M	I.W			
	2							
	3							
	4							
	5							
	6							
	7							
	8							
	9							
	10							
	11							
	12							
	13							
	14							
	15							
	16							
	17							

ENROLLMENT
OF NOS. 1 HEREON
APPROVED BY THE SECRETARY
OF INTERIOR MAR 2 - 1907

TRIBAL ENROLLMENT OF PARENTS

	Name of Father	Year	County	Name of Mother	Year	County
1	Charles Goldston			Amanda Goldston		
2						
3						
4						
5						

Wife of No.1 is on Choctaw card #339 - No.3 final roll #684. Estella Goldston
No.1 transferred from Choctaw card #D-781. See decision of Jan. 30, 1907
For child of No.1 see NB (March 3, 1905) #1307

Date of Application for Enrollment. Sept 3/02

Date of transfer to this card Jan. 31, 1907

RESIDENCE: Chickasaw Nation COUNTY. **Choctaw Nation** **Choctaw Roll** *(Not Including Freedmen)* CARD NO.
POST OFFICE: Comanche, IT FIELD NO. 6068

Dawes' Roll No.		NAME	Relationship to Person First Named	AGE	SEX	BLOOD	TRIBAL ENROLLMENT Year	County	No.
[illegible]81	1	Reed, Amanda L.	First Named	25	F	1/32	1896	Blue	4920
[illegible]82	2	" Archie	Dau	4	M				
[illegible]83	3	" Glenn	Son	1	M				
	4								
	5								
	6								
	7								
	8								
	9								
	10	ENROLLMENT							
	11	OF NOS. 1, 2 & 3 HEREON							
	12	APPROVED BY THE SECRETARY							
	13	OF INTERIOR MAR 1 1907							
	14								
	15								
	16	See 23-891							
	17	See Petition #C-52 also W [illegible]							

TRIBAL ENROLLMENT OF PARENTS

	Name of Father	Year	County	Name of Mother	Year	County
1	John H. Gamblin		Non Citz	Liza Gamblin		Non Citz
2	Arch Reed		" "	No.1		
3	A. J. Reed		" "	No.1		
4						
5	Nos 1-2 & 3 transferred from Choctaw Card No. 5059 February					
6	14-1907 - See decision of same date.					
7						
8	[Entries illegible...]					
9						
10						
11						
12						
13	NOTICE OF DEPARTMENTAL ACTION					
14	MAILED PARTIES HEREIN. APR 15 1907					
15						
16				Date of Application for Enrollment. 9/22/98		FEB 14 1907
17						

RESIDENCE: Chickasaw Nation COUNTY. **Choctaw Nation** **Choctaw Roll** *(Not Including Freedmen)* CARD NO.
POST OFFICE: Comanche, I.T. FIELD NO. 6069

Dawes' Roll No.		NAME	Relationship to Person First Named	AGE	SEX	BLOOD	TRIBAL ENROLLMENT Year	County	No.
16184	1	Scott, Louie F	First Named	28	F	1/16	1896	Atoka	11693
16185	2	" Hattie M	Dau	11	"	1/32	1896	"	11694
16186	3	" Minnie R	"	8	"	1/32	1896	"	11696
16187	4	" Archie M	Son	6	M	1/32	1896	"	11695
16188	5	" Glennis	Dau	5	F	1/32			
16189	6	" Joseph A	Son	2	M	1/32			
16190	7	" James T	"	1	M	1/32			
	8								
	9								
	10	ENROLLMENT							
	11	OF NOS 1,2,3,4,5,6&7 HEREON							
	12	APPROVED BY THE SECRETARY							
	13	OF INTERIOR MAR 1 1907							
	14								
	15	March 1, 1909 Department requests report hereon							
	16	~~April 29, 1909 Report to Department~~ *							
	17	See Petition #C-52 and for record see [?]-6068							

TRIBAL ENROLLMENT OF PARENTS

	Name of Father	Year	County	Name of Mother	Year	County
1	Jim Jones	dead	Non Citz	Malinda Jones		Non Citz
2	G.W. Scott		" "	No.1		
3	" "		" "	No.1		
4	" "		" "	No.1		
5	" "		" "	No.1		
6	" "		" "	No.1		
7	" "		" "	No.1		
8						
9	Nos. 1 to 7 inclusive transferred from Choctaw Card No 5054					
10	Feby 14-1907 - See decision of same date.					
11						
12						
13						
14						
15						
16						
17				Date of Application for Enrollment.	9/22/98	FEB 14 1907

RESIDENCE: Chickasaw Nation COUNTY. **Choctaw Nation** Choctaw Roll (Not Including Freedmen) CARD NO.
POST OFFICE: Comanche, I.T. FIELD NO. 6070

Dawes' Roll No.		NAME	Relationship to Person First Named	AGE	SEX	BLOOD	TRIBAL ENROLLMENT Year	County	No.
16191	1	Gamblin, Eliza Ann	First Named	48	F	1/16	1896	Blue	4915
	2								
	3								
	4								
	5								
	6								
	7								
	8								
	9								
	10								
	11	ENROLLMENT OF NOS. 1 HEREON APPROVED BY THE SECRETARY OF INTERIOR MAR 1 1907							
	12								
	13								
	14								
	15								
	16								
	17	For record see 7-6068	See petition #C-52						

TRIBAL ENROLLMENT OF PARENTS

	Name of Father	Year	County	Name of Mother	Year	County
1	James Jones	Dead	Non Citz	Eliza Jones	Dead	Non Citz
2						
3						
4						
5						
6	No.1 transferred from Choctaw card No. 5284 February 14-1907					
7	See decision of same date					
8						
9						
10						
11						
12						
13						
14						
15						
16						FEB 14 1907
17				Date of Application for Enrollment.	10/17/98	Date of transfer to this card

RESIDENCE: Chickasaw Nation COUNTY. **Choctaw Nation** **Choctaw Roll** (*Not Including Freedmen*) CARD NO.
POST OFFICE: Comanche I.T. FIELD NO. **6071**

Dawes' Roll No.		NAME	Relationship to Person First Named	AGE	SEX	BLOOD	TRIBAL ENROLLMENT Year	County	No.
16192	1	Gamblin, Joseph W.		28	M	1/32	1896	Blue	4916
IW 1651	2	" Emma	Wife	42	F	I.W	1896	"	4917
16193	3	" Indianola	Dau	6	"	1/64	1896	"	4918
	4								
	5								
	6								
	7								
	8								
	9								
	10								
	11	ENROLLMENT							
	12	OF NOS 1,2,& 3 HEREON							
	13	APPROVED BY THE SECRETARY							
	14	OF INTERIOR MAR 1 1907							
	15								
	16								
	17	For record see 7-6068 See Petition #C-52							

TRIBAL ENROLLMENT OF PARENTS

	Name of Father	Year	County	Name of Mother	Year	County
1	John Gamblin		Non Citz	Ann Gamblin		Non Citz
2	Bob Pruett	dead	" "	Emily Pruett	dead	" "
3	No.1			No.2		
4						
5						
6	Nos 1,2 & 3 transferred from Choctaw Card No 528[?] February 14-1907					
7	See decision of same date.					
8						
9						
10						
11						
12						
13						
14						
15						
16						
17				10/17/98		Date of Application for Enrollment.

[redacted]asaw Nation COUNTY. **Choctaw Nation** Choctaw Roll (Not Including Freedmen) CARD NO.
P[redacted]Comanche, I.T. FIELD NO. 6072

D[redacted] R[redacted]		NAME	Relationship to Person First Named	AGE	SEX	BLOOD	TRIBAL ENROLLMENT Year	County	No.
16[redacted]	1	Gamblin, James W		33	M	1/32	1896	Blue	4919
16195	2	" Hattie L	Sis	22	F	1/32	1896	"	4921
16196	3	" Benny	Son	1	M	1/64			
IW1652	4	" Lillie	Wife	20	F	I.W.			
	5								
	6								
	7								
	8								
	9								
	10								
	11	ENROLLMENT OF NOS. 1,2,3 & 4 HEREON							
	12	APPROVED BY THE SECRETARY							
	13	OF INTERIOR MAR 1 1907							
	14	Decision of Commissioner to [illegible...]							
	15	in accordance with opinion of [illegible...]							
	16	Nos. 1,2,3 & 4 denied by Department [illegible...]							
	17	For record see 7-6068 See petition #C[illegible...]							

TRIBAL ENROLLMENT OF PARENTS

	Name of Father	Year	County	Name of Mother	Year	County
1	John H. Gamblin			Liza A. Gamblin		
2	" "			" "		
3	No.1			No.4		
4	W.A. Skelton		Non Citz	Sallie Skelton		Non Citz
5						
6	Nos 1-2 & 3 transferred from Choctaw card No. 5058 February 14-1907					
7	See decision of same date					
8	No.4 transferred from Choctaw card No. D-430 February 14-1907					
	See decision of same date					
9						
10						
11						
12						
13						
14						
15						
16						FEB 14 1907 Date of transfer
17						to this card

:
CE: Calvin I.T. COUNTY. **Choctaw Nation** **Choctaw Roll** *(Not Including Freedmen)* CARD NO. FIELD NO. **6073**

	NAME	Relationship to Person First Named	AGE	SEX	BLOOD	TRIBAL ENROLLMENT Year	County	No.
1	M^c^Gee, Henry		29	M	1/8	1885	Atoka	516

ENROLLMENT
OF NOS. 1 HEREON
APPROVED BY THE SECRETARY
OF INTERIOR MAR 4- 1907

TRIBAL ENROLLMENT OF PARENTS

	Name of Father	Year	County	Name of Mother	Year	County
1	George M^c^Gee	Dead	Chick	Paralee Jones	Dead	Non Citz

No.1 placed hereon under order of the Commissioner to the Five Civilized Tribes of Feb 2-1907 holding that application was made for his enrollment within the time provided by the act of Congress approved April 26-1906

on this card
Feby 2-1907

RESIDENCE: COUNTY. **Choctaw Nation** **Choctaw Roll** *(Not Including Freedmen)* CARD NO.

POST OFFICE: Fort Smith, Ark. FIELD NO. **6074**

Dawes' Roll No.	NAME	Relationship to Person First Named	AGE	SEX	BLOOD	TRIBAL ENROLLMENT Year	County	No.
16197	1 Smith, Mary E		52	F	1/8	1896	Tobucksy	C.C.R.#2 423
16198	2 " Mary D	Dau	16	"	1/16	1896	"	"
16199	3 " Margurite[sic]	"	14	"	1/16	1896	"	"
16200	4 " George	Son	8	M	1/16	1896	"	"

ENROLLMENT OF NOS. 1,2,3 and 4 HEREON APPROVED BY THE SECRETARY OF INTERIOR Mar 4 1907

TRIBAL ENROLLMENT OF PARENTS

	Name of Father	Year	County	Name of Mother	Year	County
1	Alfred Toole	Dead	Non Citizen	Belinda Toole	dead	Choctaw Roll
2	No.1			No.2		
3	No.1			No.2		
4	No.1			No.2		

Nos. 1-2-3 & 4 transferred from Choctaw card No D-87 in accordance with Departmental instructions of Feby 15-1907

For parents of Nos. 2,3, and 4 see Choctaw Census Card No. D-87
Noted hereon 6-14-1929 - J.D.F.

Oct 20/98

Date of transfer to this card Feb. 15, 1907

RESIDENCE: Choctaw Nation COUNTY. **Choctaw Nation** **Choctaw Roll** *(Not Including Freedmen)* CARD NO.
POST OFFICE: Canadian I.T. FIELD NO. 6075

Dawes' Roll No.	NAME	Relationship to Person First Named	AGE	SEX	BLOOD	TRIBAL ENROLLMENT Year	County	No.
16210	1 Standley, Albert	First Named	28	M	1/8	1885	Gaines	

ENROLLMENT OF NOS. 1 HEREON APPROVED BY THE SECRETARY OF INTERIOR MAR 4- 1907

TRIBAL ENROLLMENT OF PARENTS

Name of Father	Year	County	Name of Mother	Year	County
1 Franz Standley	Dead	Gaines	Silva Standley	Dead	Non Coit

No.1 placed hereon under order of the Commissioner to the Five Civilized Tribes of Feb 16-1907 holding that application was made for his enrollment within the time provided by the act of Congress approved April 26-1906

GRANTED FEB 19 1907

Date of Application for Enrollment.

placed on this card FEB 18 1907

RESIDENCE: COUNTY. **Choctaw Nation** **Choctaw Roll** (Not Including Freedmen) CARD NO.
POST OFFICE: Paoli I.T. FIELD NO. 6076

Dawes' Roll No.	NAME	Relationship to Person First Named	AGE	SEX	BLOOD	TRIBAL ENROLLMENT Year	County	No.
IW 1659	1 Stanhope, Florence		30	F	I.W.			
	2							
	3							
	4							
	5							
	6							
	7							
	8							
	9							
	10							
	11							
	12							
	13							
	14							
	15							
	16							
	17							

ENROLLMENT OF NOS. One HEREON APPROVED BY THE SECRETARY OF INTERIOR MAR 4- 1907

TRIBAL ENROLLMENT OF PARENTS

	Name of Father	Year	County	Name of Mother	Year	County
1	J. P. Collins		Non Citz	Hettie Baker	dead	Non Citz
2						
3						
4						
5						

6 No.1 was formerly wife of Johnson Frazier No 1 on card 3265 Roll #9424

7

8 No.1 placed hereon under order of the Commissioner to the Five Civilized Tribes of Feb 18-1907 holding that application was made for her enrollment within the time provided by the act

9 of Congress approved April 26-1906

GRANTED

FEB 18 1907

place on this card

RESIDENCE: COUNTY. **Choctaw Nation** **Choctaw Roll** *(Not Including Freedmen)* CARD NO.
POST OFFICE: Woolsey I.T. FIELD NO.

Dawes' Roll No.	NAME	Relationship to Person First Named	AGE	SEX	BLOOD	TRIBAL ENROLLMENT Year	County	No.
IW 1660	1 Pitman, Nora	First Named	30	F	I.W.			
	2							
	3							
	4							
	5							
	6							
	7							
	8							
	9							
	10							
	11							
	12							
	13							
	14							
	15							
	16							
	17							

ENROLLMENT OF NOS. One HEREON APPROVED BY THE SECRETARY OF INTERIOR MAR 4- 1907

TRIBAL ENROLLMENT OF PARENTS

Name of Father	Year	County	Name of Mother	Year	County
1 A. Bivins		Non Citz	Martha C. Bivins	Dead	Non Citz

No.1 was formerly the wife of Sam Martin No.1 on Card 5675 Roll #14995

No.1 placed hereon under order of the Commissioner to the Five Civilized Tribes of Feb 15-1907 holding that application was made for her enrollment within the time provided by the act of Congress approved April 26-1906

GRANTED

~~on this card~~
~~FEB 15 1907~~
~~age as of this~~ year

RESIDENCE: Chickasaw Nation COUNTY. **Choctaw Nation** **Choctaw Roll** *(Not Including Freedmen)* CARD NO. 6078
POST OFFICE: Purcell I.T. FIELD NO.

Dawes' Roll No.	NAME	Relationship to Person First Named	AGE	SEX	BLOOD	TRIBAL ENROLLMENT Year	County	No.
	1 ~~Nail, Abraham H~~	~~Named~~	~~84~~	~~M~~	~~1/8~~			
	2 ~~" Matilda J~~	~~Wife~~	~~77~~	~~F~~	~~I.W.~~			
	3 ~~" John~~	~~Son~~	~~44~~	~~M~~	~~1/16~~			
	4 ~~" Aaron L~~	~~"~~	~~34~~	~~"~~	~~1/16~~			
	5							
	6							
	7							
	8							
	9							
	10							
	11							
	12							
	13							
	14							
	15							
	16							
	17 For record see 7-6078	See Petition #C-131						

TRIBAL ENROLLMENT OF PARENTS

	Name of Father	Year	County	Name of Mother	Year	County
1	William Nail	Dead		Delilah Nail	Dead	Non Citz
2	Isaac Roberson	"	Non Citz	Elvira Roberson	"	" "
3	No.1			No.2		
4	No.1			No.2		
5						

6 Nos 1-2-3 & 4 transferred from Choctaw Card No. 5308 (C-353) February
7 21-1907. See decision of same date.

8 ACTION APPROVED BY MAR 4- 1907 FEB 27 1907
9 SECRETARY OFS INTERIOR. REFUSED

10 ~~NOTICE OF DEPARTMENTAL ACTION~~ ~~RECORD FORWARDED DEPARTMENT.~~
11 FORWARDED ATTORNEYS FOR CHOCTAW
12 ~~AND CHICKASAW NATIONS.~~ APR 9 1907 FEB 27 1907

13 NOTICE OF DEPARTMENTAL ACTION
FORWARDED ATTORNEY FOR APPLICANT APR 9 1907

14 ~~NOTICE OF DEPARTMENTAL~~
15 ACTION MAILED APPLICANT. APR 9 1907

16 Date of Application for Enrollment. 10/21/98 Date of transfer on this card
17 FEB 27 1907

RESIDENCE: Chickasaw Nation COUNTY. **Choctaw Nation** **Choctaw Roll** (Not Including Freedmen) CARD NO.
POST OFFICE: Chickasha I.T. FIELD NO. 6079

	NAME	Relationship to Person First Named	AGE	SEX	BLOOD	TRIBAL ENROLLMENT Year	County	No.
	Nail, James P	First Named	38	M	1/16			
	" Lizzie	Wife	40	F	I.W.			
11								
12								
13								
14								
15								
16								
17	For record see 7-6078	See Pet #C-131						

TRIBAL ENROLLMENT OF PARENTS

	Name of Father	Year	County	Name of Mother	Year	County
1	Abraham H Nail			Matilda J Nail		
2	Dan'l G. Iman		Non Citz	Martha Iman	dead	Non Citz

Nos 1&2 transferred from Choctaw card No. 5309 (C-354) February 21 1907
See decision of same date.

FEB 27 1907

ACTION APPROVED BY SECRETARY OF INTERIOR. MAR 4- 1907

REFUSED

NOTICE OF DEPARTMENTAL ACTION FORWARDED ATTORNEYS FOR CHOCTAW AND CHICKASAW NATIONS. APR 9 1907

RECORD FORWARDED DEPARTMENT. FEB 27 1907

NOTICE OF DEPARTMENTAL ACTION FORWARDED ATTORNEY FOR APPLICANT. APR 9 1907

NOTICE OF DEPARTMENTAL ACTION MAILED APPLICANT. APR 9 1907

Date of Application for Enrollment. 10/21/98

transfer date to this card FEB 27 1907

RESIDENCE: Choctaw Nation COUNTY. **Choctaw Nation** **Choctaw Roll** *(Not Including Freedmen)* CARD NO. 608
POST OFFICE: Sutter I.T. FIELD NO.

Dawes' Roll No.	NAME	Relationship to Person First Named	AGE	SEX	BLOOD	TRIBAL ENROLLMENT Year	County	No.
16227	1 Luckly, Louvenia		10	F	1/4	1896	Sansbois[sic]	7678
	2							
	3							
	4							
	5							
	6							
	7							
	8							
	9							
	10							
	11							
	12							
	13							
	14							
	15							
	16							
	17							

ENROLLMENT
OF NOS. One HEREON
APPROVED BY THE SECRETARY
OF INTERIOR MAR 4- 1907

TRIBAL ENROLLMENT OF PARENTS

Name of Father	Year	County	Name of Mother	Year	County
1 Joe Luckly	Dead		Ginsey Luckly		
2					
3					
4					
5					
6 No1 transferred from Choctaw Freedman card No. 1196 Feby 25-1907					
7 See decision of same date					
8					
9					
10					
11					
12					
13					
14					
15					
16					
17					

Date of transfer to this card FEB 25 1907

Date of Application for Enrollment. 10/11/98

RESIDENCE: Chickasaw Nation COUNTY. **Choctaw Nation** **Choctaw Roll** (Not Including Freedmen) CARD NO.
POST OFFICE: Pauls Valley I.T. FIELD NO. 6081

Dawes' Roll No.		NAME	Relationship to Person First Named	AGE	SEX	BLOOD	TRIBAL ENROLLMENT Year	County	No.
✓	1	Burks, Henry E	First Named	42	M				
	2								
	3								
	4								
	5								
	6	REFUSED	OCT 2 1906						
	7	COPY OF DECISION FORWARDED ATTORNEYS FOR CHOCTAW AND							
	8	CHICKASAW NATIONS.	OCT 2 1906						
	9	NOTICE OF DECISION FORWARDED							
	10	ATTORNEY FOR APPLICANTS.							
	11			OCT 2 1906					
	12	COPY OF DECISION FORWARDED							
	13	APPLICANT	OCT 2 1906						
	14								
	15								
	16								
	17								

TRIBAL ENROLLMENT OF PARENTS

	Name of Father	Year	County	Name of Mother	Year	County
1	W. S. Burks			Nancy Burks	Dead	
2						
3						
4						
5	No.1 transferred from Choctaw Card No. D 50 Feby 27-1907.					
6	See decision of same date.					
7	ACTION APPROVED BY					
8	SECRETARY OF INTERIOR. MAR 1 1907					
9	NOTICE OF DEPARTMENTAL ACTION					
10	FORWARDED ATTORNEYS FOR CHOCTAW APR 17 1907					
11	AND CHICKASAW NATIONS.					
12	NOTICE OF DEPARTMENTAL ACTION					
13	FORWARDED ATTORNEY FOR APPLICANT. APR 17 1907					
14	NOTICE OF DEPARTMENTAL					
15	ACTION MAILED APPLICANT. APR 17 1907					
16						Date of transfer
17				Date of Application for Enrollment.	Sept 24/98	to this card FEB 27 1907

CE: Chickasaw Nation COUNTY. **Choctaw Nation** **Choctaw Roll** (Not Including Freedmen) CARD NO.
FICE: Roff I.T. FIELD NO. 6082

	NAME	Relationship to Person First Named	AGE	SEX	BLOOD	TRIBAL ENROLLMENT Year	County	No.
1	Taylor, Nancy H	First Named	34	F	1/8			
2	" Willie B	Son	15	M	1/16			
3	" Sarah E	Dau	10	F	1/16			
4	Hale, Stephen A	Nephew	17	M	1/8			

ENROLLMENT OF NOS. 1,2,3 & 4 HEREON APPROVED BY THE SECRETARY OF INTERIOR MAR 4- 1907

TRIBAL ENROLLMENT OF PARENTS

	Name of Father	Year	County	Name of Mother	Year	Cou
1	J. A. Husband		Non Citz	Frances E. Husband		Non
2	J. H. Taylor		" "	No.1		
3	" "		" "	No.1		
4	John C. Hale		" "	Milessa Hale	dead	Cho

~~Nos 1 to 4 inclusive transferred from Choctaw Card No. 5318 (C-363)~~
Feby 27-1907. See decision of same date.

Date of Application for Enrollment. 9/7/98

~~Date of tr~~ to this FEB 2

Choctaw By Blood Enrollment Cards 1898-1914

RESIDENCE: Chickasaw Nation COUNTY. **Choctaw Nation** **Choctaw Roll** *(Not Including Freedmen)* CARD NO.
POST OFFICE: Roff I.T. FIELD NO.

Dawes' Roll No.		NAME	Relationship to Person First Named	AGE	SEX	BLOOD	TRIBAL ENROLLMENT Year	County
16223	1	Husbands, Thomas J	First Named	39	M	1/8		
16224	2	" Johnie M	Dau	4	F	1/16		
16225	3	" James Alexander	Son	2	M	1/16		
	4	" Sarah Malissa	Dau	1	F	1/16		
	5	" Catherine J	Wife	26	F	I.W.		
	6							
	7							
	8							
	9							
	10							
	11							
	12							
	13							
	14							
	15							
	16							
	17							

ENROLLMENT OF NOS. 5 HEREON APPROVED BY THE SECRETARY OF INTERIOR MAR 4 - 1907

ENROLLMENT OF NOS. 1,2,3 & 4 HEREON APPROVED BY THE SECRETARY OF INTERIOR MAR 4 - 1907

TRIBAL ENROLLMENT OF PARENTS

	Name of Father	Year	County	Name of Mother	Year	County
1	J.A. Husbands		Non Citz	Frances E. Husbands		
2	No.1			Catherine J. Husbands		
3	No.1			" "		
4	No.1			" "		
5	Jas. A. Law		Non Citz	Law	Dead	"
6						
7						

Nos. 1 to 5 inclusive transferred from Choctaw Card No.5319 (C-364)
Feby 27-1907. See decision of same date.

Date of Application for Enrollment. 9/7/98

Date of transfer to this card FEB 27 1907

Choctaw By Blood Enrollment Cards 1898-1914

RESIDENCE: Tobucksy Co COUNTY. **Choctaw Nation** **Choctaw Roll** *(Not Including Freedmen)* CARD NO.
POST OFFICE: Ft Smith Ark FIELD NO. 6084

Dawes' Roll No.	NAME	Relationship to Person First Named	AGE	SEX	BLOOD	TRIBAL ENROLLMENT Year	County	No.
16213	1 Critz, Olive B	First Named	25	F	1/16	1896	Tobucksy	11316
16214	2 " Elizabeth E	dau	4	F	1/32			
	3							
	4							
	5							
	6							
	7							
	8							
	9							
	10							
	11							
	12							
	13							
	14							
	15							
	16							
	17							

ENROLLMENT
OF NOS. 1 and 2 HEREON
APPROVED BY THE SECRETARY
OF INTERIOR MAR 4 1907

TRIBAL ENROLLMENT OF PARENTS

Name of Father	Year	County	Name of Mother	Year	County
1 G. W. Smith		Tobucksy	Mary E Smith		Tobucksy
2 J.D. Critz			No.1		
3					
4					
5					
6					
7					
8					
9					
10					
11					
12					
13					
14					
15					
16					
17					

The enrollment of Nos 1&2 was directed by the Department
Feby 26" 1907

Nos 1&2 transferred from Choctaw Card No. D 503 Feby 28-07.

Sept 15/99 Date of Application for Enrollment.

~~Date of transfer~~ to this card
FEB 28 1907

RESIDENCE: COUNTY. **Choctaw Nation** **Choctaw Roll** *(Not Including Freedmen)* CARD NO.
POST OFFICE: FIELD NO. 6085

Dawes' Roll No.	NAME	Relationship to Person First Named	AGE	SEX	BLOOD	TRIBAL ENROLLMENT Year	County	No.
IW 1668	1 Crawford, George	First Named	47	M	I.W.			
	2							
	3							
	4							
	5							
	6							
	7							
	8							
	9							
	10							
	11 ENROLLMENT OF NOS. 1 HEREON APPROVED BY THE SECRETARY OF INTERIOR Mar 4 1907							
	12							
	13							
	14							
	15							
	16							
	17 Stratford							

TRIBAL ENROLLMENT OF PARENTS

Name of Father	Year	County	Name of Mother	Year	County
1					
2					
3					
4					
5					
6 No1 Enrolled by Department		1907			
7					
8					
9					
10					
11					
12					
13					
14					
15					
16					
17					

RESIDENCE: COUNTY. AUG 1 1914 **Choctaw Nation** **Choctaw Roll** *(Not Including Freedmen)* CARD NO.

POST OFFICE: Valliant, Oklahoma FIELD NO. **6086**

Dawes' Roll No.	NAME	Relationship to Person First Named	AGE	SEX	BLOOD	TRIBAL ENROLLMENT Year	County	No.
	1 Charles, Abram		9	M	Full			
	2	Age as of Aug 1-1914						
	3							
	4							
	5							
	6							
	7							
	8							
	9							
	10							
	11							
	12							
	13							
	14							
	15							
	16							
	17							

TRIBAL ENROLLMENT OF PARENTS

Name of Father	Year	County	Name of Mother	Year	County
1 William Charles			Sayanis Willie (dec'd)		
2					
3					
4					
5					
6 Mother of #1 enrolled as Sayanis Willis Choc Roll # 13481					
7					
8 No.1 Birthdate February 1, 1905					
Father's Roll No. 3142			Mothers Roll No. 13481		
9 ~~Father's Choctaw Roll Card No. 1158~~			~~Mother's Choctaw Roll Card No. 4932~~		
10					
11 Enrollment of No. 16228 Approved By Secretary of Interior Sep. 25-1914					
12					
13					
14					
15					
16					
17					

Choctaw By Blood Enrollment Cards 1898-1914

RESIDENCE: COUNTY. AUG 1 1914 **Choctaw Nation** **Choctaw Roll** *(Not Including Freedmen)* CARD NO.

POST OFFICE: Glover, Oklahoma FIELD NO. 6087

Dawes' Roll No.	NAME	Relationship to Person First Named	AGE	SEX	BLOOD	TRIBAL ENROLLMENT Year	County	No.
	1 Carn, David	Named	2	M	Full			
	2	Age as of March 4, 1905						
	3							
	4							
	5							
	6							
	7							
	8							
	9							
	10							
	11							
	12							
	13							
	14							
	15							
	16							
	17							

TRIBAL ENROLLMENT OF PARENTS

Name of Father	Year	County	Name of Mother	Year	County
1 Harlis Carn			Mary Carn		
2					
3					
4					
5					

6 ~~No.1 died August 23-1908. Age calculated to date of death.~~

7 Mother of No1 enrolled as Mary Oklamhambi.

11 No.1 Birthdate Feby 26-1906

~~Father's Roll No. 2882~~ ~~Mothers Roll No. 3388~~

12 ~~Father's Choctaw Roll Card No. 1082~~ ~~Mother's Choctaw Roll Card No. 1248~~

14 Enrollment of No. 16229 Approved By Secretary of Interior Sep. 25-1914

RESIDENCE: COUNTY. AUG 1 1914 **Choctaw Nation** **Choctaw Roll** *(Not Including Freedmen)* CARD NO.
POST OFFICE: Kullituklo, Oklahoma FIELD NO. 6088

Dawes' Roll No.	NAME	Relationship to Person First Named	AGE	SEX	BLOOD	TRIBAL ENROLLMENT Year	County	No.
	1 Fisher, Dicey		9	F	Full			
	2	Age as of Aug 1-1914						
	3							
	4							
	5							
	6							
	7							
	8							
	9							
	10							
	11							
	12							
	13							
	14							
	15							
	16							
	17							

TRIBAL ENROLLMENT OF PARENTS

Name of Father	Year	County	Name of Mother	Year	County
1 Hicks Fisher			Elizabeth Fisher (dec'd)		
2					
3					
4					
5					
6					
7					
8					
9					
10 No.1 Birthdate April, 1905					
11 Father's Roll No. 3342			Mothers Roll No. 3343		
Father's Choctaw Roll Card No. 1233			Mother's Choctaw Roll Card No. 1233		
12					
13 Enrollment of No. 16230 Approved By Secretary of Interior Sep. 25-1914					
14					
15					
16					
17					

Choctaw By Blood Enrollment Cards 1898-1914

AUG 1 1914

RESIDENCE: COUNTY. **Choctaw Nation** **Choctaw Roll** *(Not Including Freedmen)* CARD NO.

POST OFFICE: Blue, Oklahoma FIELD NO. [6089]

Dawes' Roll No.	NAME	Relationship to Person First Named	AGE	SEX	BLOOD	TRIBAL ENROLLMENT Year	County	No.
	1 Fobb, Mary		10	F	Full			
	2	Age as of Aug 1-1914						
	3							
	4							
	5							
	6							
	7							
	8							
	9							
	10							
	11							
	12							
	13							
	14							
	15							
	16							
	17							

TRIBAL ENROLLMENT OF PARENTS

Name of Father	Year	County	Name of Mother	Year	County
1 Joseph Fobb			Incy Fobb		
2					
3					
4					
5					
6 Application for enrollment of Mary Fobb, by Frank Anderson guardian					
7					
8					
9					
10					
11 No.1 Birthdate Aug. 9-1904					
12 Father's Roll No. 9965			Mothers Roll No. 9966		
~~Father's Choctaw Roll Card No. 3501~~			~~Mother's Choctaw Roll Card No. 3501~~		
13					
14 Enrollment of No. 16231 Approved By Secretary of Interior Sep. 25-1914					
15					
16					
17					

AUG 1 1914

RESIDENCE: COUNTY. **Choctaw Nation** Choctaw Roll (Not Including Freedmen) CARD NO.

POST OFFICE: Nashoba, Oklahoma FIELD NO. [6090]

Dawes' Roll No.	NAME	Relationship to Person First Named	AGE	SEX	BLOOD	TRIBAL ENROLLMENT Year	County	No.
	1 Garland, Lizzie		8	F	Full			
	2	Age as of Aug 1-1914						
	3							
	4							
	5							
	6							
	7							
	8							
	9							
	10							
	11							
	12							
	13							
	14							
	15							
	16							
	17							

TRIBAL ENROLLMENT OF PARENTS

Name of Father	Year	County	Name of Mother	Year	County
1 Hickman Anderson			Minnie Garland		
2					
3					
4					
5					
6 Illegitimate.					
7					
8					
9					
10					
11 No.1 Birthdate October 17-1905					
12 Father's Roll No.			Mothers Roll No. 5358		
~~Father's Choctaw Roll Card No.~~			~~Mother's Choctaw Roll Card No.~~ 1878		
13					
14 Enrollment of No. 16232 Approved By Secretary of Interior Sep. 25-1914					
15					
16					
17					

RESIDENCE: COUNTY. **Choctaw Nation** **Choctaw Roll** *(Not Including Freedmen)* CARD NO.
POST OFFICE: Lukfata, Oklahoma FIELD NO. [6091]

Dawes' Roll No.	NAME	Relationship to Person First Named	AGE	SEX	BLOOD	TRIBAL ENROLLMENT Year	County	No.
	1 Haiakonobi, Amos		17	M	Full			
	2	Age as of Aug 1-1914						
	3							
	4							
	5							
	6							
	7							
	8							
	9							
	10							
	11							
	12							
	13							
	14							
	15							
	16							
	17							

TRIBAL ENROLLMENT OF PARENTS

	Name of Father	Year	County	Name of Mother	Year	County
1	Wilson Haiakonobi			Louisa Haiakonobi		
2						
3						
4						
5						
6						
7						
8						
9						
10						

11 No.1 Birthdate About 1897
12 Father's Roll No. 1106 Mothers Roll No. Died prior Sept 25-02
Father's Choctaw Roll Card No. 529 Mother's Choctaw Roll Card No.
13
14 Enrollment of No. 16233 Approved By Secretary of Interior Sep. 25-1914
15
16
17

RESIDENCE: COUNTY. **Choctaw Nation** **Choctaw Roll** *(Not Including Freedmen)* CARD NO.
POST OFFICE: FIELD NO. [6092]

Dawes' Roll No.	NAME	Relationship to Person First Named	AGE	SEX	BLOOD	TRIBAL ENROLLMENT Year	County	No.
	1 Hodges, Melissa	First Named	17	F	3/4			
	2	Age as of Aug 1-1914						

TRIBAL ENROLLMENT OF PARENTS

Name of Father	Year	County	Name of Mother	Year	County
1 Hannibal Hodges			Sarah Pisachubbe		

It appears from testimony submitted in this case that Melissa Hodges is an illegitimate child of Sarah Pisachubbe and Hannibal Hodges.

No.1 Birthdate
Father's Roll No. 5470 Mothers Roll No. 3471
Father's Choctaw Roll Card No. Mother's Choctaw Roll Card No. 1277

Enrollment of No. 16234 Approved By Secretary of Interior Sep. 25-1914

AUG 1 1914

RESIDENCE: COUNTY. **Choctaw Nation** **Choctaw Roll** (Not Including Freedmen) CARD NO.

POST OFFICE: Garvin, Oklahoma FIELD NO. [6093]

Dawes' Roll No.	NAME	Relationship to Person First Named	AGE	SEX	BLOOD	TRIBAL ENROLLMENT Year	County	No.
	1 Jackson, Sallie		80	F	Full			
	2							
	3							
	4							
	5							
	6							
	7							
	8							
	9							
	10							
	11							
	12							
	13							
	14							
	15							
	16							
	17							

TRIBAL ENROLLMENT OF PARENTS

	Name of Father	Year	County	Name of Mother	Year	County
1	Unknown			Unknown		
2						
3						
4						
5						
6	No.1 died Oct. 14, 1910. Age calculated to date of death.					
7						
8						
9						
10						
11	No.1 Birthdate					
12	Father's Roll No. ~~~~~			Mothers Roll No. ~~~~~		
13	Father's Choctaw Roll Card No.			Mother's Choctaw Roll Card No.		
14	Enrollment of No. 16235 Approved By Secretary of Interior Sep. 25-1914					
15						
16						
17						

Choctaw By Blood Enrollment Cards 1898-1914

AUG 1 1914

RESIDENCE: COUNTY. **Choctaw Nation** **Choctaw Roll** *(Not Including Freedmen)* CARD NO.
POST OFFICE: Bethel Okla. FIELD NO. [6094]

Dawes' Roll No.	NAME	Relationship to Person First Named	AGE	SEX	BLOOD	TRIBAL ENROLLMENT Year	County	No.
	1 Jackson, William	First Named	5	M	Full			
	2							
	3							
	4							
	5							
	6							
	7							
	8							
	9							
	10							
	11							
	12							
	13							
	14							
	15							
	16							
	17							

TRIBAL ENROLLMENT OF PARENTS

Name of Father	Year	County	Name of Mother	Year	County
1 Silas Jackson			Marsie Lewis		
2					
3					
4					
5					
6 No.1 died in April, 1906. Age calculated to date of death.					
7					
8					
9					
10					
11 No.1 Birthdate					
12 Father's Roll No. 14599			Mothers Roll No. 5796		
~~Father's Choctaw Census Card No. 795~~			~~Mother's Choctaw Census Card No. 2024~~		
13					
14 Enrollment of No. 16236 Approved By Secretary of Interior Sep. 25-1914					
15					
16					
17					

AUG 1 1914

RESIDENCE: COUNTY. **Choctaw Nation** **Choctaw Roll** (Not Including Freedmen) CARD NO.

POST OFFICE: Ti, Oklahoma FIELD NO. [6095]

Dawes' Roll No.	NAME	Relationship to Person First Named	AGE	SEX	BLOOD	TRIBAL ENROLLMENT Year	County	No.
	1 James, Fannie Myrtle		8	F	3/4			
	2	Age as of Aug 1-1914						
	3							
	4							
	5							
	6							
	7							
	8							
	9							
	10							
	11							
	12							
	13							
	14							
	15							
	16							
	17							

TRIBAL ENROLLMENT OF PARENTS

Name of Father	Year	County	Name of Mother	Year	County
1 Gilbert James			Sallie James dec'd		
2					
3					
4					
5					
6 Mother of No. 1 enrolled as Sallie Clay.					
7					
8					
9					
10					
11 No.1 Birthdate December 8, 1905					
12 Father's Roll No. Chickasaw 4836			Mothers Roll No. 5343		
13 ~~Father's Chick. Roll Card No. 1221~~			~~Mother's Choctaw Census Card No. 1875~~		
14 Enrollment of No. 16237 Approved By Secretary of Interior Sep. 25-1914					
15					
16					
17					

Choctaw By Blood Enrollment Cards 1898-1914

AUG 1 1914

RESIDENCE: COUNTY. **Choctaw Nation** **Choctaw Roll** *(Not Including Freedmen)* CARD NO.

POST OFFICE: Garvin, Oklahoma FIELD NO. [6096]

Dawes' Roll No.	NAME	Relationship to Person First Named	AGE	SEX	BLOOD	TRIBAL ENROLLMENT Year	County	No.
	1 Johnson, Alphrus		8	M	Full			
	2	Age as of Aug 1-1914						
	3							
	4							
	5							
	6							
	7							
	8							
	9							
	10							
	11							
	12							
	13							
	14							
	15							
	16							
	17							

TRIBAL ENROLLMENT OF PARENTS

Name of Father	Year	County	Name of Mother	Year	County
1 Anthony Johnson			Frances Johnson		
2					
3					
4					
5					
6 Mother of No.1 enrolled as Frances Billy					
7					
8					
9					
10					
11 No.1 Birthdate February 23, 1906					
12 Father's Roll No. 393			Mothers Roll No. 2989		
13 Father's Choctaw Roll Card No. 606			Mother's Choctaw Roll Card No. 1111		
14 Enrollment of No. 16238 Approved By Secretary of Interior Sep. 25-1914					
15					
16					
17					

AUG 1 1914

RESIDENCE: COUNTY. **Choctaw Nation** **Choctaw Roll** *(Not Including Freedmen)* CARD NO.
POST OFFICE: Voca, Oklahoma FIELD NO. [6097]

Dawes' Roll No.	NAME	Relationship to Person First Named	AGE	SEX	BLOOD	TRIBAL ENROLLMENT Year	County	No.
	1 King, Solomon		8	M	Full			
	2	Age as of Aug 1-1914						
	3							
	4							
	5							
	6							
	7							
	8							
	9							
	10							
	11							
	12							
	13							
	14							
	15							
	16							
	17							

TRIBAL ENROLLMENT OF PARENTS

Name of Father	Year	County	Name of Mother	Year	County
1 Jesse King			Alice King		
2					
3					
4					
5					
6 Mother #1 enrolled as Alice Nicholas Choc Roll #9837					
7					
8					
9					
10					
11 No.1 Birthdate December 24, 1905					
12 Father's Roll No. 10778			Mothers Roll No. 9837		
Father's Choctaw Roll Card No. 3822			Mother's Choctaw Roll Card No. 3452		
13					
14 Enrollment of No. 16239 Approved By Secretary of Interior Sep. 25-1914					
15					
16					
17					

Choctaw By Blood Enrollment Cards 1898-1914

AUG 1 1914

RESIDENCE: COUNTY. **Choctaw Nation** **Choctaw Roll** *(Not Including Freedmen)* CARD NO.

POST OFFICE: FIELD NO. [6098]

Dawes' Roll No.	NAME	Relationship to Person First Named	AGE	SEX	BLOOD	TRIBAL ENROLLMENT Year	County	No.
	McKinney, Benj. Franklin		1	M	Full			
		Age as of Aug 1-1914						

TRIBAL ENROLLMENT OF PARENTS

Name of Father	Year	County	Name of Mother	Year	County
John McKinney			Dora Amos		

No1 died Aug. 8, 1906. Age caculated[sic] to date of death.

No.1 Birthdate February 2, 1905

Father's Roll No. 12229 Mothers Roll No. Miss Choc. 785

Father's Choctaw Roll Card No. 4381 Mother's Choctaw Roll Card No. Miss. Choc. 489

Enrollment of No. 16240 Approved By Secretary of Interior Sep. 25-1914

Choctaw By Blood Enrollment Cards 1898-1914

AUG 1 1914

RESIDENCE: COUNTY. **Choctaw Nation** **Choctaw Roll** *(Not Including Freedmen)* CARD NO.

POST OFFICE: Cade, Oklahoma FIELD NO. 6099

Dawes' Roll No.	NAME	Relationship to Person First Named	AGE	SEX	BLOOD	TRIBAL ENROLLMENT Year	County	No.
	1 Polk, Willis		8	M	Full			
	2	Age as of Aug 1-1914						
	3							
	4							
	5							
	6							
	7							
	8							
	9							
	10							
	11							
	12							
	13							
	14							
	15							
	16							
	17							

TRIBAL ENROLLMENT OF PARENTS

Name of Father	Year	County	Name of Mother	Year	County
1 Cephus Kepo			Mary Polk		
2					
3					
4					
5					
6 The father goes by the name of Polk but is enrolled opposite Chickasaw Roll No. 3630					
7 as Cephus Kepo.					
8					
9					
10					
11 No.1 Birthdate November 19, 1905					
12 Father's Roll No. Chickasaw 3630			Mothers Roll No. 10852		
~~Father's Chickasaw Roll Card No. 1246~~			~~Mother's Choctaw Roll Card No. 3847~~		
13					
14 Enrollment of No. 16241 Approved By Secretary of Interior Sep. 25-1914					
15					
16					
17					

[Picture of family on following page (350)]

[This photograph was found in the Dawes Packet for this particular family while researching the family names. With over 6100 cards in this series another photograph hasn't been found while doing this work and it was just felt this picture should be added with this card for the reason that if some family member ever wondered what this person looked like this just might be a special moment; a rare moment in their family history.
Willis Polk is the child standing with the "X" over him. Father's and mother's names are also on the card.]

AUG 1 1914

RESIDENCE: COUNTY. **Choctaw Nation** Choctaw Roll (Not Including Freedmen) CARD NO.
POST OFFICE: Doyle, Oklahoma FIELD NO. [6100]

Dawes' Roll No.	NAME	Relationship to Person First Named	AGE	SEX	BLOOD	TRIBAL ENROLLMENT Year	County	No.
	1 Robinson, William F	Named	53	M	3/8			
	2 " Alice		17	F	3/16			
	3 " Alpha		"	"	"			
	4 " Ada B		15	"	"			
	5 " James William		13	M	"			
	6	Ages as of Aug 1-1914						
	7							
	8							
	9							
	10							
	11							
	12							
	13							
	14							
	15							
	16							
	17							

TRIBAL ENROLLMENT OF PARENTS

Name of Father	Year	County	Name of Mother	Year	County
1 James Robinson			Emiline E Robinson		
2 William F. Robinson			Levonia Robinson		non-citizen
3 " "			" "		" "
4 " "			" "		" "
5 " "			" "		" "

6 No.1 Birthdate July 29, 1861
7 No.2 Birthdate March 15, 1897
No.3 Birthdate " " "
8 ~~No.4 Birthdate December 1, 1898~~
9 No.5 Birthdate July 3, 1901
10
11
12 No.1 Father's Roll No. ~~~~~ No.1 Mother's Roll No. 743
13 No.1 Father's Choctaw Roll Card No. Mother's Choctaw Roll Card No.
14 ~~Enrollment of No. 16242 to 16246 Approved By Secretary of Interior Sep. 25-1914~~
15
16
17

AUG 1 1914

RESIDENCE: COUNTY. **Choctaw Nation** **Choctaw Roll** *(Not Including Freedmen)* CARD NO.

POST OFFICE: Doyle, Oklahoma FIELD NO. [6101]

Dawes' Roll No.	NAME	Relationship to Person First Named	AGE	SEX	BLOOD	TRIBAL ENROLLMENT Year	County	No.
	1 Robinson, Emeline		11	F	3/16			
	2 " Mary Ola		8	"	"			
	3	Age as of Aug 1-1914						
	4							
	5							
	6							
	7							
	8							
	9							
	10							
	11							
	12							
	13							
	14							
	15							
	16							
	17							

TRIBAL ENROLLMENT OF PARENTS

Name of Father	Year	County	Name of Mother	Year	County
1 William F. Robinson			Levonia Robinson		non-citizen
2 " " "			" "		" "
3					
4					
5					
6 ~~No.1 Birthdate August 5, 1903~~					
7 No.2 Birthdate November 6, 1905					
8					
9					
10					
11 Father's Roll No.			Mothers Roll No.		
12 Father's Choctaw Roll Card No.			Mother's Choctaw Roll Card No.		
13 ~~Enrollment of No. 16247 - 16248 Approved By Secretary of Interior Sep. 25-1914~~					
14					
15					
16					
17					

Choctaw By Blood Enrollment Cards 1898-1914

AUG 1 1914

RESIDENCE: COUNTY. **Choctaw Nation** **Choctaw Roll** *(Not Including Freedmen)* CARD NO.

POST OFFICE: Double Springs, Okla. FIELD NO. [6102]

Dawes' Roll No.	NAME	Relationship to Person First Named	AGE	SEX	BLOOD	TRIBAL ENROLLMENT Year	County	No.
	1 Wright, Joseph James		9	M	3/4			
	2	Age as of Aug 1-1914						
	3							
	4							
	5							
	6							
	7							
	8							
	9							
	10							
	11							
	12							
	13							
	14							
	15							
	16							
	17							

TRIBAL ENROLLMENT OF PARENTS

Name of Father	Year	County	Name of Mother	Year	County
1 Eslam Wright			Francis[sic] Wright		
2					
3					
4					
5					
6 Mother enrolled as Francis Wade					
7					
8					
9					
10					
11 No.1 Birthdate July 9-1905					
12 Father's Roll No. 12859			Mothers Roll No. 120		
13 ~~Father's Choctaw Roll Card No.~~			~~Mother's Choctaw Roll Card No.~~		
14 Enrollment of No. 16249 Approved By Secretary of Interior Sep. 25-1914					
15					
16					
17					

Choctaw By Blood Enrollment Cards 1898-1914

AUG 1 1914

RESIDENCE: COUNTY. **Choctaw Nation** **Choctaw Roll** *(Not Including Freedmen)* CARD NO.

POST OFFICE: Coalgate, Okla FIELD NO. [6103]

Dawes' Roll No.	NAME	Relationship to Person First Named	AGE	SEX	BLOOD	TRIBAL ENROLLMENT Year	County	No.
	1 King, Mary			F	Full			
	2	Age as of Aug 1-1914						
	3							
	4							
	5							
	6							
	7							
	8							
	9							
	10							
	11							
	12							
	13							
	14							
	15							
	16							
	17							

TRIBAL ENROLLMENT OF PARENTS

Name of Father	Year	County	Name of Mother	Year	County
1 Jesse King			Alice King nee Nicholas		
2					
3					
4					
5					
6 Mother of #1 enrolled as Alice Nicholas on Choctaw Card #3452 Roll #9837					
7					
8					
9					
10					
11 No.1 Birthdate September 17, 1902					
12 Father's Roll No. 10778			Mothers Roll No. 9837		
~~Father's Choctaw Roll Card No. 3822~~			~~Mother's Choctaw Roll Card No. 3452~~		
13					
14 Enrollment of No. 16250 Approved By Secretary of Interior Sep. 25-1914					
15					
16					
17					

Choctaw By Blood Enrollment Cards 1898-1914

AUG 1 1914

RESIDENCE: COUNTY. **Choctaw Nation** **Choctaw Roll** *(Not Including Freedmen)* CARD NO.

POST OFFICE: Scipio, Oklahoma FIELD NO. [6104]

Dawes' Roll No.	NAME	Relationship to Person First Named	AGE	SEX	BLOOD	TRIBAL ENROLLMENT Year	County	No.
I.W.	1 Bevill, Joe T		57	M	I W			
	2	Age as of March 4, 1906						
	3							
	4							
	5							
	6							
	7							
	8							
	9							
	10							
	11							
	12							
	13							
	14							
	15							
	16							
	17							

TRIBAL ENROLLMENT OF PARENTS

	Name of Father	Year	County	Name of Mother	Year	County
1			Non-citizen			Non-citizen
2						
3						
4						
5						

6 Testimony on file showing marriage of Joe T. Bevill to Alice E. Pitchlynn in

7 Bokhoma County Indian Territory on December 23-1875.

11 No.1 Birthdate

12 Father's Roll No. Mothers Roll No.

Father's Choctaw Roll Card No. Mother's Choctaw Roll Card No.

14 Enrollment of No. 1673 Approved By Secretary of Interior Sep. 25-1914

RESIDENCE: COUNTY. **Choctaw Nation** **Choctaw Roll** *(Not Including Freedmen)* CARD NO.
POST OFFICE: Comanche, Okla. FIELD NO. [6105]

Dawes' Roll No.	NAME	Relationship to Person First Named	AGE	SEX	BLOOD	TRIBAL ENROLLMENT Year	County	No.
16251	1 Nichols, James B	First Named	66	M				9807
16252	2 " Nancy V	Dau		F				9811
	3		Age as of Aug 1-1914					
	4							
	5							
	6							
	7							
	8							
	9							
	10							
	11							
	12							
	13							
	14							
	15							
	16							
	17							

ENROLLMENT OF NOS. 16251-16252 HEREON APPROVED BY THE SECRETARY OF INTERIOR Sep 25-1914

TRIBAL ENROLLMENT OF PARENTS

	Name of Father	Year	County	Name of Mother	Year	County
1	Wilson Nichols	Dead	Non Citz	Delitha Nichols	Dead	Choctaw
2	No.1			Nancy C. Nichols		
3						
4						
5						
6						
7						
8						
9						
10						
11						
12						
13						
14						
15						
16					AUG	1 1914
17						

AUG 1 1914

RESIDENCE: COUNTY. **Choctaw Nation** Choctaw Roll (Not Including Freedmen) CARD NO.
POST OFFICE: Comanche, Okla. FIELD NO. [6106]

Dawes' Roll No.	NAME	Relationship to Person First Named	AGE	SEX	BLOOD	TRIBAL ENROLLMENT Year	County	No.
16253	1 Scott, Della May	First Named	29	F	1/16	1896	Blue	98[??]
16254	2 " Nema May	Dau	11	F	1/32			
16255	3 " Lita Lois	Dau	8	F	1/32			
	4	Age as of Aug 1-1914						
	5							
	6							
	7							
	8							
	9							
	10							
	11							
	12							
	13							
	14							
	15							
	16							
	17							

ENROLLMENT inc.
OF NOS. 16253 to 16255 HEREON
APPROVED BY THE SECRETARY
OF INTERIOR Sep 25-1914

TRIBAL ENROLLMENT OF PARENTS

Name of Father	Year	County	Name of Mother	Year	County
1 James B. Nichols	1896	Choctaw	Nancy C Nichols		I.W. Choc.
2 Burris Scott	Non	Citz	No.1		
3 " "	"	"	No.1		
4					
5					
6 [Entry illegible]					
7 No.2 Born May 15, 1903					
No.3 Born Feb. 1, 1906					
8 ~~Nos 2&3 previously listed on Choc. Minor Card #924~~					
9					
10					
11					
12					
13					
14					
15					
16					
17					

RESIDENCE: COUNTY. **Choctaw Nation** **Choctaw Roll** *(Not Including Freedmen)* CARD NO.
POST OFFICE: Comanche, Okla. FIELD NO. [6107]

Dawes' Roll No.	NAME	Relationship to Person First Named	AGE	SEX	BLOOD	TRIBAL ENROLLMENT Year	County	No.
16256	1 Nichols, James W		33	M			Blue	
I.W.	2 " Osa	Wife	31	F				
16257	3 " Cora Lee	Dau	3	F	1/32			
	4	Nos. 1 & 2 Ages as of Aug 1-1914						
	5	[No.3 Age as of March 4, 1906]						
	6							
	7							
	8							
	9							
	10							
	11							
	12							
	13							
	14							
	15							
	16							
	17							

ENROLLMENT inc.
OF NOS. 16256 - 16257 HEREON
APPROVED BY THE SECRETARY
OF INTERIOR Sep 25-1914

TRIBAL ENROLLMENT OF PARENTS

Name of Father	Year	County	Name of Mother	Year	County
1 Orin Nichols		Choc	Amanda M Nichols		I.W. Choc
2 Richards		Non Citz	Tennessee Richards		Non Citz
3 No.1			No.2		
4					
5					
6 [Entry illegible]					
7 No.1 previously [illegible…]					
8 No.2 " [illegible…]					
~~No.3 " [illegible] Choc Minor [New Born #926]~~					
9					
10					
11					
12					
13					
14					
15					
16					
17					AUG 1 1914

Choctaw By Blood Enrollment Cards 1898-1914

RESIDENCE: Tida Okla COUNTY. **Choctaw Nation** **Choctaw Roll** (Not Including Freedmen) CARD NO. 6108
POST OFFICE: ~~Comanche, Okla.~~ FIELD NO.

Dawes' Roll No.	NAME	Relationship to Person First Named	AGE	SEX	BLOOD	TRIBAL ENROLLMENT Year	County	No.
16258	1 Nichols, John W. B.		39	M	1/16			
I.W.	2 " Bessie	Wife	33	F	I.W.			
16259	3 " Louie Herman	Son	13	M	1/32			
16260	4 " Goldie Allie	Dau		F	1/32			
16261	5 " Sylvie Jewel	Dau	3	F	1/32			
	6	Nos. 1 - 4 Ages as of Aug 1-1914						
	7	[No.5 Age as of March 4, 1905]						

ENROLLMENT, inc. OF NOS. 16258-16261 HEREON APPROVED BY THE SECRETARY OF INTERIOR Sep 25-1914

TRIBAL ENROLLMENT OF PARENTS

	Name of Father	Year	County	Name of Mother	Year	County
1	James B. Nichols		Choctaw	Nancy C Nichols		I.W. Choc.
2	Deaton		Non Citz			Non Citz
3	No.1			No.2		
4	No.1			No.2		
5	No.1			No.2		

Nos 1&2 [illegible] June 11, [illegible]
No. [illegible]
~~No.4 " [illegible...]~~
~~Nos. 1 to [?] previously on [illegible] 5097 [illegible...]~~
No.5 Born Aug. 26, 190[5?]
" " previously listed on Choc. Minor Card No. 925

AUG 1 1914

RESIDENCE: COUNTY. **Choctaw Nation** **Choctaw Roll** *(Not Including Freedmen)* CARD NO. 6109
POST OFFICE: Comanche, Okla FIELD NO.

	NAME	Relationship to Person First Named	AGE	SEX	BLOOD	TRIBAL ENROLLMENT Year	County	No.
1	Nichols, Orin M		59	M	1/8	1896	Blue	
2	" Amanda M	Wife	53	F	I.W.	1896	"	
3	" Maggie M	Dau	27	F	1/16	1896	"	
4	" Mettie Myrtle	Dau	23	F	1/16	1896	"	
5	" Lonie A.	Dau	19	F	1/16	1896	"	
6		Age as of Aug 1-1914						
7								
8								
9								
10								
11								
12								
13								
14								
15								
16								
17								

TRIBAL ENROLLMENT OF PARENTS

	Name of Father	Year	County	Name of Mother	Year	County
1	Wilson Nichols		Non Citz	Delitha Nichols		Choctaw
2	J. L. Skelton or Shelton		Non Citz	Mary Skelton or Shelton		Non Citz
3	No.1			No.2		
4	No.1			No.2		
5	No.1			No.2		
6						
7	Nos 1&2 married Oct 26, [illegible]					
8	Nos 1 to [illegible...]					
9						
10						
11						
12						
13						
14						
15						
16						
17						AUG 1 1914

www.ingramcontent.com/pod-product-compliance
Lightning Source LLC
Chambersburg PA
CBHW030234030426
42336CB00009B/93
* 9 7 8 1 6 4 9 6 8 1 1 6 4 *

Other Books and Series by Jeff Bowen

1901-1907 Native American Census Seneca, Eastern Shawnee, Miami, Modoc, Ottawa, Peoria, Quapaw, and Wyandotte Indians (Under Seneca School, Indian Territory)

1932 Census of The Standing Rock Sioux Reservation with Births And Deaths 1924-1932

Census of The Blackfeet, Montana, 1897- 1901 Expanded Edition

Eastern Cherokee by Blood, 1906-1910, Volumes I thru XIII

Choctaw of Mississippi Indian Census 1929-1932 with Births and Deaths 1924-1931 Volume I
Choctaw of Mississippi Indian Census 1933, 1934 & 1937, Supplemental Rolls to 1934 & 1935 with Births and Deaths 1932-1938, and Marriages 1936-1938 Volume II

Eastern Cherokee Census Cherokee, North Carolina 1930-1939
Census 1930-1931 with Births And Deaths 1924-1931 Taken By Agent L. W. Page Volume I
Eastern Cherokee Census Cherokee, North Carolina 1930-1939
Census 1932-1933 with Births And Deaths 1930-1932 Taken By Agent R. L. Spalsbury Volume II
Eastern Cherokee Census Cherokee, North Carolina 1930-1939
Census 1934-1937 with Births and Deaths 1925-1938 and Marriages 1936 & 1938 Taken by Agents R. L. Spalsbury And Harold W. Foght Volume III

Seminole of Florida Indian Census, 1930-1940 with Birth and Death Records, 1930-1938

Texas Cherokees 1820-1839 A Document For Litigation 1921

Starr Roll 1894 (Cherokee Payment Rolls) Districts: Canadian, Cooweescoowee, and Delaware Volume One
Starr Roll 1894 (Cherokee Payment Rolls) Districts: Flint, Going Snake, and Illinois Volume Two
Starr Roll 1894 (Cherokee Payment Rolls) Districts: Saline, Sequoyah, and Tahlequah; Including Orphan Roll Volume Three

Cherokee Intruder Cases Dockets of Hearings 1901-1909 Volumes I & II

Indian Wills, 1911-1921 Records of the Bureau of Indian Affairs Books One thru Seven
Native American Wills & Probate Records 1911-1921

Turtle Mountain Reservation Chippewa Indians 1932 Census with Births & Deaths, 1924-1932

Other Books and Series by Jeff Bowen

Chickasaw By Blood Enrollment Cards 1898-1914 Volume I thru V

Cherokee Descendants East An Index to the Guion Miller Applications Volume I
Cherokee Descendants West An Index to the Guion Miller Applications Volume II (A-M)
Cherokee Descendants West An Index to the Guion Miller Applications Volume III (N-Z)

Applications for Enrollment of Seminole Newborn Freedmen, Act of 1905

Eastern Cherokee Census, Cherokee, North Carolina, 1915-1922, Taken by Agent James E. Henderson
Volume I (1915-1916)
Volume II (1917-1918)
Volume III (1919-1920)
Volume IV (1921-1922)

Complete Delaware Roll of 1898

Eastern Cherokee Census, Cherokee, North Carolina, 1923-1929, Taken by Agent James E. Henderson
Volume I (1923-1924)
Volume II (1925-1926)
Volume III (1927-1929)

Applications for Enrollment of Seminole Newborn Act of 1905 Volumes I & II

North Carolina Eastern Cherokee Indian Census 1898-1899, 1904, 1906, 1909-1912, 1914 Revised and Expanded Edition

1932 Hopi and Navajo Native American Census with Birth & Death Rolls (1925-1931) Volume 1 - Hopi
1932 Hopi and Navajo Native American Census with Birth & Death Rolls (1930-1932) Volume 2 - Navajo

Western Navajo Reservation Navajo, Hopi and Paiute 1933 Census with Birth & Death Rolls 1925-1933

Cherokee Citizenship Commission Dockets 1880-1884 and 1887-1889 Volumes I thru V

Applications for Enrollment of Chickasaw Newborn Act of 1905 Volumes I thru VII

Cherokee Intermarried White 1906 Volume I thru X

Applications for Enrollment of Creek Newborn Act of 1905 Volumes I thru XIV